More praise for *Americ...*
and Edmund S. Mo...

"If there is something missing from much history writing today, it is the very same quality that makes Morgan's writing so great. He is able to situate the past in dual contexts, both human and historical, and to use each to elucidate the other. The result is history of a rare kind, written with bravado, intelligence, and imagination."
— Kevin Hartnett, *Christian Science Monitor*

"A powerful historical mind at work over an amazingly long and influential career." — Annette Gordon-Reed, *The Daily Beast*

"To read these essays is to be reminded not only of just how fertile and graceful a career Morgan has had, but to understand what he and the great historians of his generation accomplished. . . . But whether in gentle praise or cutting criticism, Morgan's utter immersion in the world of the seventeenth and eighteenth centuries is so palpable as to be a gift to those who experience it through him."
— Jim Cullen, *History News Network*

"Outstanding. . . . This uniformly strong collection boasts an insightful, even startling observation—'Government requires make-believe'—on nearly ever page." — *Kirkus Reviews*, starred review

"This book is a perfect gem. . . . Highly recommended."
— *Literary Journal*

"Intelligent, opinionated essays." — *Publishers Weekly*, starred review

"Edmund Morgan is arguably the finest living American historian, an adornment to the tradition that includes Francis Parkman, George Bancroft, Charles Beard, and Perry Miller."
— Bruce Kuklick, *Christianity Today*

AMERICAN HEROES

OTHER BOOKS BY EDMUND S. MORGAN

The Genuine Article: A Historian Looks at Early America

Benjamin Franklin

*Inventing the People: The Rise of Popular Sovereignty in
England and America*

*The Puritan Family: Religion and Domestic Relations in
Seventeenth-Century New England*

Virginians at Home: Family Life in the Eighteenth Century

The Stamp Act Crisis: Prologue to Revolution (with Helen M. Morgan)

The Birth of the Republic, 1763–89

The Puritan Dilemma: The Story of John Winthrop

The Genius of George Washington

*The Meaning of Independence: John Adams, George Washington,
and Thomas Jefferson*

The Challenge of the American Revolution

American Slavery, American Freedom: The Ordeal of Colonial Virginia

The Gentle Puritan: A Life of Ezra Stiles, 1727–1795

Visible Saints: The History of a Puritan Idea

Roger Williams: The Church and the State

So What About History?

EDITED WORKS

Not Your Usual Founding Father: Selected Readings from Benjamin Franklin

Prologue to Revolution: Sources and Documents on the Stamp Act Crisis, 1764–1766

The Diary of Michael Wigglesworth, 1653–1657: The Conscience of a Puritan

Puritan Political Ideas, 1558–1794

The Founding of Massachusetts: Historians and the Sources

The American Revolution: Two Centuries of Interpretation

AMERICAN HEROES

PROFILES OF MEN AND
WOMEN WHO SHAPED
EARLY AMERICA

Edmund S. Morgan

W. W. NORTON & COMPANY
NEW YORK   LONDON

These essays are reprinted with the kind permission of the following: "Dangerous Books," *The Michigan Alumnus Quarterly Review*; "The Unyielding Indian," courtesy of the John Carter Brown Library of Brown University; "John Winthrop's Vision," Huntington Library Press; "The Puritans and Sex," *The New England Quarterly*; "The Problems of a Puritan Heiress," Colonial Society of Massachusetts; "The Case against Anne Hutchinson," *The New England Quarterly*; "The Puritan's Puritan: Michael Wigglesworth," Colonial Society of Massachusetts; "The Contentious Quaker: William Penn," *Proceedings of the American Philosophical Society*; "Ezra Stiles and Timothy Dwight," Massachusetts Historical Society; "The End of Franklin's Pragmatism," Yale University Press; "The Founding Fathers' Problem: Representation," *The Yale Review*; "The Genius of Perry Miller," courtesy of the American Antiquarian Society.

Copyright © 2009 by Edmund S. Morgan

For information about permission to reproduce selections from this book,
write to Permissions, W. W. Norton & Company, Inc.,
500 Fifth Avenue, New York, NY 10110

For information about special discounts for bulk purchases, please contact
W. W. Norton Special Sales at specialsales@wwnorton.com or 800-233-4830

Manufacturing by RR Donnelley, Bloomsburg
Book design by Helene Berinsky
Production manager: Julia Druskin

Library of Congress Cataloging-in-Publication Data

Morgan, Edmund S. (Edmund Sears), 1916–
American heroes : profiles of men and women who shaped
early America / Edmund S. Morgan.
p. cm.
Includes bibliographical references and index.
ISBN 978-0-393-07010-1 (hardcover)
1. United States—History—Colonial period, ca. 1600–1775—Biography.
2. United States—History—Revolution, 1775–1783—Biography.
3. United States—History—1783–1815—Biography. 4. Heroes—
United States—Biography. I. Title.
E187.5.M67 2009
973.2—dc22

2009000714

ISBN 978-0-393-30454-1 pbk.

W. W. Norton & Company, Inc.
500 Fifth Avenue, New York, N.Y. 10110
www.wwnorton.com

W. W. Norton & Company Ltd.
Castle House, 75/76 Wells Street, London W1T 3QT

1 2 3 4 5 6 7 8 9 0

TO THE MEMORY OF
BARBARA EPSTEIN

CONTENTS

PREFACE

AMERICAN HEROES. Probably most of the people in this book would have disclaimed or disdained the title. Through most of the eighteenth century, while Americans remained colonists of Great Britain, the word carried its ancient meaning of great warrior, with connotations of membership among the gods or demigods who first bore the title in ancient Greece. Among the Puritans of New England it might have been thought sacrilegious to apply the word to any human being, least of all to some godlike warrior. As late as 1748 Benjamin Franklin, writing as Poor Richard, turned the tables on the word's implication of veneration for warriors. "There are three great destroyers of mankind," he wrote in his almanac, "*Plague, Famine,* and *Hero*. Plague and Famine destroy your persons only, and leave your goods to your Heirs; but Hero, when he comes, takes life and goods together; his business and glory it is, to destroy man and the works of man. . . . *Hero*, therefore, is the worst of the three."

Franklin may have been engaged in one of his humorous sallies, playing with popular beliefs by upending them. But he was not insulting anyone his readers would have known. There were no great American warriors then. When Americans gained one in George Washington, he did not fit Franklin's description. Franklin was nevertheless second to none in admiration of him and had no trouble knowing whom the Marquis of Lafayette meant in 1779 when speaking of "the godlike American hero." But no American since Washington has gained remotely comparable acclaim, and Washing-

ton's continuing preeminence among our heroes probably owes as much to
his presidency as to his generalship. The heroes elevated to a place beside
him as founding fathers, including Franklin himself, Thomas Jefferson,
James Madison, and John Adams, were not warriors. Alexander Hamilton
aspired to be one and played a minor role at Yorktown, but gained heroic
status, if he has it, as secretary of the treasury.

Even before the Revolution, Americans found their heroes in men
who had led contests that stopped short of battle: a John Hampden, who
would not pay an unlawful tax in the 1630s, but not an Oliver Cromwell,
who led a civil war in the same cause. In the 1760s Americans named
many towns after heroes who had supported their cause only in parliamentary debate: Pittsburgh, Conway, Barre, Wilkes-Barre. When they
became independent, they looked to their own past for heroes and found
a collection of them in the "Pilgrim Fathers," remembered for their religious faith and popularly depicted on a solemn walk to church. They
celebrated William Penn as a peacemaker. And they began to discover
their affinity for nameless heroes among themselves who went their own
way against the grain, regardless of custom, convenience, or habits of
deference to authority. Many were to be found among the people just
then pulling up stakes to strike out over the mountains to Kentucky and
Tennessee and Ohio. They were the Americans who sassed their betters
and got into trouble, the people for whom the Bill of Rights was written, people not generally recognized as heroes but heroes nevertheless.
There was Samuel Maverick, appropriately named, who settled himself
in happy solitude on Massachusetts Bay six years before the Puritans got
there. When they arrived, he fled from their prayers to an island of his
own. There were the two Boston carters, my personal favorites, who
stood down the royal governor of Massachusetts on a wintry day in 1705.
They were carrying a heavy load of wood on a narrow road, drifted with
snow, when they encountered the governor coming from the opposite
direction. Since they did not turn off the road to let the governor's coach
pass, he leapt out and bade them give way. One of them then, according
to the governor's own testimony, "answered boldly, without any other
words, 'I am as good flesh and blood as you; I will not give way, you
may goe out of the way.'" When the governor then drew his sword and

advanced to teach the man a lesson, the carter "layd hold on the governor and broke the sword in his hand," a supreme gesture of contempt for authority and its might.

Historians have been studying such heroes and the people around them for two centuries, but I think they can still surprise us. The people I have selected here, whether public heroes or simply my own favorites, have all surprised me in one way or another. Something about them has sent me looking at the records they left behind, often looking for a second time, having second thoughts. Many of these pieces are the result of second thoughts about what I had said earlier in biographies or biographical sketches.

An example. The Puritans of New England were so sure of their historic significance that they preserved with loving care the voluminous records of everything they did. After a number of years immersed in those records, I came up for air with a biography of a man who figures largely in them, Governor John Winthrop of Massachusetts. One important document was the transcript of a speech he delivered to his shipmates on the voyage to found the colony in 1630. In it he told them that they would be as a "city upon a hill." The phrase has resounded through subsequent American history, appropriated by patriots and politicians for the whole United States as a special place in the eyes of God and of the entire world. Winthrop himself dwelt at length on the "special commission" God had given the settlers of Massachusetts, a commission that obliged them to be "knitt together in the work as one man." In *The Puritan Dilemma: The Story of John Winthrop*, I focused on the speech in explicating the Puritans' view of their mission in the New World. I think I was right to do so. The Puritans certainly thought that they were up to something special. But many years after writing that biography, in reading accounts of earlier English voyages to the New World, I came across things that made me question whether Winthrop's speech was as special as I had supposed. I have explained why in the brief essay called "John Winthrop's Vision."

Another example. After studying the extant writings of Benjamin Franklin, I had to write a biography of him, too. When you spend years with your head buried in a man's papers, you get a strong urge to tell others about him, especially when you have found him doing and think-

ing things that you admire. Some reviewers called my biography a tribute, and I guess it was. Franklin is truly my hero, and so is Washington,
two men for whom my admiration never stops growing. Recently, while
rereading some of Franklin's correspondence, I was impressed by the way
he had continually to decline doing things that the public wanted him to
do. There was a striking resemblance between the two men that I had
not noticed before: they both knew when and why to say no. "The Power
of Negative Thinking" tries to explain that characteristic. Another, "The
End of Franklin's Pragmatism," assesses more closely the situations where
Franklin, famous for the practical intelligence he brought to public problems, would draw a line in the sand and say "no farther."

Franklin, Washington, and Winthrop were heroes because of their
leadership. The same is true of William Penn, who like Winthrop
founded an American colony. He could not personally guide his colony
as Winthrop guided his, but the contours of his life help to explain much
of what happened there. Penn was another surprise to me when I began
to study his collected writings and correspondence. I was used to Quakers
who endured their sufferings stoically. This one was the son of an admiral
and a friend of the royal family, someone who was not to be meddled with
lightly. It was refreshing to observe his behavior when he was arrested in
London for preaching in the streets. Instead of appealing to the "inner
light," he patronized the judges, lectured them on the law, and left the
court with a sneer when sentenced to a term in Newgate Prison, where
he knew he could not be kept for long. He was a strange sort of leader
for a humble people. And he was able to provide a refuge for them when
he collected a large parcel of America in payment for sums his father had
lent the king.

Many of the other people celebrated here were heroes or heroines, at
least for me, by virtue of the same ability to say no that I find in Washington and Franklin. But they said it, not from positions of leadership or
command, but in resistance to what society or its custodians demanded of
them. That is the point of the essay "Dangerous Books" and, in a different
way, of the one that follows, "The Unyielding Indian." The Antifederalists, who opposed ratification of the Constitution, provide another case
in point. They deserve to be called heroes because their opposition led

to the adoption of the first ten amendments of the Constitution, our Bill of Rights. But the fundamental source of their opposition, I believe, lay in a basically insoluble problem to which the Constitution offered what was not really a solution but a workable bypass. I have preceded the piece on the Antifederalists with one analyzing that problem, the problem of representing the people, in the traditional American sense of representation, in a national government. I hope that this will make the Antifederalist opposition more comprehensible and that it may have some resonance for the operation and meaning of our federal system today.

Several pieces deal with the Puritans and their descendants in the decades after Winthrop led them ashore. They were heroes for me because they had the courage of their convictions, but not all the essays deal with their heroism. One tries to rescue them from the cartoonish prudishness of their "historical" image. Following it is the story of a Puritan heiress that exemplifies their frank recognition of the role of sex in the validation of marriage. My essay on Michael Wigglesworth suggests that the caricature may not be all wrong, but tries to clarify the patterns of thought behind their seemingly killjoy behavior.

The Salem witch trials are doubtless the most infamous episode of Puritan history. I have tried to explain here how the trials happened and how they produced a hero and heroine, both Puritan, who had the courage to say no at the cost of their lives. And because witch trials have had their counterpart in later American history, I have offered the aftermath of Salem in Massachusetts as a challenge to our complacency and complicity in the witch hunts and judicial murders of later days.

That two Puritans had the courage to defy other Puritans should not surprise us. Taking a stand on matters of principle was a Puritan trademark. But the force of popular belief in witchcraft and its powers, after the laws ceased to recognize it, did surprise this historian. The eighteenth century was the century of the Enlightenment, when (we are told) reason triumphed over superstition, when the natural displaced the supernatural, when the rights of the people threatened the thrones of kings. To the philosophers of the Enlightenment, the creation of the American republic embodied the application of reason to politics. And the greatest exemplar of the Enlightenment in America, if not in the world, Benjamin

Franklin, was present at the creation. Also present in Philadelphia was witchcraft, the murder of a supposed witch by a mob in the streets outside the hall where the apostles of reason were creating the United States Constitution. When I stumbled upon this incident, it astounded me. It was a shock that it could have happened, but more of a shock that none of the famous men inside the hall thought it worthy of notice in any of their surviving papers—no expressions of revulsion, no anger, no reaction at all. I have reproduced the only records of the incident in the piece I have called "Postcript." And I remain puzzled by this unremarked survival of gross superstition in action alongside enlightenment in action.

Only one hero in my gallery comes close to fitting Franklin's unflattering description: Christopher Columbus, subject of the first selection. Except in his daring to go where others feared to, he does not meet my criteria for a hero. But how could I leave him out? My own heroes were in some sense beneficiaries of his and his successors' taking "life and goods together" from the people they encountered in the New World. We are accessories after the fact, however remotely.

The last essay, like so many of the others, is an appreciation, a tribute. Perry Miller transformed modern understanding of the Puritans and, as mentor and friend, transformed me. I hold him personally responsible for whatever is new and true that I may have learned or taught about early America, in these essays or anywhere else.

—*Edmund S. Morgan*
New Haven, Connecticut
July 2008

Part One

———————————

THE CONQUERORS

CHAPTER ONE

———

The Conquerors

IN THE YEAR 1513 a group of men led by Vasco Núñez de Balboa marched across the Isthmus of Panama and discovered the Pacific Ocean. They had been looking for it—they knew it existed—and, familiar as they were with oceans, they had no difficulty in recognizing it when they saw it. On their way, however, they saw a good many things they had not been looking for and were not familiar with. When they returned to Spain to tell what they had seen, it was not a simple matter to find words for everything.

For example, they had killed a large and ferocious wild animal. They called it a tiger, although there were no tigers in Spain and none of the men had ever seen one before. Listening to their story was Peter Martyr, member of the King's Council for the Indies and possessor of an insatiable curiosity about the new land that Spain was uncovering in the west. How, the learned man asked them, did they know that the ferocious animal was a tiger? They answered "that they knewe it by the spottes, fiercenesse, agilitie, and such other markes and tokens whereby auncient writers have described the Tyger." It was a good answer. Men, confronted with things they do not recognize, turn to the writings of those who have had a wider experience. And in 1513 it was still assumed that the ancient writers had had a wider experience than those who came after them.

Columbus himself had made the assumption. His discoveries posed for him, as for others, a problem of identification. It seemed to be a question not so much of giving names to new lands as of finding the proper old names, and the same was true of the things that the new lands contained. Cruising through the Caribbean, enchanted by the beauty and variety of what he saw, Columbus assumed that the strange plants and trees were strange only because he was insufficiently versed in the writings of men who did know them. "I am the saddest man in the world," he wrote, "because I do not recognize them."

By 1524, when Gonzalo Fernández de Oviedo, a Spanish royal official, sat down to write about the wonders of the new land, explorers were assuming a more skeptical attitude toward the knowledge that could be gained from the ancients. Oviedo had just returned to Spain from several years in Darien, on the isthmus earlier crossed by Balboa. He, too, had encountered the alleged tiger, but he was not so sure that it was in fact a tiger. "I will not obstinately stand in opinyon," he said, "whether these beastes bee tygers or Panthers, or of the number of any other such beastes of spotted heare." It was quite possible, he thought, that this was "sum other newe beaste unknowen to the owlde wryters," for by 1524 it had become clear that "thys great parte of the worlde was unknowen to the antiquitie."

As the century wore on and the caravels of Spain probed the dimensions of the new land, it gradually expanded into a New World, and the challenge to traditional ideas expanded with it. The Jesuit missionary José de Acosta, sailing to Peru in 1570, still thought it proper to prepare himself by reading what the old writers had said of lands in that latitude, and having read he feared the worst. The heat, they said, would be too great for human life, the sun too hot to bear. But arriving in Peru in what was summer there, the month of March, he found the weather so cold that he welcomed the chance to bask in the sun. "What could I else do then," he asked, "but laugh at Aristotle's . . . Philosophie, seeing that in that place and at that season, whenas all should be scorched with heat, according to his rules, I, and all my companions were a colde?"

America released Father Acosta from Aristotle's error, and it almost released him from the Bible, too. A better botanist than Columbus, he recognized that many of the plants and animals of the New World were unique, unlike anything known to the ancients from their experience of Europe, Asia, and Africa. And he asked himself how this could be. How did they get to America and not to Europe? It occurred to him that they might have come into existence there. But if this was the case, he realized, it made the whole story of Noah's ark a little shaky; "neither was it then necessary to save all sorts of birds and beasts, if others were to be created anew. Moreover, wee could not affirme that the creation of the world was made and finished in six days, if there were yet other kinds to make, and specially perfit beasts, and no lesse excellent than those that are knowen unto us."

Father Acosta, discerning a few of the consequences of his daring thought, drew back from it, as did everyone else. He concluded at length that the universal deluge had been followed by an immediate dispersal from the ark and that some animals went in one direction and some in another. Thus he preserved Noah and the deluge and left the Bible unassailed as a source of historical knowledge.

We need not deride Father Acosta's reluctance to give up the world that he knew from books. Only idiots escape entirely from the world that the past bequeaths. The discovery of America opened a new world, full of new things and new possibilities for those with eyes to see them. And Father Acosta saw many of them. But the New World did not erase the Old. Rather, the Old World for several centuries determined what men saw in the New and what they did with it. What America became after 1492 depended both on what men found there and on what they expected to find, both on what America actually was and on what old writers and old experience led men to think it was or ought to be or could be made to be.

I cannot attempt here to give an account of what America became or was made to become by the men who invaded the continent after 1492, but I hope to tell a small early part of the story, a first chapter that may stand as an emblem or symbol of the whole. I want to describe Europe's first encounter with America on the island of Española, known also as Hispaniola and as Haiti. I want to suggest how the ideas that Columbus brought with him shaped the lives of the people of Española, which I believe will also suggest how those ideas were to affect the history of the nearby continents of North and South America.

DURING THE DECADE before 1492, as Columbus nursed a growing urge to sail west to the Indies, he was studying the old writers to find out what the world and its people were like. He read the *Ymago Mundi* of Pierre d'Ailly, a French cardinal of the early fifteenth century, the travels of Marco Polo and of Sir John Mandeville, Pliny's *Natural History*, and the *Historia Rerum Ubique Gestarum* of Aeneas Sylvius Piccolomini (Pope Pius II). Columbus was not a scholarly man. He could take a ship where no one had dared go before and bring it back again, but he did so by the dead reckoning of the practical sailor, not by the scholarly methods of celestial navigation. He probably learned to read only after he had grown up. And while he had the genius of simplicity, the nerve to act on a thought, he never shone at the things one learned from books. Yet he studied *these* books, made hundreds of marginal notations in them, and came out with ideas about the world that were characteristically simple and strong and sometimes wrong, the kind of ideas that the self-educated person gains from independent reading and clings to in defiance of what anyone else tries to tell him.

The strongest one was a wrong one—namely, that the distance between Europe and the eastern shore of Asia was short. According to Cardinal d'Ailly, Columbus noted, Aristotle and Seneca both thought that the ocean separating Spain from China could be traversed in a few days. And his own erroneous calculations of the small size of the earth led him to a similar conclusion. Although he was familiar enough with the waters of the eastern Atlantic to know that the distance could not be quite as short as the cardinal said, he thought it was much less than most of his own contemporaries supposed. He believed that Spain was closer to China westward than eastward.

Columbus never abandoned this conviction. And before he set out to prove it by sailing west from Spain, he studied his books to find out all he could about the lands that he would be visiting: China, Japan, and India, the lands known to Europe as the Indies. From Marco Polo, the Venetian who had traveled there two centuries earlier, he learned that the Indies were rich in gold, silver, pearls, jewels, and spices. The Great Khan, whose empire stretched from the Arctic to the Indian Ocean, had displayed to Marco Polo a wealth and majesty that dwarfed the splendors of the courts of Europe. The khan's family of four thousand retainers dined together in one great hall from golden dishes; his twelve thousand barons were dressed in cloth of gold with belts of gold. When traveling, he slept in tents that could hold two thousand men and that were wrought with gold and lined with ermine and sable.

Marco Polo also had things to say about the ordinary people of the Far East. Those in the province of Mangi, where they grew ginger, were averse to war and so had fallen an easy prey to the khan. On Nangama, an island off the coast, described as having "great plentie of spices," the people were far from averse to war: they were anthropophagi—man-eaters—who devoured their captives. There were, in fact, man-eating people in several of the offshore islands, and in many islands both men and women dressed themselves with only a small scrap of cloth over their genitals. On the island of Discorsia, in spite of the fact that they made fine cotton cloth, the people went entirely naked. In one place there were two islands where men and women were segregated, the women on one island, the men on the other.

Marco Polo occasionally slipped into fables like this last one, but most of what he had to say about the Indies was the result of actual observation. Sir John Mandeville's travels, on the other hand, were a hoax—there was no such man—and the places he claimed to have visited in the 1300s were fantastically filled with one-eyed men and one-footed men, dog-faced men, men with two faces, and men with no faces. But the author of the hoax did draw on the reports of enough genuine travelers to make some of his stories plausible, and he also drew on a legend as old as human dreams, the legend of a golden age when men were good. He told of an island where the people lived without malice or guile, without covetousness or lechery or gluttony, wishing for none of the riches of this world. They were not Christians, but they lived by the golden rule. A man who had decided to see the Indies for himself could hardly have failed to be stirred by the thought of finding such a people.

Columbus learned from books what to expect of the Indies. But besides his expectations of gold and silver and spices, of man-eating monsters and guileless men, he also carried with him some ideas of what he would do about these things when he found them. He surely expected to bring back some of the gold that was supposed to be so plentiful. The spice trade was one of the most lucrative in Europe, and he expected to bring back spices. But what did he propose to do about the people in possession of these treasures?

Since he did not know that the Tartar dynasty of khans had fallen more than a century before, he probably intended to establish trading relations with countries belonging to the Great Khan. But he also intended to take possession himself of at least some of the lands he encountered. When he set out, he carried with him a commission from the king and queen of Spain, empowering him "to discover and acquire certain islands and mainland in the ocean sea" and to be "Admiral and Viceroy and Governor therein." If the king and Columbus expected to assume dominion over any of the Indies or other lands en route, they must have had some ideas, not only about the Indies but also about themselves, to warrant the expectation. What had they to offer that would make their dominion welcome? Or if they proposed to impose their rule by force, how could they justify such a step, let alone carry it out? The answer is that they had two things: they had Christianity and they had civilization.

Christianity has meant many things to many men, and its role in the European conquest and occupation of America was varied. But in 1492 to Columbus there was probably nothing very complicated about it. His simplicity of mind would have reduced it to a matter of corrupt human beings, destined for eternal damnation, redeemed by a merciful savior. Christ saved those who believed in him, and it was the duty of Christians to spread his gospel and thus rescue the heathens from the fate that would otherwise await them.

Although Christianity was in itself a sufficient justification for dominion, Columbus would also carry civilization to the Indies; and this, too, was a gift that he and his contemporaries considered adequate recompense for anything they might take. When people talked about civilization—or civility, as they usually called it—they seldom specified precisely what they meant. Civility was closely associated with Christianity, but the two were not identical. Whereas Christianity was always accompanied by civility, the Greeks and Romans had had civility without Christianity.

One way to define civility was by its opposite, barbarism. Originally the word "barbarian" had simply meant "foreigner," to a Greek someone who was not Greek, to a Roman someone who was not Roman. By the fifteenth or sixteenth century, it meant someone not only foreign but with manners and customs of which civil persons disapproved. North Africa became known as Barbary, a sixteenth-century geographer explained, "because the people be barbarous, not onely in language, but in manners and customs." Parts of the Indies, from Marco Polo's description, had to be civil, but other parts were obviously barbarous, for example, the lands where people went naked. Whatever civility meant, it meant clothes.

But there was a little more to it than that, and there still is. Civil people distinguished themselves by the pains they took to order their lives. They organized their society to produce the elaborate food, clothing, buildings, and other equipment characteristic of their manner of living. They had strong governments to protect property, to protect good persons from evil ones, to protect the manners and customs that differentiated civil people from barbarians. It was conceded that barbarians might have governments of a sort but insufficient to curb their depraved habits or to nurture better ones. The superior clothing, housing, food, and protection that attached to civilization made it seem to the European a gift worth giving to the ill-clothed, ill-housed, and ungoverned barbarians of the world.

The Europeans' knowledge of barbarians did not all come from books. They had had contact with nearby Barbary itself and also with the much more barbarous Canary Islands, which they had rediscovered in the fourteenth century. By 1492 the Spaniards had subdued every island but Tenerife to Christianity, civilization, and slavery.

Slavery was an ancient instrument of civilization, and in the fifteenth century it had been revived as a way to deal with barbarians who refused to accept Christianity and the rule of civilized government. Through slavery they could be made to abandon their bad habits, put on clothes, and reward their instructors with a lifetime of work. The Spanish government frowned on the enslavement of submissive natives, and in the Canaries it was mostly the recalcitrant who became slaves. But not all Europeans, or indeed all Spaniards, discriminated between submissive and nonsubmissive barbarians. Throughout the fifteenth century, as the Portuguese explored the coast of Africa, large numbers of well-clothed sea captains brought civilization to naked savages by carrying them off to the slave markets of Seville and Lisbon.

Since Columbus had lived in Lisbon and sailed in Portuguese vessels to the Gold Coast of Africa, he was not unfamiliar with barbarians. He had seen for himself that the torrid zone could support human life, clothed as well as unclothed, and he had observed how pleased barbarians were with trinkets on which civilized Europeans set small value, such as the little bells that falconers placed on hawks. Before setting off on his voyage, he laid in a store of hawk's bells. If the barbarous people he expected to find in the Indies should think civilization and Christianity an insufficient reward for submission to Spain, perhaps hawk's bells would help.

Columbus sailed from Palos de la Frontera on Friday the third of August, 1492, reached the Canary Islands six days later, and stayed there for a month to finish outfitting his ships. He left on September 6, and five weeks later, in about the place he expected, he found the Indies. What else could it be but the Indies? There on the shore were the naked people. With hawk's bells and beads he made their acquaintance and found some of them wearing gold nose plugs. It all added up. He had found the Indies. And not only that. He had found a land over which he would have no difficulty in establishing Spanish dominion, for the people showed him an immediate veneration. He had been there only two days, coasting along the shores of the islands, when he was able to hear the natives crying in loud voices, "Come and see the men who have come from heaven; bring them food and drink." If Columbus thought he was able to translate the language in two days' time, it is not surprising that what he heard in it was what he wanted to hear or that what he saw was what he wanted to see—namely, the Indies, filled with people eager to submit to their new admiral and viceroy.

Columbus made four voyages to America, during which he succeeded in exploring an astonishingly large area of the Caribbean and a part of the northern coast of South America. Everything he saw fitted his conception of the Indies. Cuba, he believed, was a peninsula on the mainland of China, a part of the province of Mangi; he named the easternmost point of it Cape Alpha et Omega and contemplated the awesome fact that the entire landmass of the world stretched continuously westward between him and Cape St. Vincent in Portugal, the westernmost extension of Europe.

From the moment of his first landfall, Columbus was looking for spices and gold. The reason he was so distraught at not recognizing trees and plants was that he thought that some of them must be valuable spices, which he ought to bring back with him in quantity. But gold was unquestionably more important than spices or even than pearls and precious stones, and Columbus had his heart set on finding gold. "Gold," he rhapsodized, "is most excellent . . . and he who possesses it may do what he will in the world, and may so attain as to bring souls to paradise." At every island the first thing he inquired about was gold, taking heart from every trace of it he found. And at Haiti he found enough to convince him that this was Ophir, the country to which Solomon and Jehosophat had sent for gold and silver. Since its lush vegetation reminded him of Castile, he renamed it Española, the Spanish island, which was later latinized as Hispaniola.

Española appealed to Columbus from his first glimpse of it. From aboard ship it was possible to make out rich fields waving with grass. There were good harbors, lovely sand beaches, and "trees of a thousand kinds, all laden with fruit, which the admiral believed to be spices and nutmegs, but they were not ripe and he did not recognize them." The people were shy and fled whenever the caravels approached the shore, but Columbus gave orders "that they should take some, treat them well and make them lose their fear, that some gain might be made, since, considering the beauty of the land, it could not be but that there was gain to be got." And indeed there was. Although the amount of gold worn by the natives was even less than the amount of clothing, it gradually became apparent that there was gold to be had. One man possessed some that had been pounded into gold leaf. Another appeared with a gold belt. Some produced nuggets for the admiral. Española accordingly became the first European colony in America. Although Columbus had formally taken possession of every island he found, the act was mere ritual until he reached Española. Here he began the European occupation of the New World, and here his European ideas and attitudes began their transformation of land and people.

The people of Española were the handsomest that Columbus had encountered in the New World and so attractive in character that he found it hard to praise them enough. "They are the best people in the world," he said, "and beyond all the mildest." They cultivated a bit of cassava for bread and made a bit of cottonlike cloth from the fibers of the gossampine tree. But most of the day they spent like children idling away their time from morning to night seemingly without a care in the world. Once they saw that Columbus meant them no harm, they outdid one another in bringing him anything he wanted. Never had there been such generosity. It was impossible to believe, he reported, "that anyone has seen a people with such kind hearts and so ready to give the Christians all that they possess, and when the Christians arrive, they run at once to bring them everything."

To Columbus the people of Española seemed like relics of the golden age. On the basis of what he told Peter Martyr, who recorded his voyages, Martyr wrote, "If we shall not bee ashamed to confesse the Trueth, they seeme to live in that golden worlde of the which olde writers speake so much, wherein menne lived simply and innocently without enforcement of lawes, without quarreling, judges, and libelles, content onely to satisfie nature, without further vexation for knowledge of things to come."

As the idyllic Arawak Indians of Española conformed to one ancient picture, their enemies the Caribs conformed to another that Columbus had read of, the anthropophagi. According to the Arawaks, the Caribs or Cannibals were man-eaters, and as such their name eventually entered the English language. The Caribs lived on islands of their own and met every European approach with poisoned arrows, which men and women together fired in showers. They not only were fierce but, by comparison with the Arawaks, also seemed more energetic, more industrious, and, it might even be said, sadly enough, more civil. After Columbus succeeded in entering one of their settlements on his second voyage, a member of the expedition reported, "This people seemed to us to be more civil than those who were in the other islands we have visited, although they all have dwellings of straw, but these have them better made and better provided with supplies, and in them were more signs of industry, both of men and women."

Columbus had no doubts about how to proceed, either with the lovable but lazy Arawaks or with the hateful but industrious Cannibals. He had come to take possession and to establish dominion. The Arawaks of Española would obviously make good subjects. He had no sooner set eyes on them than he began making plans. In almost the same breath he described their gentleness and innocence and then went on to assure the king and queen of Spain, "They have no arms and are all naked and without any knowledge of war, and very cowardly, so that a thousand of them would not face three. And they are also fitted to be ruled and to be set to work, to cultivate the land and to do all else that may be necessary, and you may build towns and teach them to go clothed and adopt our customs."

So much for the golden age. Columbus had not yet prescribed the method by which the Arawaks would be set to work, but he had a pretty clear idea of how to handle the Caribs. On his second voyage, after capturing a few of them, he sent them in slavery to Spain, as samples of what he hoped would be a regular trade. They were obviously intelligent, and in Spain they might "be led to abandon that inhuman custom which they have of eating men, and there in Castile, learning the language, they will much more readily receive baptism and secure the welfare of their souls." The way to handle the slave trade, Columbus suggested, was to send ships from Spain loaded with cattle (there were no native domestic animals on Española), and he would return the ships loaded with Cannibals. This plan of replacing Cannibals with cattle was never put into operation, partly because the Spanish sovereigns did not approve it and partly because the Cannibals did not approve it. They defended themselves so successfully with their poisoned arrows that the Spaniards decided to withhold the blessings of civilization from them and to concentrate their efforts on the seemingly more amenable Arawaks of Española.

The process of civilizing the Arawaks got under way in earnest after the *Santa Maria* ran aground, Christmas Day, 1492, off Caracol Bay. The local leader in that part of Española, Guacanagari, rushed to the scene and with his people helped the Spaniards to salvage everything aboard. Once again Columbus was overjoyed with the remarkable natives. They are, he wrote, "so full of love and without greed, and suitable for every purpose, that I assure your Highnesses that I believe there is no better land in the world, and they are always smiling." While the salvage operations were going on, canoes full of Arawaks from other parts of the island came in bearing gold. Guacanagari "was greatly delighted to see the admiral joyful and understood that he desired much gold." Thereafter it arrived in amounts calculated to console the admiral for the loss of the *Santa Maria*, which had to be scuttled. He decided to make his permanent headquarters on the spot and accordingly ordered a fortress to be built, with a tower and a large moat.

What followed is a long, complicated, and unpleasant story. Columbus returned to Spain to bring the news of his discoveries. The Spanish monarchs who had backed his expedition were less impressed than he with what he had found, but he was able to round up a large expedition of Spanish colonists to return with him and help exploit the riches of the Indies. At Española the new settlers built forts and towns and began helping themselves to all the gold they could find among the natives. These creatures of the golden age remained generous. But precisely because they did not value possessions, they had little to turn over. When gold was not forthcoming, the Europeans began killing. Some of the natives struck back and hid out in the hills. But in 1495 a punitive expedition rounded up fifteen hundred of them, and five hundred were shipped off to the slave markets of Seville.

The natives, seeing what was in store for them, dug up their own crops of cassava and destroyed their supplies in hopes that the resulting famine would drive the Spaniards out. It was a shrewd strategy because a civil man reportedly ate more in one day than a whole family of barbarians in a month. But it did not work. The Spaniards were not to be shaken off. They were sure there was more gold in the island than the natives had yet found, and they determined to make them dig it out. Columbus built more forts throughout the island and decreed that every Arawak of fourteen years or over was to furnish a hawk's bell full of gold dust every three months. The various local leaders were made responsible for seeing that the tribute was paid. In regions where gold was not to be had, twenty-five pounds of woven or spun cotton could be substituted for the hawk's bell of gold dust.

Unfortunately Española was not Ophir, and it did not have anything like the amount of gold that Columbus thought it did. The pieces that the natives had at first presented him were the accumulation of many years. To fill their quotas by washing in the riverbeds was all but impossible, even with continual daily labor. But the demand was unrelenting, and those who sought to escape it by fleeing to the mountains were hunted down with dogs taught to kill. A few years later Peter Martyr was able to report that the natives "beare this yoke of servitude with an evill will, but yet they beare it."

The tribute system, for all its injustice and cruelty, preserved something of the Arawaks' old social arrangements: they retained their old leaders under control of the king's viceroy, and royal directions to the viceroy might ultimately have worked some mitigation of their hardships. But the Spanish settlers of Española did not care for this centralized method of exploitation. They wanted a share of the land and its people, and when their demands were not met they revolted against the government of Columbus. In 1499 they forced him to abandon the system of obtaining tribute through the Arawak chieftains for a new one in which both land and people were turned over to individual Spaniards for exploitation as they saw fit. This was the beginning of the system of "repartimientos" or "encomiendas" later extended to other areas of Spanish occupation. With its inauguration Columbus's economic control of Española effectively ceased, and even his political authority was revoked later in the same year when the king appointed a new governor.

For the Arawaks the new system of forced labor meant that they did more work, wore more clothes, and said more prayers (their owners were supposed to convert them). Peter Martyr could rejoice that "so many thousands of men are received to bee the sheepe of Christes flocke." But these were sheep prepared for slaughter. If we may believe Bartolomé de Las Casas, a Dominican who spent many years among them, they were tortured, burned, and fed to the dogs by their masters. They died from overwork and from new European diseases. They killed themselves. And they took pains to avoid having children. Life was not fit to live, and they stopped living. From a population of 100,000 at the lowest estimate in 1492, there remained in 1514 about 32,000 Arawaks in Española. In 1542, according to Las Casas, only 200 were left. In their place had appeared slaves imported from Africa. The people of the golden age had been exterminated.

Why? What is the meaning of this tale of horror? Why is the first chapter of American history an atrocity story? Bartolomé de Las Casas, who watched it happen had a simple answer, greed: "The cause why the Spanishe have destroyed such an infinitie of soules, hath been onely, that they have helde it for their last scope and marke to gette golde." The answer is true enough. But we shall have to go further than Spanish greed to understand why American history began this way. The Spanish had no monopoly on greed. There is very little reason to suppose that if the English or French had been first on the scene the results would have been different. Enslavement, torture, and murder on a large scale, not to mention catastrophic epidemics, have often accompanied Western occupation of countries inhabited by people lacking in Christianity, civility, and guns. In most cases the cause may be identified as greed. Perhaps we can begin to understand not only Spanish greed but Western greed in general, not only this first atrocity story of American history but a number of later, less spectacular atrocities, if we look at the victims through the eyes of the victors.

As I have already mentioned, from the moment they set foot on Española, the Spaniards noted that the Indians were surprisingly unattached to the things of this world. They were content to eat almost anything that happened to come along, including spiders, lizards, and worms. But by Spanish standards they ate very little of anything. They spun and wove a little cotton, but preferred to go naked. Even their houses were flimsy, temporary structures. Because they had no desire to acquire or keep anything for which they felt no present need, they were generous beyond belief; and, without the covetousness or acquisitiveness attendant upon worldly appetites, they seemed able to live together happily and peacefully, unassisted by the restraints of government.

The Indians' austere way of life could not fail to win the admiration of the invaders, for self-denial was an ancient virtue in Western culture. The Greeks and Romans had constructed philosophies and the Christians a religion around it. The man who would imitate Christ had to deny himself, give his all to the poor, love his neighbor as himself, curb his natural appetites, and set his heart on God alone. The monastic life was an organized effort to live this way. The Indians, and especially the Arawaks, gave no sign of thinking much about God, but otherwise they seemed to have attained the monastic virtues. They had also attained an impressive freedom. Plato had emphasized again and again that freedom was to be reached by restraining one's needs, and the Arawaks had done just that. According to Peter Martyr, who sometimes despaired of his own countrymen's debilitating self-indulgence, the Indians' "contentation with the benefites of nature doth playnly declare that men may lead a free and happye life without tables, table clothes, carpettes, napkins, and towels, with suche other innumerable. . . ." Europeans would do well to learn from these children of nature, who scorned superfluities, he said, "as hindrances of their sweete libertie."

But even as they admired the Indians' simplicity, the Europeans were troubled by it, troubled and offended. Innocence never fails to offend, never fails to invite attack, and the Indians seemed the most innocent people anyone had ever seen. Their freedom from acquisitive instincts was delightful to behold but disturbingly effortless. Without the help of Christianity or of civilization, they had attained virtues that Europeans liked to think of as the proper outcome of Christianity and civilization. The fury with which the Spaniards assaulted the Arawaks even after they had enslaved them must surely have been in part a blind impulse to crush an innocence that seemed to deny the Europeans' cherished assumption of their own civilized, Christian superiority over naked, heathen barbarians.

The affront went deep, and the cruelty and greed it provoked were symptoms of a conflict that has lasted in one form or another to the present day and can end only when the West has achieved what is now known as "modernization" of the entire world. The life of the Arawaks, for all its admirable simplicity and austerity, was incompatible with the kind of existence that Europeans, for all their praise of self-denial, thought right. The self-denial that civilized Christians were supposed to practice did not eventuate in nakedness. Christians might deny themselves silks and velvets, but they must not deny themselves clothes; they might embrace poverty but not idleness; they might fast, but they must not neglect to work for bread. Europeans, while telling themselves to curb their appetites, had organized a civilization that required them to extract from nature a greater abundance of goods than the Arawaks cared to have.

The Arawaks were actually skilled agriculturists; with a minimum of

labor, they made their island support an enormous population, and with
their apparent intelligence, they could certainly have produced more
food, more clothing, better shelters. But their needs were small, and they
wanted no more than they needed. They preferred to spend their days in
what seemed to the European mere play and idleness. When European
confronted Indian, then, friction could scarcely have failed to develop.

We must, of course, remember that European production in the fifteenth century was nowhere near as efficient as it has since become.
By modern standards Europeans of Columbus's time lived an unorga-
nized and ineffective life. Indeed, the upper classes, when they were not
busy fighting holy wars, aspired to a way of life that required no more
work than an Arawak would do. But by comparison with the Arawaks,
fifteenth-century Europeans made spectacularly high demands, if not
on themselves, at least on those who stood in the lower ranks of society.
They had developed ideas about work that were wholly incompatible
with the seeming fecklessness of the Arawaks of Española. Behind the
Spanish assault on the Indians lay a conviction that men must work, if
not for themselves then for their betters, in the interests of civility and
Christianity. It was this conviction that allowed Peter Martyr to hymn
the Indians' asceticism and love of liberty but then go on to censure
them because the object of both virtues was mere "play and idleness."
For the same reason Columbus could admire the Indians even while he
made plans to enslave them.

The Spanish government was not unmindful of what was going on in
its new lands across the sea and made periodic efforts to control the abuse
of the Indians. It even authorized a few abortive experiments in setting
the Indians free. But it could not condone a liberty that resulted in idleness. The only way to keep Indians at work, it seemed, was to make them
work for Spaniards. In 1517 when a team of Jeronymite friars quizzed the
oldest Spanish inhabitants of Española about the capacities and capabili-
ties of the natives, there was unanimous agreement that the Arawaks were
unwilling to work unless forced to. They must be made to work for Spain,
as the Spanish government had proclaimed in 1513, "to prevent their living in idleness and to assure their learning to live and govern themselves
like Christians."

   The Spanish determination that the Indians should not live in idleness was reinforced in Española by Columbus's expectations of the country he thought he had reached and by the similar expectations of other Spaniards. The true Indies were already geared to the European economy: merchants for centuries had been sending the products of European labor eastward to the Orient in exchange for spices and other treasures. Española in the role of Ophir was expected to yield its riches to Columbus as it had to Solomon. When it became evident that Española was not Ophir and that America was not the Indies but a new world, that whole new world had to be transformed. It had to be organized and exploited to produce the things expected of it.

   Columbus's first method of exploiting Española, when the natives failed to produce what was expected of them, was crude: to ship the inhabitants to Spain as slaves was to make no more effective use of the island than the neighboring Caribs did in occasionally harvesting a crop of Arawaks to eat. To put them to work under their chieftains was far more productive. To give them at last to Spanish masters who could extract more work than the chieftains could was still more effective—except that the Arawaks died. Probably more died from other causes than from overwork, but it would be hard to say how much work was overwork for an Arawak. Work had not been an important part of human life in Española before Columbus.

   That the Indians were destroyed by Spanish greed is true. But greed is simply one of the uglier names we give to the driving force of modern civilization. We usually prefer less pejorative names for it. Call it the profit motive, or free enterprise, or the work ethic, or the American way, or, as the Spanish did, civility. Before we become too outraged at the behavior of Columbus and his followers, before we identify ourselves too easily with the lovable Arawaks, we have to ask whether we could really get along without greed and everything that goes with it. Yes, a few of us, a few eccentrics, might manage to live for a time like the Arawaks. But the modern world could not have put up with the Arawaks any more than the Spanish could. The story moves us, offends us, but perhaps the more so because we have to recognize ourselves not in the Arawaks but in Columbus and his followers.

The Spanish reaction to the Arawak was Western civilization's reaction to the barbarian: the Arawaks answered the Europeans' description of men, just as Balboa's tiger answered the description of a tiger, and being men they had to be made to live as men were supposed to live. But the Arawaks' view of man was something different, and they were unable to recognize themselves as men in the role in which the invaders cast them. They were offered civility in the shape of clothing that they did not want, in return for work that they did not wish to perform.

Civility and Christianity in the form of a cotton shirt and baptism were not adequate recompense for the liberty without which they had no will to live. They died not merely from cruelty, torture, murder, and disease but also, in the last analysis, because they could not be persuaded to fit the European conception of what they ought to be. Since they would not or could not accept the place assigned them in the Old World scheme for America, they had to give place to new men, African or European, who would make the country yield what was expected of it. The Arawaks of Española were the first to be pushed aside in this way but by no means the last. Although their story was only a small early incident in the Europeans' total transformation of the Western Hemisphere, and ultimately of the world, it epitomized that transformation. It was indeed the first chapter of American history, as we know it, the first chapter of *our* history.

—*Previously unpublished*

Part Two

———————

PURITANS, WITCHES, AND QUAKERS

CHAPTER TWO

Dangerous Books

SEVERAL YEARS AGO, at a meeting of book collectors, I was brought up short by the remark of a man who valued books as most of us do. It was at Brown University's John Carter Brown Library, and one of the luminaries present was a gentleman, considerably older than I, whom I respected and revered but frequently quarreled with. We were both members of several historical societies at which I had read papers. At the conclusion of each of my talks, he had risen to denounce me for a young radical and had pointed out with characteristic vigor that my papers were full of the most utter nonsense. "I admire," he used to say, "the thoroughness of Mr. Morgan's research, which is matched only by the absurdity of his conclusions."

I don't think he thought I was a communist or an anarchist, but perhaps that I believed in free love or the New Deal or something on that scale of monstrosity. There had, nevertheless, grown up between us, at least I like to think there had, a certain affection and respect of the kind that may take place between people who recognize each other as opposites.

On this occasion I was in a happy position of neutrality. I had not delivered the paper, and consequently he did not feel obliged to denounce me. I therefore thought that this might be a rare opportunity for conversation in which we might find ourselves in agreement. I discovered him examining a case of books in which was displayed a particularly handsome copy of *Purchas his Pilgrims* (1625). He was intent on his examination of the book and made a fine figure as he bent over the case, for he had a leonine head of long white hair that contrasted dramatically with the dark woodwork. I stood beside him for a time in silence, and then ventured the only remark that I could think of and one that seemed thoroughly innocuous—namely, that this copy of *Purchas* was remarkably clean, looking as though it had just come off the press.

As soon as I had spoken, he turned on me with eyes blazing and said yes, indeed it was, and he hoped that it would remain in that condition, unlike the books in the Harvard Library. "That's the tragic thing about the Harvard Library," he said, "that fellow Jackson* lets those professors go in there and *read* those books any old time they have a mind to."

I beat a hasty retreat. But it has often occurred to me since that my friend, who gave a great deal to the Harvard Library, the John Carter Brown, and many other libraries, was more right than he knew. He was a man who hated change in any form. And there is no more insidious instrument of change than a library in which professors or students or people in general are allowed to *read* the books.

In fact, in view of what books have done to change the world, it is strange that those who fear change have not succeeded in burning them all long since. The trouble with books is that people *will* read them. And when they do, they are bound to get new and dangerous ideas. Libraries are the great hothouses of change, where new ideas are nursed into being and then turned loose to do their work. And the ideas are not always benign. One thinks at once of Karl Marx, laboring through the musty volumes of the British Museum and emerging with those notions that turned the world upside down. Or the Bibliothèque Nationale in Paris—how much, one wonders, did its volumes contribute to the French Revolution?

But we need go no farther for examples than to your library or mine. First, I should like to say a little about the extraordinary way the Yale Library in the eighteenth century took command of the college, subverted the purposes for which it was founded, and transformed it into something utterly different (something, in my opinion, infinitely better, but I am not sure that the founders would agree).

Yale and the Yale Library were founded in 1701 by a group of Con-

* William Jackson, Harvard's distinguished curator of rare books, 1938–64.

necticut ministers who thought it was high time for the colony to have a college of its own. Connecticut Puritans had been talking about a college for years, for Puritanism was a bookish faith, and the Puritans thought that their leaders, whether in church or in state, ought to have a college education. In the seventeenth century Harvard had served the purpose, but Harvard was inconveniently located for Connecticut boys, and toward the end of the century uncomfortable rumors began to circulate about its orthodoxy. The Harvard faculty, it seemed, and notably the senior tutors, were reading the wrong kind of books and recommending them to the students, and everybody in Cambridge was getting fond of ideas that New Englanders were not supposed to be fond of.

The Puritans were not afraid of books. They had too much confidence in the rightness of their own views to worry about anyone's refuting them in print. And they were sure that neglect of reading was an invitation to that old deluder Satan, who might gain control of the souls of ignorant men. But if they were not afraid of books, the Puritans were afraid to let impressionable youth be taught by men who lacked the perspicacity to see that books by Anglicans were shallow and misleading, if not actually wicked. For it was Anglican books that the Harvard tutors had recommended—Anglican books that presumably espoused the insidious heresy known as Arminianism. Arminianism was the doctrine that man could help himself toward salvation. It implied that a man could alter God's eternal decrees and get to heaven on his own merits.

The Puritans, always prone to self-righteousness, were peculiarly susceptible to this heresy, and they were always on the alert for it. When they heard that it had penetrated Harvard, they became uneasy. Cotton Mather and Increase Mather tried their best to purge the college of it. When their efforts proved unsuccessful, they turned hopefully to the west, where Connecticut was at last roused to action. With the support of the Mathers and of other Bostonians who had been shocked by the turn of events at Harvard, Connecticut began a new college, dedicated to the preservation of both learning and orthodoxy.

It started at Killingworth, Connecticut, with two faculty members and not more than a dozen students. For the first six years there were no college buildings other than the rector's house. But there *was* a library.

The men who founded the college had realized that it might exist without buildings but not without a library, and they had contributed from their own private holdings enough volumes to get it started. It was not much of a library, consisting as it did of old dog-eared volumes that had come over with the first settlers and had already served two generations of ministers in Connecticut without generating new ideas in anybody. For thirteen years these books continued to serve, but in 1714 one of the well-wishers of the college arranged an extraordinary donation.

Jeremiah Dummer, a New England boy and a Harvard graduate, moved to England in 1708 and acted there as agent for the colonies of Massachusetts and Connecticut. Although his official duties did not require it, he also became an ardent propagandist and solicitor for both Harvard and Yale. Dummer recognized that what Yale needed more than anything else was books, and, since England was full of authors and patrons of authors, he undertook to persuade them to donate some of their favorite works to the college in the New World. There was an exotic attractiveness to the idea of planting civilization in the wilderness, and the English intellectuals were so moved by Dummer's appeal that no fewer than 180 of them contributed, including such leading figures as Sir Isaac Newton, Edmund Halley, Sir Hans Sloane, and Richard Steele. They sent more than 500 volumes, of which the first shipment, packed in nine boxes, arrived in September 1714.

The unpacking of the crates must have been a moment of singular excitement and curiosity for students and faculty. Here was an enormous variety of riches: Newton, Locke, and Boyle, Defoe, Addison and Steele, Sherlock, Tillotson, Chillingworth, Stillingfleet—names that had hitherto meant nothing in Connecticut and not much in the rest of New England were suddenly present in the original. None of those who first opened the volumes and leafed through them could have recognized the full dimensions of what had happened. A century of English literature, science, philosophy, and theology was spread before them. It was as though a group of men today had studied nothing but the textbooks of a hundred years ago and were suddenly confronted for the first time with Darwin, Marx, Hegel, Freud, and Einstein, all at one blow.

For many, of course, it was simply too much to comprehend. To be handed a hundred years' work to do may not be an altogether pleasing experience. And it was a long time before the full effect of the new books was felt. But New England was never the same after their arrival, and we can see the leaven beginning to work at once.

We can see it, for example, in a boy who rode down from Windsor to enter college two years later. In his sophomore year he discovered John Locke's *Essay concerning Human Understanding*. By his own account, he found "more satisfaction and pleasure in studying it than the most greedy miser in gathering up handfuls of silver and gold from some new discovered treasure." This was Jonathan Edwards, who would probably have changed any world he lived in. But the starting point of the revolution that Edwards made in New England religion was that volume of Locke. He saw that New England theology, as he had learned it from his father's sermons at Windsor, would not stand before the new philosophy of John Locke.

He went on to recast the Calvinism of his father to fit the new philosophy, and the result was a wholly different theology, which came to be known in New England as the New Divinity. It won Edwards worldwide fame, and it split New England Puritanism wide open. It lost Edwards his pulpit at Northampton, and it won him the presidency of Princeton. A hundred years later people were still arguing hotly about what it meant.

It took Edwards a lifetime to work out his theology after reading Locke, but within eight years of their arrival the new books produced a more spectacular result in a different group of readers. One of these was Samuel Johnson, a Guilford boy. Johnson graduated from college the year before the books arrived; but alumni could use the library, and Johnson read avidly in the new books. As an undergraduate he had studied the old system of logic taught from books that the founding fathers of New England had brought with them. His college notebooks survive, filled with the complicated propositions that summed up the whole of human knowledge for the academic mind of the seventeenth century. At the end of one of these notebooks he has written, "And by next Thanksgiving, November 16, 1715, I was wholly changed to the New Learning." By which he meant that he had been reading John Locke and had decided to forget everything he thought he knew before.

Johnson stayed on at the college as a tutor from 1716 to 1719, and then, the college having moved to New Haven, he took a position as the minister of the nearby West Haven Church. He could have had better jobs at a greater distance from New Haven, but he wanted to stay near those new books. The head of the college after its removal to New Haven was the Reverend Timothy Cutler, and he, too, spent his spare minutes in the library. Cutler and Johnson and another tutor, Daniel Browne, together with a number of the ministers of New Haven and the neighboring towns, formed a discussion group that met regularly in the library to talk over what they had been reading and to help each other master the new learning.

As they read and talked and read again, they found themselves warming to ideas that they recognized as dangerous, the very ideas that Yale had been founded in order to overcome. They were becoming Arminians, and they were finding the Anglican writers appallingly attractive. And so, like the good Puritans they were, they kept reading, confident, no doubt, that they would arrive at the correct, orthodox position in the end. Instead, they were carried farther from it. What was worse, they could not confine their new ideas to themselves. In the realm of ideas, it is difficult to lead a double life. Few men who care about ideas at all have the talent for hypocrisy—to say what they do not believe. Consequently, the new ideas began to leak out. By the spring of 1722, the rumor was going round that "Arminian books are cryed up in Yale College for Eloquence and Learning, and Calvinists despised for the contrary; and none have the courage to see it redressed."

By September 1722 the rumor had grown to alarming proportions, but it is doubtful that anyone was quite prepared for what happened next. At the commencement ceremonies in that year, Rector Timothy Cutler closed his prayer with the words "And let all the people say Amen." This must have made the audience gasp, for it was the form followed in the Anglican Church. The next day, as the trustees met in the library, Rector Cutler and six of his friends appeared at the scene of their crime and confessed: they had not only become Arminians but had all decided to join the Church of England and were going to leave for England at once to take orders.

The consternation would not have been greater if the president of

an American college, at the height of the Cold War, had told his trustees that he and his faculty and a number of leading local citizens had
been reading Karl Marx together, had decided to become communists,
and were departing for Moscow to receive instructions. In just twenty-
one years from the date of its founding, the Yale Library had completely
subverted the purpose for which the college was established. The Yale
trustees, of course, promptly fired Rector Cutler and Tutor Browne, and
everyone tried to talk the converts out of their conversion. In the course
of the next month, three were persuaded back to Puritanism. But Rector
Cutler, Tutor Browne, Samuel Johnson, and James Wetmore, the pastor,
now the former pastor, of North Haven, were adamant. The books in the
library were more persuasive to them than anything their friends could
say. They departed for England, where they were ordained as ministers
of the Anglican Church and, with the exception of Browne, who died in
England, returned to form the spearhead of a drive to convert the rest of
New England to Anglicanism.

Yale meanwhile set about to recover its dignity. The trustees hired a
series of rectors notable for their orthodoxy, culminating in the terrible-
tempered Thomas Clap, who in 1745 assumed the title of president and
kept the college firmly in the orthodox path. But neither Clap nor the
trustees ventured to close the library. In fact, they accepted more books
for it from Bishop Berkeley and from Isaac Watts. Seditious volumes lay
still available to innocent minds, ready to lure them to new and perhaps
still worse heresies.

The faculty at this time consisted of the president and two or three
tutors. The president read lectures on various subjects, and the tutors
heard the recitations of the various classes in the assigned reading. One
of the tutors whom Clap hired in 1749 appeared to be a safe young man.
Ezra Stiles was the son of Isaac Stiles, the North Haven minister who took
the place of the Anglicized and departed James Wetmore. Isaac Stiles was
a friend of Clap's, and Isaac's son Ezra made a good record in college as
an undergraduate. After graduation in 1746, Ezra Stiles remained in New
Haven, reading in the library and casting about for a career. There was
only one thing wrong with this young man: he had an insatiable curiosity. If necessity is the mother of invention, curiosity is surely the father

of it, and invention is heresy by another name. It was probably inevitable that Ezra Stiles, placed in reach of the Yale Library, would sooner or later arrive at a number of heretical ideas.

He had been reading for three years after graduation when Clap hired him; and, though he himself may not have realized it at the time, he was already well launched toward a heresy worse than Cutler's or Johnson's. It seems to have begun with a book whose title sounded harmless: Samuel Clarke's *Demonstration of the Being and Attributes of God*, printed in London in 1705. Clarke was a pious man, and much of his book was directed against the deists, who believed that divine revelation through the Scriptures was not necessary for the discovery and enforcement of moral precepts. Revelation, Clarke insisted, *was* necessary. You could go a long way with unaided human reason toward discovering God's will, but you could not go far enough. Clarke's admonitions had an effect on Stiles similar to that of warning a child not to stuff beans up his nose. His curiosity was whetted rather than satisfied.

He went on to read Shaftesbury's *Characteristics* and Pope's *Essay on Man*. He was so impressed with Pope that he committed long passages to memory and entertained himself with recitations as he walked abroad or paced the floor of his room. He did not recognize either of these works as deistic, but he admired in them the same quality that deists admired, their rationality. They were doing for moral philosophy what Newton had done for natural philosophy. Newton's method, Stiles had learned in college, was "to discard the authority of great names and ingenious Hypotheses in philosophy, and to rely instead wholly upon reason." Why not do the same in religion? The ethical and religious writings of a Shaftesbury seemed to proceed on this principle; Shaftesbury looked to no scriptural writers for authority but argued his case from pure reason.

As soon as Ezra Stiles examined his own religious beliefs in the light of these ideas, something had to give. The first thing to go was the Westminster Confession of Faith, a creed drawn up by an assembly of Puritan divines in the 1640s and generally regarded in New England as the authoritative statement of Christian doctrine. What made it authoritative? That a group of learned and pious ministers had written it? That the colony of Connecticut approved it? Stiles decided not; even though he may still have believed most of its doctrines, it was "no authoritative Standard of Truth."

This brought him up against another and more difficult question. If you rejected the Westminster Confession as an authoritative statement, why accept the Bible? Stiles never doubted the existence of God. Neither did the deists. But if he was rejecting the authority of great names, was there anything about the Bible to stamp it as the product of divine revelation? The mere fact that its authors said it was could hardly be sufficient proof.

Ezra Stiles knew that if he decided the Bible to be something less than the word of God, he was a deist. And to be a deist was a pretty drastic and daring thing in New England. There were deists, especially among the lawyers, who seem to have been a notoriously ungodly lot, but they were *not* supposed to be tutors at Yale, corrupting the youth of Connecticut with ideas worse than Anglicanism.

Ezra Stiles wrestled long and hard with his problem, and he did most of his wrestling in the library. He had read himself to the edge of deism with Shaftesbury, and he now tried to read himself back again with John Taylor, Joseph Butler, John Scott, and Isaac Watts. From these and other authors and from the Bible itself, he was able to conclude that the Bible, whoever wrote it, was a "most rational and sublime Scheme far exceeding natural Religion," far exceeding, that is, any religion that was unaided by revelation. This was still not quite proof that the Bible was the word of God, but Stiles eventually convinced himself from the consistency of different apostles in relating the same facts, and from the fulfillment of Old Testament prophecies, that the Bible was indeed divinely inspired. By further reading in the writings of the early Puritans, he later developed into a thoroughgoing Calvinist.

It might seem, therefore, that Ezra Stiles fully recovered from his bout with the library. But the books he read left a lasting mark upon him and, through him, on others. Having met temptation and survived, he concluded, perhaps too easily, that others who met it, as he had, would also survive. Though firmly committed to revelation, he continued to believe in reason. Let men read and think freely, he maintained, and they would come to truth in the end, just as he had. He had the same confidence as the old Puritans whom he admired, a confidence that reason would lead men to his opinions.

But Ezra Stiles went a step beyond the Puritans. If reason did not bring other men to his opinions, he was content to let them hold their wrong opinions in peace. When he recovered his confidence in the Bible, he did not resume the proper New England stance with regard to the Westminster Confession. For him that was still no authoritative standard of truth. In fact, he retained a phobia against all creeds and tests in religious matters. Once he had established the authenticity of the Bible, he made it an excuse for not recognizing the authority of any man-made creed.

While he was a tutor, Stiles's rampant curiosity led him to write to authors all over the world, begging copies of their works for the college library. He went right on begging after he moved to Newport, Rhode Island, as pastor of the Second Congregational Church there. One of the men whom he solicited successfully was Henry Collins, a Newport Baptist, and among the books that Collins wished to give Yale were some by James Foster, a controversial but respected English theologian, who favored unitarianism and opposed infant baptism. Collins actually had no hopes of making Baptist converts through Foster's writings. He merely wanted to make the learned world acquainted with the fact that Baptists could write learned books. But Clap had grown suspicious of heretical books, however learned. He had recently removed from the library some of those he considered most subversive, including one by Samuel Clarke, the author who had started Stiles on the road to skepticism. Having got these out of the way, Clap did not propose now to start filling the library with new evils. Rather than expose the students to Foster's works, Clap refused the Collins gift. He had evidently become convinced that a library is a dangerous place.

Ezra Stiles had not. Pained by Clap's suppression of free inquiry, he wrote a letter suggesting that liberty offered a clearer road to truth than the kind of control that Clap was now exercising. "It is true," Stiles admitted, "with this liberty error may be introduced; but turn the tables, the propagation of truth may be extinguished. Deism has got such head in this age of licentious liberty, that it would be in vain to try to stop it by hiding the Deistical Writings: and the only Way left to conquer and demolish it, is to come forth in the open Field and dispute the matter on an even Footing."

This letter has a significance that extends beyond the circumstances of its composition, because in a little less than twenty years after he wrote it, Ezra Stiles became president of Yale College. Had he by this time overcome his youthful confidence in reason, he might have been a fit man to keep the students free from heresy. But he still had not altered from the sentiments expressed in his letter to Clap. He not only let the students read what they wanted but encouraged them to discuss controversial questions in every field of thought.

His liberal policy escaped serious criticism during the Revolution and the early post-Revolutionary years, when the intellectual climate throughout America was effervescent. In Connecticut, however, conservative reaction gradually set in. People witnessed the growth of infidelity undermining their religion, and the new ideas of democracy assaulting their social and political habits of thought. They watched the French Revolution, from hopeful beginnings, boil over into the excesses of mob violence and regicide. They saw the formation of democratic clubs in America as a sure sign that the germs of the French Revolution had crossed the ocean and were about to breed a revolution of social classes in the land of the free. And so when their sons came home from Yale College with nicknames such as Rousseau and Voltaire, and with an admiration for such subversive Frenchmen, small wonder if eyebrows and tempers rose. President Stiles obviously let the students read and discuss these French infidels.

Indeed, in spite of his firm belief in Calvinist Christianity, his sympathy for the French was notorious. Fifty years later, David Daggett, a New Haven lawyer, could recall Stiles accosting him on the street:

"Have you heard the glorious news?" cried Stiles.

"What news, Mr. President?"

"The French have entered Holland—they have planted the Tree of Liberty before the Stadtholder's palace. They will plant it before the palaces of all the princes of Europe. The people will live under its shade—I rejoice at it—I am a democrat—yea, I am a Jacobin—I glory in the name."

At a time when most men in Connecticut shuddered at the word Jacobin, Ezra Stiles gloried in the name, because he continued to believe that it spelled liberty. His faith endured that the way to truth "is to come forth in the open Field and dispute the matter on an even Footing." If free inquiry led to the death of kings, that did not alarm or surprise him, for only tyrants, he believed, need fear the truth. His last book, published just before his death, in 1795, was a history of the men who condemned Charles I. It contained an impassioned defense not merely of that action but also of the execution of Louis XVI, and from there it rose to a white-hot polemic in favor of freedom of thought and the right of democratic clubs to hold and propagate their subversive doctrines in the United States.

Ezra Stiles, as you can see, was a dangerous man. But the danger lay less in his own radical views than in the freedom he wanted for others, the freedom to read and from reading to think and speak the thoughts that dissolve old institutions and create new ones. That kind of freedom is as dangerous today as it was then. If we allow young men and women to read and think, we must expect that their thoughts will not be our thoughts and that they will violate much that we hold dear.

The danger may appear remote that such innovating thoughts could arise from the study of rare books and manuscripts in a library dedicated to the American past. There exists among many persons today an assumption that the knowledge of our past will engender among its possessors a reverence for the status quo. Partly as a result of this assumption, there has arisen a widespread demand that young Americans know more about their history. Examination of our high-school and college graduates has in fact revealed a shocking ignorance of American history.

Though I am perhaps a prejudiced observer, since I make a trade of studying and teaching American history, I share the general dismay at this ignorance, and I applaud all efforts to overcome it. In particular I applaud the attack at the root of the matter carried on in libraries. But I am not sure that the effect of wider knowledge will be what some of its advocates suppose. Several years ago one of our educational pundits sent out a questionnaire to college administrators with a question to this effect: Do you think that a better knowledge of American history would make American students less susceptible to other ideologies? I had not previously realized that American history was supposed to be itself an ideology, but that is clearly how this man thought of it, as a religion, of which the founding fathers were the prophets. I suggest that the study of American history could prove as productive of heresy in this religion of American history as the study of religious and philosophical treatises was in the Calvinist religion of eighteenth-century New England.

Let us take just one article in the creed of our American ideology, the article that reads, "All men are created equal." Ever since the Declaration of Independence, these words have enjoyed an almost sacred devotion from Americans. But history will reveal that Americans sometimes interpreted the words in ways that would not be greeted happily in all quarters today.

Would anyone, for example, care to have the student derive from a study of American history the idea that all men should have an equal amount of property? Such an idea sounds like one of those "other" ideologies. But listen to the Reverend Benjamin Trumbull, a sober and respected New England parson, advising the freemen of Connecticut how to vote in 1773:

> It should also be the particular care of every civil community to keep their rulers as much as possible dependent on them, and intimately connected with them. For this purpose it will be highly politic, in every free state, to keep property as equally divided among the inhabitants as possible, and not to suffer a few persons to amass all the riches and wealth of a country: and also to have a special care how they adopt any laws, customs, or precedents, which have a tendency this way. For when men become possessors of the Wealth of a state, it will be in their power to purchase, or by undue influence . . . to thrust themselves into all places of honour and trust. This will put it in their power, by fraud or force to keep themselves in those important posts, and to oppress and tyrannize over their fellow-men. It will teach the people to look up to them, as to lords and masters, make them servile, and by little and little it will despoil them of all true liberty and freedom. But on the other hand, the keeping of property, as equally divided as possible among a people, will make elections more free, the rulers more dependent, and the liberty and privileges of the ruled vastly more secure.

The Reverend Trumbull was speaking three years before Jefferson penned his famous words. He was arguing for the preservation of a condition that he believed to exist already. For he thought that property, in his own state at least, was pretty evenly divided. He wanted to keep it that way, and he believed in governmental action to preserve an even division. No one rebuked him. Indeed, many other examples of his sentiment can be found in the Revolutionary period.

But suppose the student escapes the heresy that might grow from a projection of Trumbull's sentiments. Suppose he examines the ideas of Jefferson himself. Jefferson's affirmation of human equality has informed the most profound and most needed changes in American society for more than two centuries. Yet Jefferson could lead the student to a very novel application of equality. Jefferson thought that the earth belongs to the living, not to the dead, a stirring rhetorical concept, with a strong appeal to the young. With Jefferson it was not mere rhetoric.

He thought that all men, of whatever generation, were created equal, and that therefore one generation was not bound by the actions of the preceding one. From tables of mortality he calculated that the majority of the adult inhabitants in a country at a given time would be dead in about twenty years. A generation, therefore, might be taken as lasting twenty years and should have authority only for its own duration. No government should have authority, for example, to contract debts for its successor. A people, therefore, could repudiate debts contracted by their government more than twenty years previously. Such a doctrine, if applied today, would dissolve, among other institutions, the United States government.

Benjamin Trumbull was a respected clergyman, and Thomas Jefferson was president of the United States. The study of the American past would lose some of its richness and excitement if we confined our study to such respectable and eminent persons. We cannot neglect the various movements for reform. Some of these were so extreme or eccentric that our students are not likely to be infected by them with any zeal for imitation, or if they are it will not matter. We need not, for example, worry about the kind of equality that Bronson Alcott and his followers practiced in 1843, at Fruitlands, their Utopian community in Harvard, Massachusetts, where even the cows were considered equal and not subjected to the degrading exploitation of being milked.

But there was one equalitarian movement that proved successful and that still has implications in American life, the movement for abolition of slavery. The historian's understanding of this movement was transformed in the last century by the publication of the letters of Theodore Dwight Weld in 1934. Anyone studying abolitionism must begin with these letters, and in them will be found ideas to shake any tendency to look upon American history as a source of conservatism. Theodore Weld was one of the great radicals of the nineteenth century. In fact, he was almost a caricature of a radical.

By his own confession he never combed his hair from one end of the year to the other. He never had any fixed time for shaving, but waited until his beard chafed against his collar and then shaved simply to avoid the discomfort. His appearance was so appalling that children fled in terror when he entered a room. He was completely absentminded, with a very poor memory. He was constantly meeting people who greeted him affectionately but whom he could not remember having seen before. He used to peel an apple, eat the peelings, and throw the apple away. He used to go for walks in the middle of the night, in the course of which he climbed young trees, swung the top of them down to the ground, and jumped off. As a grown man, he liked to dive off high cliffs, stand on his head, scream like a loon, run on all fours. In other words, to all outward appearances he was a complete nut.

Yet this man had one of the most commanding personalities of his time. He could truthfully say in a letter to his future wife in 1838, "Those with whom I have been associated have always *deferred* and *conceded* to me—they have spontaneously *yielded* to me. . . . And yet so far from having a desire to be looked upon as a *leader*, to *be* a leader, I always loathed and spurned it, and from a child have always refused all office and worked in the ranks as a common soldier and yet in reality did actually control and give shape to a thousand things with which I *seemed* to have nothing to do."

One of the things Weld gave shape to was the movement for abolition of slavery. He controlled it without seeming to, kept it from being sidetracked into ineffectual demands for other kinds of equality, made it a powerful instrument of reform. He believed in the fullest social and racial equality, but with a perfect sense of timing knew just how much to ask for at once. Though he stayed well ahead of both the Supreme Court and the election returns, he did not get so far ahead as to be out of sight. The United States began to catch up with him in the Emancipation Proclamation of 1863 and is still moving in his direction. It is not improbable that some of us may live to see it overtake him. He was and is a dangerous man, and the dangerous part of him is housed in libraries, where he may still incite men to decency.

One might go on with a list of dangerous Americans who defied the orthodoxy of their times and could teach their readers to do likewise. One can find them in every period, from Roger Williams in the seventeenth century to Henry Thoreau in the nineteenth. But there is no need to enlarge the list. My point is that those who fear change and hope to find protection against it in American history are likely to be disillusioned. If they could control the kind of history taught in our schools and colleges, they might conceivably be successful. But while libraries exist, where students and scholars can go to the original sources and discover the facts for themselves, all efforts at control will be futile. The only way to make a library safe is to lock people out of it. As long as they are allowed to read the books "any old time they have a mind to," libraries will remain the nurseries of heresy and independence of thought. They will, in fact, preserve that freedom which is a far more important part of our life than any ideology or orthodoxy, the freedom that dissolves orthodoxies and inspires solutions to the ever-changing challenges of the future. I hope that your library and mine will continue in this way to be dangerous for many years to come.

—1959

CHAPTER THREE

The Unyielding Indian

ANYONE WHO READS VERY FAR in the voluminous literature of the American Indian is likely to be impressed by the variety of the peoples described and exemplified. When Columbus opened the New World to Europeans, it was inhabited by people who lived under the most widely differing conditions. Their number was not great; current estimates range as low as a million for the whole of North America in 1492. But every part of the New World was inhabited. People were living in the arctic wastes of Hudson's Bay and in the tropical jungles of Central America, on the plains and in the mountains, in coastal swamps and desert basins.

Though we have given them all a single name, Indians, it is obvious that people existing under such divergent conditions must have displayed many different ways of life. You cannot behave the same way in Alaska and in Panama. New Mexico demands of humans something different from what New England does. It is no surprise, therefore, to find Indians in many different stages of what we commonly call civilization. Some tribes were farmers, others hunters. Some lived in stone houses, others in wigwams. Some wove cloth and made their clothes of it; others dressed in animal skins; and still others did not dress at all. Many of these differences were clearly the result of the natural environment: of the climate and the character of the land. It quickly becomes apparent, however, to anyone who looks closely at the Indians, that their variety is not simply a matter of adaptation to different habitats.

What are we to make, for example, of the bewildering number of
Indian languages? Linguists today recognize 375. One would not suppose there were that many different habitats. It would appear that many
Indians were unable to talk to their near neighbors. Actually, it seems that
most of them did not want to. Even the Indians who spoke a single language were apt to be divided into a host of independent tribes, each one
usually numbering no more than a few hundred individuals, who looked
on all the others as undesirable aliens. In many places the tribes were in a
state of open and continuous warfare.

Much of the variety displayed by the Indians might therefore be
described as political in origin, a result of centuries of living in small,
isolated units. This multiplicity of tribes, added to differences of habi-
tat, will go a long way toward explaining Indian variety, but there is still
another kind of difference, the source of much debate among anthropologists, and that is the tremendous variation in physical appearance and
conformation. The Indians not only behaved differently and lived differently; they actually *were* different in the physical characteristics by which
anthropologists have sought to differentiate the races of mankind.

I am aware that some anthropologists deny altogether the existence of
different races among men, but there are many who occupy themselves
with classifying people by shape of head, color of skin, length of jaw, and
so on. When these scientists approach the American Indian, they find
a greater variety of types than exists within the entire range of persons
called white. It seems to be agreed that Columbus was not very far off in
calling them all Indians, because they probably all came from Asia originally, by way of the Bering Strait, but the variety of physical types suggests that they did not all come at the same time or from the same place.
Archaeological evidence suggests that they came in three surges, fifteen,
ten, and five thousand years ago. The progenitors of some may have lived
for a long period in the Far East. Others may have originated elsewhere
and simply passed through Asia. The variety of languages and cultures,
then, may be not merely the product of time and local circumstance operating on a single people. Instead, we may be dealing with people who
from the beginning have differed widely.

In view of this overwhelming diversity, one may well ask whether it is at all profitable to speak, as I have proposed to do, of *the* American Indian. My first impression, after surveying the evidence was that there was no such thing as *the* American Indian and that one would do well to stop talking as though there were. But upon closer reading and further reflection, it appeared to me that the manifold peoples we call Indian did exhibit one remarkable characteristic in common: almost without exception they refused to be absorbed into the civilization offered them by the people who have appropriated the name American, the people who settled the eastern seaboard of the United States and from there pressed westward to the Pacific. For our purposes it will avoid confusion if we call these invaders the English Americans. The Indian refused to become an English American. The history of most other invasions during historic times shows invaders and invaded mingling together, the one absorbing the other, or the two joining to produce a composite civilization. The very Englishmen who became Americans were the product of many different mixtures that had resulted from the successive conquests of England by Anglo-Saxons, Romans, Danes, and Normans. The invasion of America had no such result; the Indian refused to mix. One might have supposed that among the many different tribes, some would have joined the invaders and others not, but this was not the case. The Indians were almost unanimous in preferring their own way of life to that of the new arrivals. And for the historian this is perhaps the most important single fact, the fact that justifies considering the Indian in the singular instead of the plural.

Of course, part of the Indian's refusal to mingle must be blamed on the English American: it was a failure to absorb as well as a failure to be absorbed. The French in Canada, though they never really assimilated the Indians, came closer to it than the English Americans. The French lived with the Indians, married Indian women, taught them to say prayers, and were able to bring a fair number of Indians into a moderately French manner of living. The Spanish were still more successful, though perhaps because they were dealing with a different, and for the most part more technologically advanced, set of Indians. The Spaniards were able to devise colonial institutions that incorporated these Indians. Often, to be sure, they incorporated them as slaves, but slavery can be an effective,

even though a crude and cruel, way of absorbing another people. Perhaps, then, the trouble lay with the American rather than the Indian. It
will be worth examining briefly what kind of efforts the Americans made
to absorb the people whose territories they invaded.

Absorption, if successful, would undoubtedly have meant, first of all,
Christianization. The English Americans considered Christianity to be
the most important single advantage of their civilization over the barbarism of the Indians. To convert an Indian into a Christian would be to
convert him in the most important possible way, from a savage to a civilized man. To undertake this task was the announced purpose of many
English settlers in coming to America, and there were a number who
stood fast in their intentions after arriving here. The number was small,
in comparison with those deployed by the Spanish and the French, but
the measure of success achieved was even smaller. The French and Spanish enrolled hundreds of Indians in the Catholic Church for every one
claimed by English Protestants.

The reason, according to the English, was that the French and
Spanish missionaries were content to set the Indians to kneeling, kiss-
ing the cross, and reciting a few unintelligible prayers. English Protestantism, and especially the Puritan brand of it, demanded a higher
standard of piety. The Indians must not only say the right words; they
must know what they meant. This evidently proved an insuperable
obstacle to the Puritan missionaries. It was either impossible to make
the Indians understand Puritanism, or if you did get them to understand, to make them like it. A succession of notable men from John
Eliot to Jonathan Edwards labored long and hard in the attempt but
with pitifully small results.

It was not that the Indians were intolerant or bigoted. They were
quite willing to listen to stories about the Englishman's God, but they
showed a surprising indifference to the rewards and punishments that He
was said to dole out. Henry Timberlake, a lieutenant serving with British forces in the Carolinas during the French and Indian War, says of the
Cherokees that in religious matters every one of them felt "at liberty to
think for himself," with the result that a great diversity of religious opinion existed among them. Timberlake tells of the efforts of a Reverend

Mr. Martin to convert this tribe. Martin, he says, having preached "till both his audience and he were heartily tired, was told at last, that they knew very well, that, if they were good, they should go up; if bad, down; that he could tell no more; that he had long plagued them with what they no ways understood, and that they desired him to depart the country." It was this attitude that led Benjamin Gale of Connecticut, at about the same time, to say that he would as soon undertake to convert a wolf as an Indian, unless the Indian were first civilized.

Gale, of course, was begging the question. Christianity was the major part of the civilization that had to be imparted to the Indian. But many Americans took the same view, that Christianization should not be attempted until the Indians became familiar with other aspects of civilized life. How, then, were they to gain this familiarity?

The method most commonly suggested in the colonial period was to send the Indian to college. By passing through the purifying rigors of Harvard, Yale, Brown, or Dartmouth, the uncouth Indian would begin to look and think like an Englishman. If even a few could be persuaded to undergo this experience, they might then go back home and set the fashion for their countrymen. One of the essential steps in this collegiate method was to get the Indians indoors. If you could put them inside a house and shut the windows, they might begin to act the way other people do who live inside and sleep on beds. This possibility seems to have captured the imagination of Englishmen in the mother country who wished to contribute to the ultimate salvation of lost Indian souls. At least we find that enterprising college presidents of the seventeenth and eighteenth centuries were able to carry on successful money-raising campaigns in England in order to build dormitories for the prospective Indian students.

Unfortunately college education proved even less palatable to the Indian than Christianity. When it was possible to get an Indian boy to go to college, it would not be long before he cut his classes and lit out for the hills. Those who stayed behind seldom survived, and when they fell victims to collegiate food and overheated rooms, their parents showed an unreasonable disposition to blame the president. As a result, the buildings were quickly turned over to deserving English American boys, who could stand the strain of college life. The Indian stayed in the woods.

Another possible method of bringing civilization to the Indian was marriage. This was a mode in which, of course, the French excelled. A study of the relations between French and Indians in eastern Canada shows that the Indian girls became so eager for French husbands that they jilted the Indian boys in a wholesale manner and upset all the traditional patterns of tribal behavior. The English frequently told themselves to go and do likewise, but either they lacked the skill of the French in these matters, or else their hearts were not in it. The English government in 1719 went so far as to offer ten pounds and fifty acres of land in Nova Scotia to any Englishman who married an Indian girl or any English girl who married an Indian man. But few couples appeared to claim the reward.

When Englishmen traveled among the Indians on trading, or surveying, or hunting expeditions, they frequently accepted the hospitality of the Indians. And since the Indian notions of hospitality were generous, the guest was frequently provided with one of the comelier maidens of the tribe. Sometimes these lighthearted unions proved of more than passing duration, but if so the children of the couple usually grew up as Indians. John Lawson, himself a surveyor in North Carolina, tells us in his account of that province, that the Indians there regarded children as belonging to their mother, and therefore, he says, "it ever seems impossible for the Christians to get their Children (which they have by these Indian Women) away from them." On the other hand, he says, "we often find, that English Men and other Europeans that have been accustomed to the Conversation of these Savage Women and their Way of Living, have been so allured with that careless sort of Life, as to be constant to their Indian Wife, and her Relations, so long as they lived, without ever desiring to return again amongst the English, . . . of which sort I have known several." It seems altogether probable that marriage was an avenue along which English Americans went native more often than Indians became civilized.

The French married the Indians; the Spaniards enslaved them. If the English could not pursue the French method with enthusiasm, they were more assiduous in the Spanish one. Warfare has generally provided the justification for slavery. In the seventeenth and eighteenth centuries the victorious party in a just war—and what war is not just in the eyes of the victor?—thought itself entitled to enslave its captured enemies. On this basis the settlers of America enslaved any Indians who made unsuccessful war against them. But the Indians were as unwilling to accept this blessing as any other the white man offered them. It was a fact that Indians did not make good slaves: they were too unruly. That fact did not prevent the English Americans from enslaving them. The Puritans of New England were as ready to do so as the planters of South Carolina. But neither in New England nor in South Carolina did people want to *keep* Indian slaves. Instead, they packed them aboard ships and sold them in the West Indies like so many wooden nutmegs. And lest this traffic should recoil upon themselves, the people of Massachusetts passed a law prohibiting the importation of Indian slaves, on the grounds that Indians were all "of a malicious, surley and revengeful spirit, rude and insolent in their behaviour, and very ungovernable." Thus the enslaved Indians found no home among their captors, and slavery did not prove a successful means of introducing Indians into American civilization.

Christianity, education, marriage, and slavery—all were pressed upon the Indians, with varying degrees of enthusiasm. All except marriage they rejected, and in marriage they generally won the upper hand. In the end the only part of the white man's civilization they would accept was its material goods. They knew at a glance that guns were better than spears or arrows, iron hatchets than stone tomahawks, cloth than fur. Each of these things they cheerfully appropriated and fetched beaver skins for the English Americans in order to purchase them. In so doing, they had to alter many of their traditional ways and devote themselves more and more to trapping beaver, less and less to their customary handicrafts, but they managed to subordinate the new products to their own ends. Guns and hatchets were useful weapons for defense against their enemies, perhaps including the men who sold them to them. Cloth was only a more manageable and uniform kind of fur. The Indians thus appropriated the materials of the English and used them in their own way. They were not lured into the white man's civilization by them.

If, then, the English Americans did not exert themselves as much as they might have to assimilate the Indian, the fact remains that the Indians showed an extraordinary resistance to whatever efforts *were* made, an extraordinary refusal to accept the manners and methods of a people who were obviously more powerful than they. And we find this intransigence among Indians of every kind, among Westos and Creeks, Iroquois and Algonquians. Diverse as these different tribes may have been, they all possessed some quality that made white civilization unattractive to them.

One must, therefore, look beyond their apparent diversity and seek the common element or elements in their ways of life, the elements that led them to reject so firmly the opportunities of white civilization. If we read the early accounts with this purpose in mind, one fact immediately presents itself: the early observers were all struck by the unusual kind of government that the different tribes practiced. Europeans were accustomed to governments that claimed an absolute authority. Among the Indians absolute governments did develop in South and Central America and in a few parts of North America, but most of the tribes encountered by the English Americans lived in a state that might be described as orderly anarchy. Each tribe had its own customs, which exercised a powerful influence on the members, doubtless much more powerful than European observers realized, but the heads of the tribes, the chiefs or sachems, seem in most cases to have had no coercive authority. The Indians' resistance to white civilization was not organized and directed from above by powerful rulers, for Indian rulers were not powerful, in fact were scarcely rulers at all.

James Adair, a trader who lived among the southern Indian tribes for many years in the eighteenth century, has left us an illuminating account of their government. There was no such thing among them, he says, as an emperor or a king. Their highest title signified simply a chief, and "the power of their chiefs," according to Adair, "is an empty sound. They can only persuade or dissuade the people, either by the force of good-nature and clear reasoning, or colouring things, so as to suit their prevailing passions. It is reputed merit alone, that gives them any titles of distinction above the meanest of the people."

Henry Timberlake, whose memoirs I have already quoted, was familiar only with the Cherokee Indians. Of them he says, "Their government, if I may call it government, which has neither laws or power to support it, is a mixed aristocracy and democracy, the chiefs being chose according to their merit in war, or policy at home." Timberlake gives an interesting example of the helplessness of tribal government to control any member, even in matters of great importance. It seems that a number of British soldiers in the garrison at Fort Loudoun on the Tennessee River had taken up with some of the local Cherokee girls. Later, when the Cherokees besieged the fort (in the French and Indian War), the girls proceeded to bring food daily to their former lovers. The chief naturally forbade this breaking of the siege, but the girls, says Timberlake, "laughing at his threats, boldly told him, they would succour their husbands every day, and were sure, that, if he killed them [meaning the girls], their relations would make his death atone for theirs."

The early cartographer Lewis Evans tells us, of the Indians in Pennsylvania, "that there is no such thing as coercive power in any Nation: nor does the government ever interfere between party and party; but let every one be judge and Executioner in his own Case."

Even among the Iroquois, who appeared to have the most powerful government of all the eastern Indians, the authority of the chiefs rested only on public opinion. The New York savant Cadwallader Colden, in his history of the Five Indian Nations that made up the Iroquois, says, "Each Nation is an absolute Republick by its self, govern'd in all Publick Affairs of War and Peace by the Sachems or Old Men, whose Authority and Power is gain'd by and consists wholly in the Opinion the rest of the Nation have of their Wisdom and Integrity. They never execute their Resolutions by Compulsion or Force upon any of their People."

If we turn from the eighteenth century to the nineteenth and from the Indians of the East to those of the Great Plains, we find the same observations. George Catlin, a Pennsylvania portrait painter, was so enthralled by the sight of a group of Indians who visited his studio in Philadelphia that he packed up his paints and brushes and headed for the Far West. There, on the banks of the Missouri and the Yellowstone and the Columbia, he lived for eight years among the Indians. That was in the 1830s when the only other white men on hand were a few fur traders and soldiers, before the slaughter of the buffalo drove the Indians off the plains. Catlin recorded his experience in hundreds of paintings and drawings and in a remarkable book.

He knew the Mandan and the Minataree and the Sioux and the Comanche and the Flatheads and dozens of other tribes, knew them intimately and described the peculiar customs and characteristics and physical appearance of each. But he observed that the governments of all the tribes were much the same, under the leadership of a chief. This chief, he observed, "has no control over the life or limbs, or liberty of his subjects, nor other power whatever, excepting that of *influence* which he gains by his virtues, and his exploits in war, and which induces his warriors and braves to follow him, as he leads them to battle—or to listen to him when he speaks and advises in council."

In war as in peace, discipline imposed from above was at a minimum. Indian warfare was carried on mostly by small parties, among the eastern tribes seldom more than ten together. The leader of such a group had no more authority than the other members chose to allow him, and in the actual fighting it was every man for himself, each seeking to outdo the others in the fury of his attack. Indian warfare was not a pretty thing, no matter how one looks at it: no atrocity was too great for the Indian to commit against his opponent. Women and children were as fair game as men. But the object of war was as much to display the power and courage of the individual as it was to destroy the enemy.

The absence of coercive government, together with the horrendousness of Indian warfare, may suggest that Indian life was, as Hobbes would have maintained, nasty, brutish, and short. If we may believe the testimony of eyewitnesses, the opposite was true: the Indians who move through the pages of the early accounts display an extraordinary dignity and decorum. They appear very much indeed like the noble savages of fiction.

Nowhere is this more evident than in a body of literature composed by the Indians themselves, the Indian treaties. The Indians, of course, did not actually write the treaties, for they did not know how to write. Like other illiterate peoples, they relied heavily on their memories. And in order to establish so important an event as a treaty in the tribal consciousness, they did their peacemaking in an impressive ceremonial manner. The records of these ceremonies, taken down by white observers, were so beautiful, so moving, and withal so aesthetically satisfying, that colonial printers brought them out in pamphlet form for sale.

In the treaties we begin to get a glimpse of what contemporary writers meant when they said that the authority of the chiefs depended solely on merit and persuasive powers. The stature and eloquence of the Indian sachem at the council table speak strongly to us even at this distance in time and circumstance: a chief who relied solely on persuasion may not have been altogether helpless among men who valued dignity at a high rate. And if we look at the everyday life of the everyday Indian, we may see that it was not merely the chiefs who had dignity. For people to live together in the absence of coercive government, even in so small a unit as a tribe, it was necessary that everyone maintain a barrier of dignity around oneself and respect the same barrier in others. The English traveler John Lawson says of the southern Indians, "They never fight with one another unless drunk, nor do you ever hear any Scolding amongst them. They say the Europeans are always rangling and uneasy, and wonder they do not go out of this World, since they are so uneasy and discontented in it." The famous frontiersman Robert Rogers, who knew only the northern Indians, says much the same of them: "if any quarrels happen, they never make use of oaths, or any indecent expressions, or call one another by hard names." Indians were not long on conversation, and white guests used to find their silence quite unnerving at times. When they did speak, courtesy required that it be in a low voice. They spoke so low, in fact, that Europeans found it difficult to hear what they were saying, while the Indian was often obliged to ask white visitors if they supposed him to be deaf. No matter how angry he might be, an Indian never raised his voice.

Obviously not all Indians were faultless, even by their own standards, but when any one of them violated the customs or mores of his tribe, the treatment he received either from the chief or from the offended party was calculated to shame, rather than force, him into reform. In some tribes the most deadly weapon of authority seems to have been sarcasm. If a man was thought guilty of theft, for example, he might be commended before a large audience for his honesty. If he ran away from the enemy in battle, he would be praised for his courageous actions, each one of which would be related so as to bring out his cowardice. Adair says, "They introduce the minutest circumstances of the affair, with severe sarcasms which wound deeply. I have known them to strike their delinquents with those sweetened darts, so good naturedly and skilfully, that they would sooner die by torture, than renew their shame by repeating the actions."

The whole Indian mode of government was designed to emphasize the dignity of the individual. The same emphasis may be found elsewhere in Indian life. The Indian was so fond of his dignity and so proud of his ability to sustain it by strength of character alone, that he completely discounted the props by which the European supported his. The Indian lacked entirely the European's respect for worldly goods. In Europe, and indeed in most of the world, the acquisition and possession of riches constitutes the ultimate basis for social esteem. We may think it better to be born rich than to become rich, but in our society wealth has seldom been thought a handicap. Among the Indians, on the other hand, there existed a deliberate indifference to wealth, an indifference that could sometimes be infuriating to the white man.

Consider, for example, the Puritans of Massachusetts, who in 1643 were trying to take under their protection a group of Narragansett Indians. The immediate object was a land grab, to get the Indians' land away from Rhode Island, but Massachusetts felt obliged to conduct the transaction in such a way that the Indians would appear to be receiving a favor. Since Christianity was the greatest favor a white man could confer on a savage, the authorities of Massachusetts undertook to instruct the Indians in the Ten Commandments. There is no record of what was said about coveting neighbors' lands, but Governor Winthrop noted in his journal the Indians' response to the fourth commandment. Will you agree, the men of Massachusetts inquired, not to "do any unnecessary work on the Lord's day"? To which the Indians replied, "It is a small thing for us to rest on that day, for we have not much to do any day, and therefore we will forbear on that day."

By Puritan standards, the Indian was not only lazy; he was proud of his laziness. The settlers observed this fact at the beginning and never forgave him for it. But those observers who saw the Indian in his tribal life and made some attempt to understand him, knew that his unwillingness to labor for riches was something more than mere laziness. Rather, it was the result of a genuine scorn for the riches of this world, to which the Puritans themselves were constantly professing their own indifference. The

Indian could afford to scorn riches and to shun the industry necessary to acquire them, because in his society it was the man that counted, not what he owned. The observers are surprisingly unanimous in their statements on this subject. Let me give you a few of them. Robert Rogers, speaking of the northern Indians: "Avarice, and a desire to accumulate . . . are unknown to them; they are neither prompted by ambition, nor actuated by the love of gold; and the distinctions of rich and poor, high and low, noble and ignoble, do not so far take place among them as to create the least uneasiness, or excite the resentment of any individual; the brave and deserving, let their families or circumstances be what they will, are sure to be esteemed and rewarded." John Lawson, of the Indians of Carolina: "They are a People that set as great a Value upon themselves, as any sort of Men, in the World, upon which Account they find something Valuable in themselves above Riches. Thus, he that is a good Warriour is the proudest Creature living; and he that is an expert Hunter, is esteemed by the People and himself; yet all these are natural Vertues and Gifts, and not Riches, which are as often in the Possession of a Fool as a Wise-man." James Adair: "Most of them blame us for using a provident care in domestic life, calling it a slavish temper: they say we are covetous, because we do not give our poor relations such a share of our possessions, as would keep them from want. . . ."

Among the Indians, wealth was not merely a matter of indifference. It was, in fact, something to be avoided by anyone who prided himself on his merits. According to Cadwallader Colden, the chiefs of the Iroquois nations were generally poorer than the common people. For in order to attain their eminence they had to demonstrate their indifference to worldly goods by giving away all the presents and plunder they obtained from friends or enemies. "If," says Colden, "they should once be suspected of *Selfishness*, they would grow mean in the opinion of their Country-men and would consequently loose their authority."

It may be that some of the observers I have quoted were idealizing the Indian. Perhaps you will think that they rationalized laziness into a virtue. Yet it was a laziness that Henry Thoreau also practiced: like the Indian, Thoreau was too busy being himself to spend his time in pursuit of wealth. And if my chroniclers idealized the Indian, they were idealizing something they had seen themselves. Most of them had lived among the Indians and knew what they were talking about. Indeed, the man who knew the Indians most intimately was the one who has given us the noblest savages of all. George Catlin found in the Indians of the Far West all the attributes that our earlier observers discovered in the eastern tribes. "I have watched," says Catlin in the florid prose of his day,

> the bold, intrepid step—the proud, yet dignified deportment of Nature's man, in fearless freedom, with a soul unalloyed by mercenary lusts, too great to yield to laws or power except from God. As these independent fellows are all joint-tenants of the soil, they are all rich, and none of the steepings of comparative poverty can strangle their just claims to renown. Who (I would ask) can look without admiring, into a society where peace and harmony prevail—where virtue is cherished—where rights are protected, and wrongs are redressed— with no laws, but the laws of honour, which are the supreme laws of their land?

Here, as in the other remarks by other eyewitnesses about other Indians, we have a series of characteristics that most Indians of North America seem to have shared.

These common characteristics, I believe, indicate that Indian ways of life in North America, however diverse, all produced men who attached the highest possible value to the individual. Indeed, the diversity of Indian life was fostered and encouraged by this very exaltation of the individual. Men who valued individual freedom so highly would not create any large or effective political organization of their own, nor would they be content to live under one created by white men. They preferred their own small and ineffective organizations, preferred them because they were small and because they were ineffective. They were individualists, intransigent and incorrigible.

I do not mean that the Indian was possessed of some mysterious essence to which we can give the name "individualism." I use the word merely to tie together the different aspects of Indian life that we have been examining. They all add up to a single quality, which has been given various names. The Massachusetts General Court, for example, as we have seen, called it "a malicious, surley, and revengeful spirit." But the more positive epithet of "individualism" will also apply.

By whatever name we call it, and however it was produced, this quality was preeminent among the Indians of North America, and it may help us to understand not only why the Indian refused to join us but also why we have admired and hated him for his refusal. The Indian in his individualism displayed virtues to which Americans, and indeed all Christians, have traditionally paid homage. An indifference to the things of this world, a genuine respect for human dignity, a passionate attachment to human freedom—these are virtues we all revere. We should be flattered, I think, if someone said of us that "the great and fundamental principles of their policy are, that every man is naturally free and independent; that no one . . . on earth has any right to deprive him of his freedom and independency, and that nothing can be a compensation for the loss of it." But these words were not written about us or our ancestors. They were written about the Indians (by Robert Rogers) and published eleven years before the Declaration of Independence.

They fit the Indian better than they fit us. The Indian therefore is both a challenge and an affront to us. We see in him what we might be if we carried some of our avowed principles to their logical conclusions. And what we see is disturbing. For we do *not* wish to be like the Indian. We do *not* wish to see our nation disintegrate into a thousand petty republics; we do *not* wish to be so free that no superior authority will make us behave. Nor do we intend to abandon whatever riches we have laid up in this world. It may be as difficult for a rich man to enter heaven as for a camel to go through the eye of a needle, but most of us would welcome a chance to make the attempt. And so we are irritated, annoyed, and even infuriated by men who exhibit our values better than we do.

I do not suggest a mode of accommodation. We do not in fact have room for such incorrigible individualists within our civilization. And yet that civilization will have been impoverished beyond repair if the time ever comes when we cannot admire the Indian in his diversity, his dignity, and his intransigence, more than he ever had reason to admire us.

—1958

CHAPTER FOUR

John Winthrop's Vision

JOHN WINTHROP'S "MODELL of Christian Charity" has probably enjoyed as much attention from historians as from Winthrop's shipmates aboard the *Arbella* in 1630. It offers an explicit statement, convenient for quotation, of the idea that the Bay Colony was in covenant with God, a chosen people, a new Israel. It has accordingly become the very emblem of the Puritan quest, the manifesto in which Winthrop proclaimed the place of Massachusetts as a "city upon a hill."

The document deserves the attention it has received and perhaps a little more. Historians have generally related it to the events that followed it. It represents the ideal by which the later actuality is measured or the key by which to explain the sense of mission that engaged first New England and then the United States. The validity of this interpretation is not in question, but a look at the context in which Winthrop was operating may enrich our understanding of what he was doing in his shipboard sermon.

The "Modell of Christian Charity" was an explication of the love that flows from regeneration in Christ, and of the hope that this love would inform and sustain the holy experiment on which Winthrop and his companions were embarked. More immediately it was an appeal for subjection to authority. God himself, Winthrop said, had ordained that "some must be rich some poore, some high and eminent in power and dignitie; others meane and in subjeccion." This was the lesson, the "model," which the rest of the sermon or essay was designed to uphold.

The passengers must have expected some iteration of the lesson, for it was the central platitude of sixteenth- and seventeenth-century social and political thought, invoked whenever the occasion seemed to suggest a need for reinforcing authority. The founding of the Puritan commonwealth in Massachusetts Bay was surely such an occasion. Its success, in Winthrop's view at least, would depend on the willingness of the participants to join in loving subjection to the men they trusted to lead them. But Massachusetts Bay was not the first English colony in America, and the voyage of the *Arbella* was only one of a long line of voyages in which Englishmen boarded ship on dangerous errands that they thought would redound to the glory of God and country. By the same token it was not the first time that the leader of a voyage or colony appealed to Christian charity in order to foster subjection to authority and to discourage the dissension that must imperil the mission.

Winthrop makes no mention of the "Modell of Christian Charity" either in his journal or in his surviving correspondence, and the only known copy is not in his hand. Though there seems no doubt that the authorship is properly ascribed to him, the circumstances under which he may have delivered it aboard the *Arbella* are therefore uncertain. Given the theme, it seems likely that it preceded or accompanied the taking of the sacrament among the passengers during one of the Sunday shipboard services. Whether or not that was the case, the communion of Christians in the Lord's Supper was often the occasion for appeals to brotherly love in voyages or colonizing enterprises.

Christians were supposed to have a special love for one another, as Winthrop pointed out in the "Modell," and Christian love found its highest symbolic expression in the sacrament. It was accordingly of special importance that no one partake of the sacrament while entertaining hostile thoughts or intentions toward his neighbor. William Perkins, the standard authority for Puritans, made the point in his *Cases of Conscience* that the sacrament "is a Communion, whereby all the receivers, joyntly united together in love, doe participate of one and the same Christ. And therefore, as no man in the old law might offer his Sacrifice, without a fore-hand agreement with his brother; so no Communicant may partake with others at this Table, without reconciliation, love, and charitie."

As communion was a time for reconciliation, reconciliation might also be a time for communion. Before setting out on the high seas for strange lands, captain, crew, and passengers might take the sacrament in celebration of their mutual love and in hope of concord and amity in the voyage. Atlantic voyages in the sixteenth, as in the seventeenth, century could present a formidable challenge to anyone's charity toward those with whom he was obliged to rub elbows day and night. Men might be aboard ship without interruption for as much as three months and, of course, even longer on voyages into the Pacific or the Indian Ocean. A "voyage" might be an expedition of several ships, but most of the ships themselves were small, some of them only thirty or forty tons, and the size of the crew was extremely large by modern standards in proportion to the size of the vessel (as many as one man for every two or three tons), partly because sailing vessels of that day required large crews, partly because masters anticipated that many would die during the trip. Fifty men crowded aboard a vessel of a hundred tons barely had standing room on the decks. As the weeks aboard wore on, tempers grew short, and it required firm discipline to prevent flare-ups of violence. Yet seamen were scarcely the mildest and most tractable of men. The history of countless voyages shows that they frequently refused to take a ship where they were ordered. Indeed, it would appear that a wise master did not give orders without ascertaining in advance that his men were willing to carry them out.

Precisely because a long sea voyage pressed human patience to its limits, a successful leader had to take advantage of every possible means of maintaining harmony and agreement in his followers. The great captains of the day were men who knew how to command loyalty, obedience, and even love under the most trying conditions. When dissension did break out, they knew how to deal with it swiftly and surely. Some have suffered in reputation, and perhaps rightly, because they were capable of swift, decisive, and utterly ruthless action. Francis Drake, on his way round the world, had a friend beheaded because Drake suspected him of creating a faction.

Prevention was better than such drastic cures, and it is not unlikely that the leaders of a voyage took some pains to exhort their fellow voyagers to

peace and harmony. The records of voyages seldom tell us much about
the initial stages when such speeches would have been most appropriate.
Unless some unusual event occurred, all we get is the date of the vessel's or
fleet's departure, the winds they encountered, when they made the Azores
or Madeira or the Canaries or Cape Verde, and so on. But occasionally one
gets a glimpse of the commander instructing his men to "love one another,"
as in John Hawkins's orders to his fleet as they left the Canaries in 1564
for Guinea and the Caribbean. Sebastian Cabot's instructions to Sir Hugh
Willoughby and Richard Chancellor in their search for a northeast passage
in 1553 began with an admonition that the officers of the expedition "be
so knit and accorded in unitie, love, conformitie, and obedience in every
degree on all sides, that no dissention, variance, or contention may rise or
spring betwixt them and the mariners of this companie, to the damage or
hinderance of the voyage: for that dissention (by many experiences) hath
overthrown many notable enterprises and exploits."

There is more detail in an episode on Sir Anthony Sherley's privateering expedition to the West Indies in 1596, because Sherley fell sick
at Cape Verde and thought himself near death. Gathering his "captains,
masters, and officers" about him, he made

> a very pithie and briefe speech, tending to this purpose: That as we
> were Christians and all baptised and bred up under one and the true
> faith, so wee should live together like Christians in the feare and ser-
> vice of God: And as we were the subjects of our most excellent sov-
> ereigne, and had vowed obedience unto her: so we should tend all
> our courses to the advancement of her dignity, and the good of our
> countrey, and not to enter into any base or unfit actions. And because
> we came for his [Sherley's] love into this action that for his sake we
> would so love together as if himselfe were still living with us, and that
> we would follow (as our chiefe commander) him, unto whom under
> his hand he would give commission to succeede himself: all which
> with solemne protestation we granted to obey.

Edward Fenton on a voyage to South America in 1582–83 carried
two chaplains, and on the first Sunday aboard one of them, John Walker,

preached "of concorde and the coming of the holy ghost." Although Walker repeated his admonitions to love and concord in a later sermon, the voyage failed for lack of these virtues. Fenton was a poor leader, given to quarreling himself and unable to prevent it among his men. Robert Dudley on a voyage to Guiana a dozen years later was more successful, perhaps because he was aware of the need for love and concord. According to the account of one of his captains, Dudley inaugurated his expedition with a ceremony designed to establish harmony:

> Havinge allreadie sent his provision unto Southampton by his servants the which shoulde give attendance on him in this viage, hee sett forwarde himselfe and came unto Hampton, where retayninge a sufficient and able companie, not without his great chardge for the throughlie manninge of his shippinge for the viage, [he] gave a speciall commaundement unto all his companies that they shoulde generallie provide themselves to goe with him the Sonday followinge, beinge the thirde day of November, to the church and theare accompany him for the reverent receavinge of the Holie Communion, and after at his chardge to dine with him all togeather, as members united and knitt together in one bodie.

Dudley later became a Catholic and may already have leaned that way— he named a cape on Trinidad after the "divine Mary." John Hawkins, on the other hand, was something of a Puritan. But the need for Christian charity on a sea voyage was neither Puritan nor Catholic. It was a condition of survival.

The founding of a new colony was as hazardous an enterprise as the voyage to it, and one to which concord and amity were equally crucial. The expedition that founded the first permanent English settlement at Jamestown, in 1607, nearly foundered at the outset in the dissension among members of the governing council, but it was not for lack of exhortations to and affirmations of the kind of love that Winthrop later demanded. Before the expedition had fairly established itself at Jamestown, Captain Christopher Newport, in command of the ships, played

Winthrop's role in an attempt to foster love and unity. According to the most detailed surviving account, Newport being

> no lesse carefull of our amitye and combyned friendship then became him in the deepe desire he had of our good, vehemently with ardent affectyon wonne our harts by his fervent perswaysyon to uniformity of consent, & callmed that (out of our love to him) with ease, which I doubt, without better satisfactyon, had not contentedly been caryed. We confirmed a faythfull love one to another, and, in our hartes, subscribed an obedyence to our superyors this day [June 10, 1607].

Like many another love feast, this one did not endure for long. Two years later Robert Gray, in a sermon entitled *A Good Speed to Virginia*, was still pleading for love: "All degrees and sorts of people which have prepared themselves for this Plantation must be admonished to preserve unitie, love and concord amongst themselves: for by concord small things increase and growe to great things, but by discord great things soone come to nothing." Virginia remained on the verge of coming to nothing for a good many years. As late as the 1630s Governor Harvey and his council were continually at loggerheads. But like other Englishmen they knew that the solution must lie in Christian charity. On one occasion in 1631 when they determined to bury the hatchet, they joined in a lengthy declaration of love that began by crediting God with having "inspired the spirit of peace into our hearts and calmed those thoughts and purposes of contention and bitterness, whereby distraction hath happened to our councells and consultations." Henceforth "all jarrings, discords and dissentions" would be "wholly laid aside, love embraced, and all be unanimously reconciled." To this end, they exhorted themselves,

> lett us prepare ourselves with that Psalmist, to goe into the house of God, and after due consideration & contrition for our sinnes, seale and deliver this our concord peace and love, with the seale of that most blessed sacrament of the body and blood of our Saviour, who hath called us to the union of our fayth & made us members of his

body, that living together in peace in this world, wee may live with him in eternall peace in the world to come.

None of these exhortations and rituals in Virginia served quite as high a purpose as Winthrop's, and none reached his level of discourse. Stephen Foster has brilliantly exhibited the creative application that Winthrop made of accepted Christian doctrine in the "Modell." The point here is to suggest not only that Winthrop was developing a conventional doctrine but also that he wrote or spoke in a context where that doctrine was regularly called upon for an immediate practical purpose, a purpose that Winthrop, too, embraced even as he exalted it into something more than the success of a voyage.

The New England Puritans had a creative genius for adapting old forms to new conditions. Out of a variety of local institutions—parish, borough, manor—they created the New England town. Out of English common law and assorted biblical injunctions, they created a systematic code of laws. John Winthrop, like any good captain, knew that his expedition could founder on dissension. In New England his special gift lay in bringing disagreements to a happy issue. In the "Modell of Christian Charity" he did what he could to forestall trouble. At the same time he turned a captain's exhortation into a statesman's proclamation of the new Canaan.

—1987

CHAPTER FIVE

———

The Puritans and Sex

HENRY ADAMS ONCE OBSERVED that Americans have "ostentatiously ignored" sex. He could think of only two American writers who touched upon the subject with any degree of boldness—Walt Whitman and Bret Harte. Since the time when Adams made this penetrating observation, American writers have been making up for lost time in a way that would make Harte, if not Whitman, blush. And yet there is still more truth than falsehood in Adams's statement. Americans, by comparison with Europeans or Asiatics, are squeamish when confronted with the facts of life. My purpose is not to account for this squeamishness but simply to point out that the Puritans, those bogeymen of the modern intellectual, are not responsible for it.

At the outset, consider the Puritans' attitude toward marriage and the role of sex in marriage. The popular assumption might be that the Puritans frowned on marriage and tried to hush up the physical aspect of it as much as possible, but listen to what they themselves had to say. Samuel Willard, minister of the Old South Church in the latter part of the seventeenth century and author of the most complete textbook of Puritan divinity, more than once expressed his horror at "that Popish conceit of the Excellency of Virginity." Another minister, John Cotton, wrote,

> Women are Creatures without which there is no comfortable Living
> for man: it is true of them what is wont to be said of Governments,
> *That bad ones are better than none*: They are a sort of Blasphemers then

who dispise and decry them, and call them *a necessary Evil*, for they are *a necessary Good*.

These sentiments did not arise from an interpretation of marriage as a spiritual partnership, in which sexual intercourse was a minor or incidental matter. Cotton gave his opinion of "Platonic love" when he recalled the case of

one who immediately upon marriage, without ever approaching the *Nuptial Bed*, indented with the *Bride*, that by mutual consent they might both live such a life, and according did sequestring themselves according to the custom of those times, from the rest of mankind, and afterwards from one another too, in their retired Cells, giving themselves up to a Contemplative life; and this is recorded as an instance of no little or ordinary Vertue; but I must be pardoned in it, if I can account it no other than an effort of blind zeal, for they are the dictates of a blind mind they follow therein, and not of that Holy Spirit, which saith *It is not good that man should be alone*.

Here is as healthy an attitude as one could hope to find anywhere. Cotton certainly cannot be accused of ignoring human nature. Nor was he an isolated example among the Puritans. Another minister stated plainly that "the Use of the Marriage Bed" is "founded in mans Nature," and that consequently any withdrawal from sexual intercourse upon the part of husband or wife "Denies all reliefe in Wedlock vnto Human necessity: and sends it for supply vnto Beastiality when God gives not the gift of Continency." In other words, sexual intercourse was a human necessity and marriage the only proper supply for it. These were the views of the New England clergy, the acknowledged leaders of the community, the most Puritanical of the Puritans. As proof that their congregations concurred with them, one may cite the case in which the members of the First Church of Boston expelled James Mattock because, among other offenses, "he denied Coniugall fellowship vnto his wife for the space of 2 years together vpon pretense of taking Revenge upon himself for his abusing of her before marryage." So strongly did the Puritans insist upon the sexual character of marriage that one New Englander considered himself slandered when it was reported "that he Brock his deceased wife's hart with Greife, that he wold be absent from her 3 weeks together when he was at home, and wold never come nere her, and such Like."

There was just one limitation that the Puritans placed upon sexual relations in marriage: sex must not interfere with religion. Man's chief end was to glorify God, and all earthly delights must promote that end, not hinder it. Love for a wife was carried too far when it led a man to neglect his God:

> . . . sometimes a man hath a good affection to Religion, but the love of his wife carries him away, a man may bee so transported to his wife, that hee dare not bee forward in Religion, lest hee displease his wife, and so the wife, lest shee displease her husband, and this is an inordinate love, when it exceeds measure.

Sexual pleasures, in this respect, were treated like other kinds of pleasure. On a day of fast, when all comforts were supposed to be forgone in behalf of religious contemplation, not only tasty food and drink were to be abandoned but sexual intercourse, too. On other occasions, when food, drink, and recreation were allowable, sexual intercourse was allowable as well, though of course only between persons who were married to each other. The Puritans were not ascetics; they never wished to prevent the enjoyment of earthly delights. They merely demanded that the pleasures of the flesh be subordinated to the greater glory of God: husband and wife must not become "so transported with affection, that they look at no higher end than marriage it self." "Let such as have wives," said the ministers, "look at them not for their own ends, but to be fitted for Gods service, and bring them nearer to God."

Toward sexual intercourse outside marriage the Puritans were as frankly hostile as they were favorable to it in marriage. They passed laws to punish adultery with death, and fornication with whipping. Yet they had no misconceptions as to the capacity of human beings to obey such laws. Although the laws were commands of God, it was only natural— since the fall of Adam—for human beings to break them. Breaches must be punished, lest the community suffer the wrath of God, but no offense, sexual or otherwise, could be occasion for surprise or for hushed tones of voice.

How calmly the inhabitants of seventeenth-century New England could contemplate rape or attempted rape is evident in the following testimony offered before the Middlesex County Court of Massachusetts:

The examination of Edward Wire taken the 7th of october and alsoe Zachery Johnson. who sayeth that Edward Wires mayd being sent into the towne about busenes meeting with a man that dogd hir from about Joseph Kettles house to goody marches. She came into William Johnsones and desired Zachery Johnson to goe home with her for that the man dogd hir. accordingly he went with her and being then as far as Samuell Phips his house the man over tooke them. which man caled himselfe by the name of peter grant would have led the mayd but she oposed itt three times: and coming to Edward Wires house the said grant would have kist hir but she refused itt: wire being at prayer grant dragd the mayd between the said wiers and Nathanill frothinghams house. hee then flung the mayd downe in the streete and got atop hir; Johnson seeing it hee caled vppon the fellow to be sivill and not abuse the mayd then Edward wire came forth and ran to the said grant and took hold of him asking him what he did to his mayd, the said grant asked whether she was his wife for he did nothing to his wife: the said grant swearing he would be the death of the said wire. when he came of the mayd; he swore he would bring ten men to pul down his house and soe ran away and they followed him as far as good[y] phipses house where they mett with John Terry and George Chin with clubs in there hands and soe they went away together. Zachy Johnson going to Constable Heamans, and wire going home. there came John Terry to his house to ask for beer and grant was in the streete but afterward departed into the towne, both Johnson and Wire both aferme that when grant was vppon the mayd she cryed out severall times.

Deborah hadlocke being examined sayth that she mett with the man that cals himselfe peeter grant about good prichards that he dogd hir and followed hir to hir masters and there threw hir downe and lay vppon hir but had not the use of hir body but swore several othes that he would ly with hir and gett hir with child before she got home.

Grant being present denys all saying he was drunk and did not know what he did.

The Puritans became inured to sexual offenses, because there were so
many. The impression one gets from reading the records of seventeenth-
century New England courts is that illicit sexual intercourse was fairly common. The testimony given in cases of fornication and adultery—by far the
most numerous class of criminal cases in the records—suggests that many
of the early New Englanders possessed a high degree of virility and very
few inhibitions. Besides the case of Peter Grant, take the testimony of Elizabeth Knight about the manner of Richard Nevars's advances toward her:

> The last publique day of Thanksgiving (in the year of 1674) in the eve-
> ning as I was milking Richard Nevars came to me, and offered me abuse
> in putting his hand, under my coates, but I turning aside with much
> adoe, saved my self, and when I was settled to milking he agen took
> me by the shoulder and pulled me backward almost, but I clapped one
> hand on the Ground and held fast the Cows teatt with the other hand,
> and cryed out, and then came to mee Jonathan Abbot one of my Mas-
> ters Servants, whome the said Never asked wherefore he came, the said
> Abbot said to look after you, what you doe unto the Maid, but the said
> Never bid Abbot goe about his businesse but I bade the lad to stay.

One reason for the abundance of sexual offenses was the number of men
in the colonies who were unable to gratify their sexual desires in marriage.
Many of the first settlers had wives in England. They had come to the new
world to make a fortune, expecting either to bring their families after them
or to return to England with some of the riches of America. Although these
men left their wives behind, they brought their sexual appetites with them;
and in spite of laws that required them to return to their families, they continued to stay, and more continued to arrive, as indictments against them
throughout the seventeenth century clearly indicate.

Servants formed another group of men, and of women, too, who could
not ordinarily find supply for human necessity within the bounds of marriage. Most servants lived in the homes of their masters and could not
marry without their consent, a consent that was not likely to be given unless
the prospective husband or wife also belonged to the master's household.
This situation will be better understood if it is recalled that most servants
at this time were engaged by contract for a stated period. They were, in

the language of the time, "covenant servants," who had agreed to stay with
their masters for a number of years in return for a specified recompense,
such as transportation to New England or education in some trade (the
latter, of course, were known more specifically as apprentices). Even hired
servants who worked for wages were usually single, for as soon as a man
had enough money to buy or build a house of his own and to get married,
he would set up in farming or trade for himself. It must be emphasized,
however, that anyone who was not in business for himself was necessarily
a servant. The economic organization of seventeenth-century New England had no place for the independent proletarian workman with a family
of his own. All production was carried on in the household by the master
of the family and his servants, so that most men were either servants or
masters of servants; and the former, of course, were more numerous than
the latter. Probably most of the inhabitants of Puritan New England could
remember a time when they had been servants.

Theoretically servants had no right to a private life. Their time, day
or night, belonged to their masters, and both religion and law required
that they obey their masters scrupulously. But neither religion nor law
could restrain the sexual impulses of youth, and if those impulses could
not be expressed in marriage, they had to be given vent outside marriage.
Servants had little difficulty in finding the occasions. Though they might
be kept at work all day, it was easy enough to slip away at night. Once out
of the house, there were several ways for a man to meet with a maid. The
simplest way was to go to her bedchamber, if she was so fortunate as to
have a private one of her own. Thus Jock, Mr. Solomon Phipps's Negro
man, confessed in court

> that on the sixteenth day of May 1682, in the morning, betweene 12
> and one of the clock, he did force open the back doores of the House
> of Laurence Hammond in Charlestowne, and came in to the House,
> and went up into the garret to Marie the Negro.
>
> He doth likewise acknowledge that one night the last week he
> forced into the House the same way, and went up to the Negro Woman
> Marie and that the like he hath done at severall other times before.

Joshua Fletcher took a more romantic way of visiting his lady:

> Joshua Fletcher . . . doth confesse and acknowledge that three sev-
> erall nights, after bedtime, he went into Mr Fiskes Dwelling house
> at Chelmsford, at an open window by a ladder that he brought with
> him. the said windo opening into a chamber, whose was the lodging
> place of Gresill Juell servant to mr. Fiske. and there he kept company
> with the said mayd. she sometimes having her cloathes on, and one
> time he found her in her bed.

Sometimes a maidservant might entertain callers in the parlor while family members were sleeping upstairs. John Knight described what was
perhaps a common experience for masters. The crying of his child awak-
ened him in the middle of the night, and he called to his maid, one Sarah
Crouch, who was supposed to be sleeping with the child. Receiving no
answer, he arose and

> went downe the stayres, and at the stair foot, the latch of doore was
> pulled in. I called severall times and at the last said if shee would not
> open the dore, I would breake it open, and when she opened the
> doore shee was all undressed and Sarah Largin with her undressed,
> also the said Sarah went out of doores and Dropped some of her
> clothes as shee went out. I enquired of Sarah Crouch what men they
> were, which was with them. Shee made mee no answer for some space
> of time, but at last shee told me Peeter Brigs was with them, I asked
> her whether Thomas Jones was not there, but shee would give mee
> no answer.

In the temperate climate of New England, it was not always necessary to
seek out a maid at her home. Rachel Smith was seduced in an open field
"about nine of the clock at night, being darke, neither moone nor starrs
shineing." She was walking through the field when she met a man who

> asked her where shee lived, and what her name was and shee told
> him. and then shee asked his name, and he told her Saijing that he
> was old Good-man Shepards man. Also shee saith he gave her strong
> liquors, and told her that it was not vthe first time he had been with
> maydes after his master was in bed.

Sometimes, of course, it was not necessary for servants to go outside their master's house in order to satisfy sexual urges. Many cases of fornication are on record between servants living in the same house. Even where servants had no private bedroom, even where the whole family slept in a single room, it was not impossible to make love. In fact, many love affairs must have had their consummation upon a bed in which other people were sleeping. Take for example the case of Sarah Lepingwell. When Sarah was brought into court for having an illegitimate child, she related that one night when her master's brother, Thomas Hawes, was visiting the family, she went to bed early. Later, after Hawes had gone to bed, he called to her to get him a pipe of tobacco. After refusing for some time,

> at the last I arose and did lite his pipe and cam and lay doune one my one bead and smoaked about half the pip and siting vp in my bead to giue him his pip my bead being a trundell bead at the sid of his bead he reached beyond the pip and Cauth me by the wrist and pulled me on the side of his bead but I biding him let me goe he bid me hold my peas the folks wold here me and if it be replyed come why did you not call out I Ansar I was posesed with fear of my mastar least my master shold think I did it only to bring a scandall on his brothar and thinking thay wold all beare witnes agaynst me but the thing is true that he did then begete me with child at that tim and the Child is Thomas Hauses and noe mans but his.

In his defense Hawes offered the testimony of another man who was sleeping "on the same side of the bed," but the jury nevertheless accepted Sarah's story.

The fact that Sarah was intimidated by her master's brother suggests that maidservants may have been subject to sexual abuse by their masters. The records show that sometimes masters did take advantage of their position to force unwanted attentions upon their female servants. The case of Elizabeth Dickerman is a good example. She complained to the Middlesex County Court

> against her master John Harris senior for profiring abus to her by way of forsing her to be naught with him: . . . he has tould her that if she

tould her dame: what cariag he did show to her shee had as good be hanged and shee replyed then shee would run away and he sayd run the way is befor you: . . . she says if she should liwe ther shee shall be in fear of her lif.

The court accepted Elizabeth's complaint and ordered her master to be whipped twenty stripes.

So numerous did cases of fornication and adultery become in seventeenth-century New England that the problem of caring for the children of extramarital unions was a serious one. The Puritans solved it, but in such a way as to increase rather than decrease the temptation to sin. In 1668 the General Court of Massachusetts ordered

that where any man is legally convicted to be the Father of a Bastard childe, he shall be at the care and charge to maintain and bring up the same, by such assistance of the Mother as nature requireth, and as the Court from time to time (according to circumstances) shall see meet to Order: and in case the Father of a Bastard, by confession or other manifest proof, upon trial of the case, do not appear to the Courts satisfaction, then the Man charged by the Woman to be the Father, shee holding constant in it, (especially being put upon the real discovery of the truth of it in the time of her Travail) shall be the reputed Father, and accordingly be liable to the charge of maintenance as aforesaid (though not to other punishment) notwithstanding his denial, unless the circumstances of the case and pleas be such, on the behalf of the man charged, as that the Court that have the cognizance thereon shall see reason to acquit him, and otherwise dispose of the Childe and education thereof.

As a result of this law a girl could give way to temptation without the fear of having to care for an illegitimate child by herself. Furthermore, she could, by a little simple lying, spare her lover the expense of supporting the child. When Elizabeth Wells bore a child, less than a year after this statute was passed, she laid it to James Tufts, her master's son. Goodman Tufts affirmed that Andrew Robinson, servant to Goodman Dexter, was the real father, and he brought the following testimony as evidence:

Wee Elizabeth Jefts aged 15 ears and Mary tufts aged 14 ears doe
testyfie that their being one at our hous sumtime the last winter
who sayed that thear was a new law made concerning bastards that
If aney man wear aqused with a bastard and the woman which had
aqused him did stand vnto it in her labor that he should bee the
reputed father of it and should mayntaine it Elizabeth Wells hearing of the sayd law she sayed vnto vs that If shee should bee with
Child shee would bee sure to lay it vn to won who was rich enough
abell to mayntayne it wheather it wear his or no and shee farder
sayed Elizabeth Jefts would not you doe so likewise If it weare
your case and I sayed no by no means for right must tacke place:
and the sayd Elizabeth wells sayed If it wear my Caus I think I
should doe so.

A tragic unsigned letter that somehow found its way into the files of the
Middlesex County Court gives more direct evidence of the practice that
Elizabeth Wells professed:

der loue i remember my loue to you hoping your welfare and i hop
to imbras the but now i rit to you to let you nowe that i am a child
by you and i wil ether kil it or lay it to an other and you shal have no
blame at al for I haue had many children and none have none of them
. . . [i.e., none of their fathers is supporting any of them.]

In face of the wholesale violation of the sexual codes to which all these
cases give testimony, the Puritans could not maintain the severe penalties
that their laws provided. Although cases of adultery occurred every year,
the death penalty is not known to have been applied more than three
times. The usual punishment was a whipping or a fine, or both, and perhaps a branding, combined with a symbolical execution in the form of
standing on the gallows for an hour with a rope about the neck. Fornication met with a lighter whipping or a lighter fine, while rape was treated
in the same way as adultery. Though the Puritans established a code of
laws that demanded perfection—that demanded, in other words, strict
obedience to the will of God—they nevertheless knew that frail human
beings could never live up to the code. When fornication, adultery, rape,

or even buggery and sodomy appeared, they were not surprised, nor were they so severe with the offenders as their codes of law would lead one to believe. Sodomy, to be sure, they usually punished with death; but rape, adultery, and fornication they regarded as pardonable human weaknesses, all the more likely to appear in a religious community, where the normal course of sin was stopped by wholesome laws. Governor Bradford, in recounting the details of an epidemic of sexual misdemeanors in Plymouth in 1642, wrote resignedly,

> it may be in this case as it is with waters when their streames are stopped or dammed up, when they gett passage they flow with more violence, and make more noys and disturbance, then when they are suffered to rune quietly in their owne chanels. So wikednes being here more stopped by strict laws, and the same more nerly looked unto, so as it cannot rune in a comone road of liberty as it would, and is inclined, it searches every wher, and at last breaks out wher it getts vente.

The estimate of human capacities here expressed led the Puritans not only to deal leniently with sexual offenses but also to take every precaution to prevent such offenses, rather than wait for the necessity of punishment. One precaution was to see that children got married as soon as possible. The wrong way to promote virtue, the Puritans thought, was to "ensnare" children in vows of virginity, as the Catholics did. As a result of such vows, children, "not being able to contain," would be guilty of "unnatural pollutions, and other filthy practices in secret: and too oft of horrid Murthers of the fruit of their bodies," said Thomas Cobbett. The way to avoid fornication and perversion was for parents to provide suitable husbands and wives for their children:

> Lot was to blame that looked not out seasonably for some fit matches for his two daughters, which had formerly minded marriage (witness the contract between them and two men in *Sodom*, called therefore for his Sons in Law, which had married his daughters, Gen. 19. 14.) for they seeing no man like to come into them in a conjugall way . . . then they plotted that incestuous course, whereby their Father was so highly dishonoured. . . .

As marriage was the way to prevent fornication, successful marriage was the way to prevent adultery. The Puritans did not wait for adultery to appear; instead, they took every means possible to make husbands and wives live together and respect each other. If a husband deserted his wife and remained within the jurisdiction of a Puritan government, he was promptly sent back to her. Where the wife had been left in England, the offense did not always come to light until the wayward husband had committed fornication or bigamy, and, of course, there must have been many offenses that never came to light. But where both husband and wife lived in New England, neither had much chance of leaving the other without being returned by order of the county court at its next sitting. When John Smith of Medfield left his wife and went to live with Patience Rawlins, he was sent home poorer by ten pounds and richer by thirty stripes. Similarly Mary Drury, who deserted her husband on the pretense that he was impotent, failed to convince the court that he actually was so, and had to return to him as well as to pay a fine of five pounds. The wife of Phillip Pointing received lighter treatment: when the court thought that she had overstayed her leave in Boston, it simply ordered her "to depart the Towne and goe to Tanton to her husband." The courts, moreover, were not satisfied with mere cohabitation; they insisted that it be peaceful cohabitation. Husbands and wives were forbidden by law to strike one another, and the law was enforced on numerous occasions. But the courts did not stop there. Henry Flood was required to give bond for good behavior because he had abused his wife simply by "ill words calling her whore and cursing of her." The wife of Christopher Collins was presented for railing at her husband and calling him "Gurley gutted divill." Apparently in this case the court thought that Mistress Collins was right, for although the fact was proved by two witnesses, she was discharged. On another occasion the court favored the husband: Jacob Pudeator, fined for striking and kicking his wife, had the sentence moderated when the court was informed that she was a woman "of great provocation."

Wherever there was strong suspicion that an illicit relation might arise between two persons, the authorities removed the temptation by forbidding the two to come together. As early as November 1630, the Court of Assistants of Massachusetts prohibited a Mr. Clark from "cohabitacion and frequent keeping company with Mrs. Freeman, vnder paine of such punishment as the Court shall thinke meete to inflict." Mr. Clark and Mr. Freeman were both bound "in XX £ apece that Mr. Clearke shall make his personall appearance att the nexte Court to be holden in March nexte, and in the meane tyme to carry himselfe in good behaviour towards all people and espetially towards Mrs. Freeman, concerneing whome there is stronge suspicion of incontinency." Forty-five years later the Suffolk County Court took the same kind of measure to protect the husbands of Dorchester from the temptations offered by the daughter of Robert Spurr. Spurr was presented by the grand jury

> for entertaining persons at his house at unseasonable times both by day and night to the greife of theire wives and Relations &c
>
> The Court having heard what was alleaged and testified against him do Sentence him to bee admonish't and to pay Fees of Court and charge him upon his perill not to entertain any married men to keepe company with his daughter especially James Minott and Joseph Belcher.

In like manner Walter Hickson was forbidden to keep company with Mary Bedwell, "And if at any time hereafter hee bee taken in company of the saide Mary Bedwell without other company to bee forthwith apprehended by the Constable and to be whip't with ten stripes." Elizabeth Wheeler and Joanna Peirce were admonished "for theire disorderly carriage in the house of Thomas Watts being married women and founde sitting in other mens Laps with theire Armes about theire Necks." How little confidence the Puritans had in human nature is even more clearly displayed by another case, in which Edmond Maddock and his wife were brought to court "to answere to all such matters as shalbe objected against them concerning Haarkwoody and Ezekiell Euerells being at their house at unseasonable tyme of the night and her being up with them after her husband was gone to bed." Haarkwoody and Everell had been found "by the Constable Henry Bridghame about tenn of the Clock at night sitting by the fyre at the house of Edmond Maddocks with his wife a suspicious weoman her husband being on sleepe [*sic*] on the bedd." A similar distrust of human ability to resist temptation is evident in the following order of the Connecticut Particular Court:

> James Hallett is to returne from the Correction house to his master Barclyt, who is to keepe him to hard labor, and course dyet during the pleasure of the Court provided that Barclet is first to remove his daughter from his family, before the sayd James enter therein.

These precautions, as we have already seen, did not eliminate fornication, adultery, or other sexual offenses, but they doubtless reduced the number from what it would otherwise have been.

In sum, the Puritan attitude toward sex, though directed by a belief in absolute, God-given moral values, never neglected human nature. The rules of conduct that the Puritans regarded as divinely ordained had been formulated for men, not for angels and not for beasts. God had created mankind in two sexes; He had ordained marriage as desirable for all, and sexual intercourse as essential to marriage. On the other hand, He had forbidden sexual intercourse outside of marriage. These were the moral principles that the Puritans sought to enforce in New England. But in their enforcement they took cognizance of human nature. They knew well enough that human beings since the fall of Adam were incapable of obeying perfectly the laws of God. Consequently, in the endeavor to enforce those laws, they treated offenders with patience and understanding, and concentrated their efforts on prevention more than on punishment. The result was not a society in which most of us would care to live, for the methods of prevention often caused serious interference with personal liberty. It must nevertheless be admitted that in matters of sex the Puritans showed none of the blind zeal or narrow-minded bigotry that is too often supposed to have been characteristic of them. The more one learns about these people, the less do they appear to have resembled the sad and sour portraits that their modern critics have drawn of them.

—1942

CHAPTER SIX

The Problems of a Puritan Heiress

I N THE YEAR 1656 Anna Keayne was the most eligible debutante in Boston. At the age of sixteen she had been "very well and carefully educated," and furthermore her grandfather had just left her £900 in his will. Although the good people of Boston may have looked with some bitterness upon this dowry—for Robert Keayne had become notorious by his hard bargains—Anna was nevertheless accepted as a respectable member of society. Her grandfather, in spite of his harsh business dealings, had long been a member of the church in good standing. He had attended regularly, taken notes on the sermons, and even begun to write a commentary on the Bible. At the time of his death he had completed three precious volumes of this work, which he declared he would not part with for a hundred pounds. There could be no question that, aside from his too great attention to worldly wealth, he was a good Puritan. His grandchild would be accepted even in the most exclusive and godly circles. Besides, the old merchant had in his will partially atoned for his failings. His neighbors and customers must have been somewhat softened toward Anna by the fund of £120 he had left to the poor and the £300 he had left to the town for the erection of public buildings.

Anna's parents could not bear such close scrutiny as her grandparents. Her father, Benjamin Keayne, the only son of old Robert, had made what at first seemed to be a fortunate marriage with Sarah Dudley, daughter of Governor Thomas Dudley and sister of the poetess Anne Bradstreet. But

Sarah had turned out to be a shrew, and the match had proved "unhappy and uncomfortable." Some time after Anna's birth Benjamin accused his wife of adultery, obtained a divorce, and went off to London, leaving her to marry again and to get herself in trouble with the church by "Irregular prophecying in mixt Assemblies." Benjamin never questioned, however, that Anna was his child. Before he departed for England, he placed her in the hands of her grandparents, and they brought her up with loving care and proper discipline. Robert Keayne provided in his will that her education be continued, if necessary, in some godly family to be chosen by his executors, "where she may have hir carnall disposition most of all subdued and reformed by strict discipline." He probably did not mean to imply that Anna was particularly susceptible to the temptations of the flesh. Like all Puritans, he assumed that every human being is endowed with a "carnal disposition" that it is part of the business of education to subdue. There is no reason to believe that Anna's character at the time of her grandfather's death was in any way questionable. In spite of her mother's shady reputation, she herself was a respectable, well-bred young lady with a fortune of £900—assuredly the best match in town.

Her grandfather, whose love for her was evident to everyone, had given some instructions in his will about her prospective husband. He had advised that she marry "some man truely fearing God," and had instructed the overseers of his will "to provide some fitt and godly match proportionable to hir estate and condition that she may live comfortably and be fitt to doe good in hir place and not to suffer hir to be circumvented or to cast away hirselfe for want of counsell and watchfullness upon some swagering gentleman or others that will Looke more after the enjoying of what she hath, then liveing in the feare of God and true love to hir." In order to be sure that Anna followed the instructions of her guardians, he charged her "that she would not dare to set hir affections upon any in that kind without there advice counsell and helpe." It may seem hard that a girl should have to receive permission from her grandmother, or worse still from the overseers of her grandfather's will, before falling in love; but such was the custom in seventeenth-century Boston. Children, especially if possessed of sizable fortunes, were supposed to allow their parents or guardians to make their matches for them.

The proper man appeared a few months after her grandfather's death. Edward Lane, a London merchant reputed to be worth £1,800 (a suitor was expected to be worth at least twice as much as his future wife), thirty-six years old and single, arrived at Boston aboard the *Speedwell* on July 27, 1656. It was not long before he was making overtures to Anna's guardians, and since he seemed to be well qualified in godliness and in worldly goods, Mrs. Keayne gave him permission "to make tryall for the gayning of my Grandchilds affections as to marriage." Thereafter, following a common custom, he sent a friend often to visit Anna and to gain her affections for him. With the friend he sent many pieces of gold for her to assure her of his own affection and at the same time, doubtless, to remind her that he was a man of wealth, worthy to be her suitor. The eloquence of the friend—or of the gold—soon prevailed, and the couple became affianced.

Hitherto Lane had remained pretty much in the background. Now he stepped prominently into the picture. Mrs. Keayne, thankful for the prospect of having a man in the family once more, decided to hand over to him the job of executing her late husband's will, for she had scarcely begun the task of carrying out the manifold orders contained in that lengthy document. Since Anna was still underage and since her dowry had to be paid from the estate, Lane was easily persuaded of "the great benefitt it would bee vnto me in respect of the securitie of my wiues portion" to take over the task. After he had agreed to do so, however, he discovered that, according to the terms of the will, he would lose a part of his wife's portion if she should die before reaching the age of eighteen. Because of this and other dubious provisions of the will, Lane thought it advisable to have an express agreement drawn up concerning the exact amount due to Mrs. Keayne as the widow, so that the remainder, minus all bequests and legacies, might be entirely his.

For so grave a matter the assistance of an impartial tribunal was necessary. Accordingly Lane and Mrs. Keayne each chose two friends to meet together as an arbitrating committee and decide "what they shall judge just and equal to be payd and receiued by one or other." A week later, after perusing the 158 pages of Robert Keayne's will, this committee drew up an agreement to which Lane and the widow set their signatures: Mrs. Keayne was to receive a house and land, an annuity of £40, plus £400 in money; Lane was to have everything else, and he gave bond for £1,000 to pay all the bequests and other debts owed by the estate. In addition Mrs. Keayne left all preparations for the coming wedding up to the bridegroom. She agreed to "allow unto the said Edward Lane, the summe of fifty pounds for the more contentfull and comely apparrelling of Anna Keayne the younger [Mrs. Keayne's name was Anna, too] his intended wife together with what he sees meet to lay out for the marriage solemnity that so the said Anna the elder may be freed from all troubles in making provision for the same. . . ." With these preliminaries out of the way, the stage was at last set for the wedding, which took place on December 11, 1657, under the direction of Governor John Endecott. Since church weddings were not allowed, Anna had no chance to display her "contentfull and comely" apparel to an admiring congregation; but if she and her husband followed colonial custom, they invited their friends to a feast after the ceremony. Here Anna was able to show off her new gown, while friends toasted her with "sack-posset" and rum. Perhaps, if the authorities had not been displaying too much strictness lately, there might even have been dancing.

Had Edward Lane been a normal man, the story might have ended here, with the couple living happily ever after. But an ugly rumor soon began to be heard in Boston, and fifteen months after the wedding popular suspicion was confirmed by a petition that Mrs. Lane presented to the Court of Assistants.

To the Honoured Court of Assistants now Assembled at Boston

May it please this Honoured Court to pitty the sad and disconsolate condition of your handmaid, laboring under a bondage, from which reason and religion doth set her free, yet needing and craving the Authority to doe the same.

Your petitioner hath bin deceived in a contract of marriage with Mr. Edward Lane, to whom (upon an essentiall mistake) shee gaue her selfe as a wife, and hath not bin wanting in the duty of that relation, expecting the performance of an husband on his part, wherin he hath been from first to last altogether deficient; which for seaven monthes I bare without imparting my grief to my nearest friends, who then understanding the same; and hoping and desiring more private help, put him upon seeking remedy by physick, which he also attended making use of Mr. Snelling, who practised upon him with forcible medicines, but without successe, so that by the counsell of the overseers of my Grandfathers will (to whom he acknolidged his infirmity) he was advised to seek further help from more physitians; and accordingly he made knowne his case to Mr. Eire, Mr. Clerk, and Mr. Megeke, and hath been under their hands neer seaven monthes. And your petitioner hath by absenting herselfe with his consent, and returning to him through difficulties applied herselfe to accomodate him. All which notwithstanding the said Mr. Lane hath been and doth continue uncapable of performance of the marriage Covenant: by reason wherof, as also from the sense of the great and manifold inconveniences of the publick notice of it, your petitioner is (tho with shame and affliction) enforced to fly to your justice for succour and reliefe by declaring mee free from the sayd pretended Contract of marriage with Mr. Lane. And by ordering him to repaire the damage and wronge to my person and estate as your justice shall judg meet.

My patient silence in this condition cannot prejudice my cause with your wisdomes which will not think it meet or tolerable, for a woman after just complaint in such case made, to remaine under the power of a pretended husband, and to yield herselfe to bee the subject of vaine experements, to the dishonour of her name, danger of her person and estate which cannot bee prevented but by a present release declared by this honoured Court which is the humble and earnest petition of your handmaid

ANNA LANE

Upon receipt of this document the court sent for Lane and asked him if his wife's charge were true. "After a considerable pause his answer was that he must speake the truth he could not say he had performed the office of a husband." Accordingly, after due deliberation, the magistrates declared the marriage to be dissolved.

It soon appeared, however, that Anna was not the only one who had been deceived. The bequests and debts owed by the estate of Robert Keayne amounted to much more than the value of the estate itself. By the terms of the agreement that he had signed, Edward Lane was a loser by more than £500. He, too, now sought relief in court, pointing out that he had assumed the executorship because of the marriage. The marriage having been dissolved, he ought therefore to be relieved of the burden and reimbursed for the expenditures he had made. The court's first reaction was to appoint a committee empowered to examine all the evidence and instructed "to make a loving and amicable agreement, if it may be, to mutual satisfaction of the sajd Mr. Lane and Mrs. Anna Keajne, thereby to prevent further trouble to this court."

The court did not escape further trouble so easily. The widow Keayne had made a bargain, and like her husband she meant to see that it was kept. She refused to listen to any compromise and presented an answer to Lane's petition in which she pointed out that Lane had entered the agreement with his eyes open. If the court were to release him from his obligations, she said, it would be plain "to the world that no man or woman of what condition soeuer of sound mind or theire friends so being can make any bargaine, but the Court may vndoe it which I hope will not be asserted, much lesse practised." Mrs. Keayne was saying that business is business, but the court had heard that plea before from the lips of her late husband. To him they had replied, in a fine of £200, that business may be business, but it is not justice. They now returned the same answer to her: they discharged Lane from the executorship and ordered the overseers of the will to reimburse him with £650, plus two years' rent from most of the houses and lands in possession of the estate.

Anna Lane now began to regret her action, for it was plain that she was not so desirable a match as she had at first appeared to be. Lane told her that because of deficiencies in her grandfather's estate her dowry "must fall Short more then twoe therdes." Furthermore, he was slow about returning her personal property, which he may have been keeping as a pledge until his £650 were paid. Lane was naturally somewhat piqued at Anna's exposure of his infirmity, especially since he knew that "the phycitians that have administred vnto mee can finde no naturall Defect in mee as they have Declared and are still ready to Declare." He continued

to take treatments and after a time became convinced that his weakness
had ceased. Friends now tried to patch things up, and because of Anna's
uncertainty about her estate she was the more willing to listen to them.
Her grandmother later related, "I have severall times found my Daughter
in a roome with Mr. Lane and Mr. Cooke to my great greif and have been
angry with Mr. Cooke about it; And he hath Led me out and said lett
them alone I would have her try him for he is a man; And to Convince me
told mee some thing that was so Immodest I cannot write it."

The result of these meetings was that on December 12, 1659, two
years after their first marriage and nine months after the annulment, the
couple went once more to the governor and asked to be married again.
The episode and its sequel were later recalled by Edward Hutchinson:

> Edward Hutchinson aged 53 years or Thereabouts sworne saith That
> when Mr. Edward Lane and Anna his wife Came together the second
> Time they sent for mee to the house of Leift. Richard Cooke and
> There they Declared to Mee (I comeing ouer late to goe with them
> to the Gouernours) that they had been at the governours to Desire
> to be married againe; but the governour told them that they being
> seperated by the Court it was not for him to Joyne them together;
> but if they were both sattisfied that the Cause was remoued That
> moved the Court to Declare their Marriage a Nullity he said that
> that Declareation would not make it a Nullity; for it was not man
> that could part Those god Joyned together Therefore told them they
> should be well advised and be vpon good Grounds which they sayd
> they Declared they were. Then he Told them as they said, That it
> being Their owne act Their first Marriage was good and the Nul-
> lity was voyde; And Desired The Lord to blesse them together after
> which we being together some of vs merrily Jesting with them said
> They must have made some Tryall or elce they could not soe Declare;
> They said both of them it may be they had what was That to us vpon
> our parteing away Capt. Olliver bidding them both good night Mrs.
> Lane Answered she Questioned not as good a night as any woman In
> Boston next morning Capt. olliver and my self goeing to visitt them
> Capt. Olliver askeing her if now she had received sattisfaction so as to

be satisfied the Impediment that Mr. Lane had before was remoued; she Answered it was now otherwise with him then before; and she was sattisfied in his sufficiency as a man This is the substance of what I heard and Though I will not be perticular to all the words yett as near as my memory serves it was in these words above or words to the like effect.

To all outward appearances the whole affair was now patched up. Lane once more became executor of the will, though the agreement between him and the widow Keayne this time provided that she should have simply an annuity of twenty pounds and possession of the new house in Boston. Furthermore, he stipulated that if any more debts appeared "that hath not as yet beene taken notice of," and beyond the value of the estate, the overseers of the will should take steps to assist him in the payments. On this basis the couple lived quietly together for the next four years. Edward became well established as a Boston merchant and attested his prosperity to his neighbors by sporting a London hat with a silver hatband. Anna meanwhile demonstrated that this time her marriage was genuine by giving birth to two children, a boy and a girl. The little girl, named after her mother, died at the age of eight months, but the boy, named after Edward, lived until 1680, meeting his death at the age of eighteen in Leyden.

Early in 1664 Anna sailed for England, on what business is not known, but it was evidently understood in Boston that her husband would shortly follow. Before he could do so, however, he was dead. When Anna returned to Boston two years later, it was with a new husband, also a Bostonian who had been visiting England, Mr. Nicholas Paige. Now once more the rumors began to spread. It was said that Anna had married Paige before Lane had died, for some persons had received letters from Paige before the latter event in which he made mention of his wife. Since there were bound to be enemies in Boston of any descendant of Robert Keayne, the grand jury soon got wind of the matter and conducted an investigation, which resulted in an indictment against Anna for adultery. Before the trial took place, Anna gave herself away by proposing to the Court of Assistants a question to be resolved by the magistrates: "whether a woman may not have children by a man that is not in the eye of the

world accounted her husband and yet not be accounted an adulteresse."
The cat was now out of the bag, and in the trial that followed evidence
was produced that the boy who bore the name of the late Edward Lane
was really the son of Nicholas Paige. Richard Cooke came into court and
affirmed that "about two yeares since upon Mrs. Hannah Lanes going for
England this deponent was desired to come unto the house of Mr. Edward
Lane . . . at which time this deponent did heare Mrs. Lane acknowledge
that the Children which She then had had were Mr. Page his Children and
not mr. Lanes." The whole truth came to light, however, when the following document, dated December 6, 1663, was brought forth:

> To all whom this present writing may concern this is to certify that
> whereas thear was a marriage between Edward Lane of Boston in
> the County of Suffolke in New England and Anna Keayne of the
> said Boston living together sometime, I the said Edward Lane being
> wholly insufficient through weakness and infirmity never in the least
> manner to performe the duty or office of a husband to the said Anna
> nor never knew her carnally: Upon Petition to the Court of Assis-
> tance held at Boston March, '58, The Court upon good consider-
> ations pronounced the marriage a nullity wee wear bouth free from
> each other nine months after upon some considerations wee came
> to live togather and have so continued togather four yeares but the
> same weaknes and insuffitiency continuing to this day I thinke it not
> convenient for her any longer to bare the name of my wife who in
> truth before God is none. Therefore I utterly disown her and dis-
> seize her never more to maintain her or looke at her as any relation
> to me more then a friend from the date hereof for though we have
> made one house our habitation yet we have made use of tow beds
> therefore this is to atest the cause and truth of our seperation as is
> done by a coppy taken out of the Records As witnes my hand And in
> part of requitall for that great wrong I have done her I freely give her
> the pasture which was her Granfathers which lys behind the house of
> Goodman Pells.

Confronted with the situation that was now apparent, the magistrates
and the jury could not agree whether or not Anna Paige, formerly Anna

Lane, should be punished for adultery. The matter was therefore brought before the General Court of the colony, where, as the record reads,

> . . . vpon a full hearing of the case, the Court found hir guilty of much wickednes, but vpon a motion from hirself, the Court gaue hir opportunity to make acknowledgment of such hir great offences which were charged vpon hir, which accordingly she hath donne to the satisfaction of this Court, who doe hereby declare their acceptation of it, so as she make the like acknowledgment in open Court when called thereto; that as the Court hath seene the fruits of her repentance, so it may be declared to others also. The sajd Anna Page came into the Court, and openly made acknowledgment, in like manner, to the Courts acceptance, who ordered that Mrs. Page pay the charge of the witnesses, and so is discharged.

Apparently the General Court was as puzzled by the case as the inferior court had been; but just as Governor Endecott had decided that Anna's first marriage had not been truly annulled, the court now, in 1666, must have decided that neither the first nor the second marriage had been truly a marriage. Thus although it was clear that Anna had committed "much wickedness," the court was not ready to say that she was guilty of adultery, and so she escaped virtually scot-free.

Having thus come out of danger, she and her husband began to take cognizance of her former estate. Besides the pasture he had granted her in the paper renouncing her as his wife, Lane had assigned her, in a paper dated four days earlier, the mansion house of Robert Keayne "wherein I the said Edward Lane now Dwell." This grant was made on condition that she make no further claims whatever to his estate. Twelve days later Lane, who was evidently a sick man, made out another paper. Stating that he did not know "what condition he the said Edward Lane may fall into or what Providences as concerning himselfe may fall out in one regard or in an other &c.," he transferred his property to Richard Cooke and John Wiswall of Boston, merchants, in return for his maintenance and for payments of all his debts.

Accordingly when Anna and her new husband returned from Eng-

land, they found Richard Cooke and John Wiswall installed in the possession of most of her grandfather's property. Now the whole thing became
apparent to Anna: it had all been a plot on the part of Richard Cooke
from the very beginning. It was he who had persuaded her to marry Lane
in the first place, he who had carried to her the pieces of gold and the
messages of affection. After the annulment it was he who had persuaded
her of Lane's sufficiency and had brought them together again. He had
even been present when the paper was drawn up in which Lane assigned
her the mansion house in return for a resignation of all other claims to
the estate. She had been so desperate at the time to free herself that she
had not thought of what she was so blithely resigning; and yet twelve days
later Cooke, with his accomplice Wiswall, had it all in his own hands,
even the rich farm at Rumney Marsh that had been her grandfather's
pride. And then when she returned home from England, Cooke, wearing
her grandfather's big ring and Lane's hat with the silver band, had furnished the principal evidence against her in the trial for adultery. It was
only too clear that the whole business had been deliberately, diabolically
planned.

She had good evidence of Cooke's malice toward her now that he had
her estate. Several people were ready to report his reaction when he heard
that she and her husband were returning from England. On the day when
the news reached Boston, Ursula Cole and Alice Tilly both informed
Cooke about it and warned him that she was coming to recover her lost
property. Cooke replied that he would see her hanged if she tried to do it.
John and Mary Mansfield told Anna how Cooke had stormed about the
matter, how he had accused her of poisoning her husband, how he had
sworn to "vse all the meanes he Could to have her hanged, and had said
that if he failed to get her hanged in Boston, "he had a sonn in Barbadi-
ous: that should goe from thence to England: to prosecute the Lawe to
hange hir there."

The case seemed to be open and shut, and Anna promptly petitioned
the General Court to recover from Cooke and Wiswall all the property
that Lane had given them. She demonstrated that her marriage to Lane
had been a conspiracy on the part of Cooke to get her property and her
grandfather's into Lane's hands so that Cooke might eventually have it for

himself. He had known that Lane was impotent and that therefore there could be no heirs; he had also known that Lane was sick and could not live long. He had even offered that fact to her grandmother as a reason for allowing the second marriage. The widow Keayne—who had since become Mrs. Samuel Cole—came into court and testified that Cooke had told her that Lane "was very sickley and would not live aboue Three or four years and Therefore fear not but Lett your Daughter have him and she may Quickley have an other husband." Mrs. Cole was convinced that Cooke from the very start had "not only Indeavored to ruin my Daughter but mee."

Anna rested her case not just on this evidence of conspiracy but likewise on the claim that her second marriage with Lane was not valid, because it had never been consummated. Therefore, she said, the contract which depended upon that marriage and which put the estate again into Lane's hands was likewise invalid. It was "Founded vpon the same mestake of a marriage as the former and upon the same Ground: Cann not bee of aney force to the prejudice of your petetioner."

But the General Court was weary of this eternal squabble over Robert Keayne's property and refused to believe the story that to Anna was so obvious. To her melodramatic pleas the icy reply was given that it was not thought "suiteable to reuive troubles to the Court" in a matter that had already been settled once before. Having herself failed, Anna persuaded the overseers of the will to make a similar plea the following year (1667), but they, too, were denied. With this rebuke she gave up the struggle for a while and settled down to a happy and normal life as Mrs. Nicholas Paige. Neither she nor her husband had forgotten the injury that Richard Cooke had done them, but justice was not yet to be had. They would bide their time, and someday, perhaps, the opportunity to recover their lost heritage would come. In the meantime there was no use crying over spilt milk. Nicholas had some capital of his own, and by careful investments and hard work gradually increased it. Before many years passed, he had become one of the leading merchants of Boston and recouped by his ships and shops as much as he and Anna had lost through the machinations of their enemies.

Anna's new husband was a bold and likable man, of generous impulses but shrewd in all his public actions. Though not disposed to reckon over-much with religious scruples in his commercial dealings, he had sense enough never to offend Puritan sensibilities. He did his best to gain the friendship and respect of his community, especially of those men who seemed best qualified to help him. As a result, each new turn of events found him more firmly established in public favor and personal security. When King Philip's War threatened the colony's existence in 1675, Captain Paige won esteem by commanding a cavalry troop that helped to whip the savages into submission. A year later, when Edward Randolph came to enforce the Navigation Acts in Boston, Paige gained the commendations of his fellow merchants by threatening to knock Randolph on the head if the latter attempted to board his ships. Before long, however, Nicholas saw that the wind was not blowing in that direction. He and a number of other prominent citizens, including Joseph Dudley (Anna's uncle), made friends with Randolph so that by 1685 the customs officer was writing letters to Dudley in which he sent his respects to "Mr. Page and his lady."

In the ensuing revolutions that rocked the colony, Paige played his hand with consummate skill. When the charter was revoked and Joseph Dudley became president of the Council for New England, Nicholas invited him to live at Boston in the house that he and Anna had acquired there. Since Dudley's own house was in Roxbury, he gladly agreed to live with the Paiges, where his hostess would be his own niece. When Andros arrived as governor of the Dominion of New England in 1686, Paige kept in the good graces of that ruler, too; but when the people of Boston gathered together to overthrow the tyrant in 1689, Paige was on the scene, not exactly assisting the process but apparently not hindering it either. While the people called for Dudley's blood along with that of Andros, they had such confidence in Captain Paige that they placed Dudley in his hands for safekeeping. When stable government was finally established under a new charter in 1691, Paige had weathered the storm safely. What is more, he had recovered Anna's property, not only the houses and lands in Boston but the farm in Rumney Marsh as well.

The fact is that the Cookes had not played their cards so well as the Paiges. Elisha Cooke, son and successor to old Richard, had chosen the wrong side in the struggle—as far as worldly success was concerned. He had never made friends with Randolph. Instead, he had led the opposition party, the one that favored resistance to Randolph, resistance to Dudley, resistance to Andros, resistance even to the new charter that Increase Mather obtained in 1691. Consequently it had been no great matter for Paige to procure a judgment returning the lands. As soon as the old charter was revoked in 1685, the old county courts dissolved, and a new system set up under control of Dudley, the Paiges entered an action against Cooke. The jury was handpicked by Paige's friends; the judges were Paige's friends; the result was inevitable: Paige got the lands (August 5, 1686). When the verdict had been rendered, Cooke appealed to the council, presided over by Dudley, then residing in Paige's house. The result again was inevitable, and when Cooke appealed to the king in council, Dudley required him to give bond of a thousand pounds to Paige to prosecute the appeal (November 2, 1686). This was too much, and Cooke had to abandon the case (December 20, 1686). When he tried to reopen it under Andros, he met with a quick rebuff.

After the new charter had been established—over his protest—Cooke tried again, but was nonsuited. As a last resort he introduced a special bill in the General Court (February 26, 1701/02) to allow him to have the case reviewed. At the time when he introduced the bill, the governor's chair was vacant, but before the General Court took any action, Joseph Dudley was made governor. Needless to say, the bill received no further consideration.

In the meantime, since the recovery of the estate, Anna had become the great lady that she must have wished to be when she first married Edward Lane. Paige was now Colonel Paige, with a coat of arms. He had purchased a coach for her and negro servants in livery to attend upon it, a luxury that even the wealthy Samuel Sewall felt himself unable to afford. She and Nicholas moved out to the farm at Rumney Marsh and there lived in regal style, entertaining guests in the most elegant manner. Samuel Sewall, who dined there on November 4, 1690, spoke of the "sumptuous Feast" that he had enjoyed. He had already had occasion to admire Anna's coach, for he had recorded on September 12, 1688, "Rid to Cambridge Lecture, being rainy in the afternoon, Madam Paige invited me, and I came home in her Coach, with Mr. Willard and his wife, and Mrs. Paige's Boy rid my Horse."

Apparently Boston had agreed to forgive Anna for her scandalous past and to accept her as one of the elite. The Mr. Willard to whom Sewall refers was the minister of the Old South Church, which Anna had joined in 1670. Although her husband never joined, that fact was not held against him socially, for by the close of the seventeenth century a large proportion of Boston's leading citizens were in the same category.

Thus by shrewd political maneuvering Anna and Nicholas Paige overcame the social and economic handicaps with which their wedded life began and won for themselves a position of the highest rank in Boston society. Anna lived to enjoy her success until June 30, 1704. When the news of her death at Rumney Marsh reached Boston, it caused the whole colony to pause. Sewall recorded the event: "As the Governor sat at the Council-Table twas told him, Madam Paige was dead; He clap'd his hands, and quickly went out, and return'd not to the Chamber again; but ordered Mr. Secretary to prorogue the Court till the 16th of August, which Mr. Secretary did by going into the House of Deputies."

A year before she died Anna had assisted her husband in making a will, the terms of which bring this story back to where it began. The will provided that all the property of Nicholas and Anna, except for a number of small legacies, should be given to their kinswoman Martha Hobbes, who was also to be executrix. The overseers of the will, however, among whom was Governor Dudley, must "Advise and Council this our Executrix in her Marriage with any Person that she may Marry withall And we do hereby leave it as a Solemn Charge upon her and as our dying request that she do take your Advice therein And be very Carefull how she doth dispose of her self in Marryage, And that she match into a good Familly and with one that feareth God, that so neither 'She and so fair an Estate be not thrown away in her Match."

—1942

CHAPTER SEVEN

The Case against Anne Hutchinson

T HE PURITANS WHO FOUNDED the New England colonies are sometimes portrayed as having fled from persecution in order to enjoy
religious freedom. It would be fairer to say they had been unable to cap-
ture control of the English government and church in order to establish
their way as the only way of worshipping God. They believed that absolute truth, of which, they said, nature gives only a hint, was revealed to
man once and for all in the Word of God, the Bible. At the Reformation,
Calvin had rejected the interpretation of the Bible used by the Catholic
Church and had made a complete interpretation of his own. Since that
time, two generations of Puritans had been revising Calvin's interpretation, and this revision for them was absolute truth, divine and unquestion-
able. It was not merely the statement of things as they are in the world; it
was truth eternal, unlimited by time or space. It was the way of salvation.
By it the Puritans had determined to mold their daily lives, their church,
and their state. And to make this determination a reality, they had crossed
the Atlantic and had settled on the shores of Massachusetts Bay.

It is a little surprising that people so sure of themselves could have agreed
with one another long enough to establish churches and governments that
lasted for generations. They had been dissenters in England, but they did
not regard dissent itself as valuable in the way that we have come to do. We
tend to sympathize with the people they expelled for disagreeing with them.
One who stands out is Anne Hutchinson, whose disagreement gathered fol-

lowers to threaten the Massachusetts enterprise. In 1637 they expelled her, after a trial in which, as will be seen, she actually outwitted her judges. In later centuries she was hailed as a heroine for her courage in standing up for her beliefs. But if we wish to understand what was at stake in her trial and its outcome, we must consider the other side of the story.

The founders of Massachusetts had been there only four years when Hutchinson joined them. At first she was welcomed as the godly wife of a pious and successful merchant; but before she had been long in Massachusetts, she broached a doctrine that was absolutely inconsistent with the principles upon which the colony had been founded. She began to affirm a new basis for absolute truth: immediate personal communion with the Holy Ghost. If this communion had been merely for the purposes of illuminating the meaning of Holy Scripture, the Puritans might have had no quarrel with her. The communion that she described, however, was one that resulted in immediate revelation apart from the Word. To accept her doctrine would have meant the abandonment of the fundamental belief for which the Puritans had crossed the water—the belief that truth for man was to be found in the Bible. It would have meant a complete change in their daily lives, in their church, and in their state.

As for their daily life, the Puritans saw that the new doctrine would probably encourage or condone indolence and loose living. In the communion described by Hutchinson, the believer was completely passive. He did not scrutinize his life to see whether it was in accord with the precepts of the Bible; he merely waited for the Holy Ghost. As Thomas Welde, one of her judges, put it, "he is to stand still and waite for Christ to doe all for him. . . . And if he fals into sinne, he is never the more disliked of God, nor his condition never the worse." This would remove all the rational basis for moral endeavor that the Puritan theologians had been painfully constructing since the time of Calvin. The magistrates of Massachusetts found an example of what acceptance of this heresy meant in the refusal of Hutchinson's followers to join the expedition against the Pequot Indians, who were threatening the colony.

As for the church, the Puritans must have realized that Hutchinson's dogma destroyed most of the reasons for its existence. For in the list of eighty-two errors refuted by a synod of New England ministers,

and declared by most members of the court that condemned her to have
sprung from her doctrine of revelation, are found these two statements:

> Errour 22. None are to be exhorted to beleeve, but such whom we
> know to be the elect of God, or to have his Spirit in them effectually.
> Error 53. No Minister can teach one that is anoynted by the Spirit
> of Christ, more then hee knowes already unlesse it be in some
> circumstances.

In other words, the minister and the church were no longer needed,
"unlesse it be in some circumstances," since God, according to Hutchinson, preferred to deal with His children directly.

In the same way she would have done away with the state as it then
existed. Her view might have been compatible with a state concerned only
with secular ends, but to the Puritans such a state would have seemed
a sorry affair. Their community was a spiritual association devoted primarily to spiritual ends; and it found its laws in the general principles
deducible from the Bible and from a rational observation of God's gover-
nance of the world. Her insistence on revelation apart from the Word as
the source of truth had the corollary "that the will of God in the Word,
or directions thereof, are not the rule whereunto Christians are bound
to conforme themselves, to live thereafter." Therefore, the laws that the
Puritan state was enforcing could have no divine validity for her. If the
state were to exist, it would have to be simply as a secular association; and
that was a concept which the founders could not entertain and for which
they had exiled Roger Williams the year before.

These results of Hutchinson's doctrines became apparent before the
members of the orthodox group knew for certain what those doctrines
were, for Hutchinson had carefully refrained from committing herself in
public. It was clear to the magistrates of the Bay Colony, however, that
the nub of her teaching had to consist in the idea of personal revelation,
and that its consequences were at war with the ideals of Massachusetts.
Because the Puritans had undergone great hardships in order to put those
ideals into practice, it was only to be expected that they should do their
utmost to maintain them. This we of today can readily understand. What

is more difficult for us to comprehend is that the Puritans did not regard Hutchinson's attack on their ideals as a difference of opinion. The elected governor of the colony, John Winthrop, could not regard the case as that of one opinion against another; it was personal opinion against truth. And the terrifying fact was that this personal opinion was gaining ground; the Word of God was being undermined by a woman. Winthrop saw the commonwealth that he had done much to found—which had been consecrated to absolute truth—rocked to its foundations by the seductive teachings of a clever lady. He could not help regarding that woman as an enemy of God. As governor he was bound to do his utmost to protect the Word and the state from this instrument of Satan.

To appreciate Winthrop's sense of responsibility, it is necessary to recall the Puritans' conception of the magistrate's office. This requires an examination of that classic of Protestant political theory, the *Vindiciæ Contra Tyrannos*. Here we find the origin of the state described in these terms:

> Now we read of two sorts of covenants at the inaugurating of kings,
> the first between God, the king, and the people, that the people might
> be the people of God. The second, between the king and the people,
> that the people shall obey faithfully, and the king command justly.

The *Vindiciæ* explains that in these covenants "kings swear as vassals to observe the law of God," and subjects promise to obey them within the limits thus set.

From numerous statements of the Puritans, it is clear that the theories of government outlined in the *Vindiciæ* were those followed in Massachusetts. Although the foundation of the government was the charter from the king, all who came into the community were by tacit assumption regarded as "bound by soleme covenant to walke by the rule of Gods word in all their conversation." Winthrop explained the origin of the government in this fashion:

> We A. B. C. *etc.* consented to cohabite in the Massachusetts, and
> under the government set up among us by his Majesty's patent or

grant for our mutual safety and wellfare, we agreed to walke according to the rules of the gospell. And thus you have both a christian common weale and the same founded upon the patent.

It was pursuant to this social compact that the oath administered to officers of the government provided that they should act "according to the Laws of God, and for the advancement of his Gospell, the Laws of this land, and the good of the people of this Jurisdiction."

That the compact was not merely between the people themselves and the magistrates whom they set up, but also between the people, the magistrates, and God, is indicated by the language in which the Puritans spoke of themselves. Always they were the "People of God," and frequently they referred to their commonwealth as Israel. Furthermore, they believed the consequences of their compact to be those specified by the author of the *Vindiciae*. The latter pointed out that according to the compact, "the king himself, and all the people should be careful to honour and serve God according to His will revealed in His word, which, if they performed, God would assist and preserve their estates: as in doing the contrary, he would abandon, and exterminate them." In like manner the Puritan ministers explained to the people of New England that they were a chosen people and could not "sin at so cheap a rate, or expect so few stripes for their disobedience" as those who had no covenant with the Almighty:

Whilst a covenant people carry it so as not to break covenant, the Lord blesseth them visibly, but if they degenerate, then blessings are removed and woful Judgments come in their room.

So, while the Puritans were submissive and obedient to God—that is, as long as they submitted to His will as expressed in the Word—He would prosper all their affairs. But if they strayed and fell to open sin, He would let loose His wrath upon them. As the *Vindiciae* points out, there are two respondents to God's covenant:

. . . the king and Israel, who by consequence are bound one for another and each for the whole. For as when Caius and Titus have promised jointly to pay to their creditor Seius a certain sum, each of them is bound for himself and his companion, and the creditor may demand the sum of which of them he pleases. In the like manner the king for himself, and Israel for itself are bound with all circumspection to see that the church be not damnified: if either of them be negligent of their covenant, God may justly demand the whole of which of the two He pleases, and the more probably of the people than of the king, and for that many cannot so easily slip away as one, and have better means to discharge the debts than one alone.

The implications of this theory are numerous. Probably the most important is the doctrine that subjects must rebel when the magistrates command something contrary to the Law of God. More to the point in the present instance, however, is the notion that if the ruler does not punish outward breaches of that law, the whole people may suffer punishment at the hands of the Almighty Himself. Solomon Stoddard, the minister of Northampton, put the case as late as 1703:

> Under the best government many times there will be a breaking out of sin, though Rulers and People do what they can to prevent it, yet particular persons will be guilty of flagitious crimes. But if the people doe their duty to inform Rulers, and Rulers theirs in bearing a due testimony against them, these are not the sins of the Land; God don't charge these sins upon the Country: the country is not guilty of the Crimes of particular Persons, unless they make themselves guilty; if they countenance them, or connive at them, they make themselves guilty by participation: But when they are duely witnessed against, they bring no publick guilt.

Increase Mather had the same doctrine in mind when in 1677 he exhorted the governors,

> I know you cannot change mens hearts, yet you may doe much (if God help you) towards the effecting an outward Reformation, which will procure outward blessings and prevent outward Judgments and

desolations. There is pride in the hearts of men, you cannot Reform that, but there is pride in *Apparel*, which the Lord has said he will punish for, you may cause *that* to be reformed. There is Drunkeness in the sight of God, which doth not fall under your Cognizance, but Drunkeness in the sight of men, and the occasions of it, do; which you may and ought to remove.

This was doubtless the reason that Massachusetts gave to Plymouth Colony after imprisoning John Alden for alleged complicity in a murder on the Kennebec in Maine. For Governor Bradford, after expressing dissatisfaction with the action of Massachusetts, apparently refers to such a justification:

But yet being assured of their Christian love, and perswaded what was done was out of godly zeale, that religion might not suffer, nor sinne any way covered or borne with, . . . they did indeavore to appease and satisfie them the best they could.

Bradford records also the testimony of several ministers who had been questioned concerning the duty of the magistrate in seeking out instances of disobedience of the Mosaic laws regarding adultery and sodomy. The answer of one of them is typical. He declared that the magistrate must follow up every suggestion of indulgence in these crimes in order to punish them, "or els he may betray his countrie and people to the heavie displeasure of God."

No one was more thoroughly imbued with this socioreligious theory of criminology than Governor Winthrop. At the outset of the Bay Colony experiment, he had advised his fellow immigrants that "the care of the publique must oversway all private respects." Later he reminded the colonists that the nature of their incorporation "tyes every member thereof to seeke out and entertaine all means that may conduce to the wellfare of the bodye, and to keepe off whatsoever doth appeare to tend to theire damage." Granted this, it was the social obligation of every member of the commonwealth to refrain from breaking the Lord's commandments, for by such a breach he might bring down the divine wrath on the whole community. And it was, of course, the duty of the magistrate to protect the community by punishing the individual sinner, lest the community appear to condone sin. As Winthrop put it, "better it is some member should suffer the evill they bring upon themselves, than that, by indulgence towards them, the whole familye of God in this countrey should be scattered, if not destroyed."

It was with these beliefs in mind that the magistrates of Massachusetts began the trial of Hutchinson. There were undoubtedly numerous personal animosities that led to the inauguration of the prosecution—the pique of the ministers and the jealousy of the magistrates. Theoretically, however, the trial was based on the charge that Hutchinson had broken the Law of God. Now it must be remembered that before her trial this wise woman had never publicly advanced her tenet of personal revelation. Neither had she openly professed any doctrines that could be sanely regarded as contrary to the Law of God. It was clear, nevertheless, that someone must have been urging such views privately, for the synod of ministers had found eighty-two of them to condemn. It was common rumor that that someone was Hutchinson. Accordingly in October 1637 she was summoned before the General Court to answer the scanty list of charges that the magistrates had been able to draw up.

Although she may have instigated it, Hutchinson had been wise enough not to sign a petition in favor of John Wheelwright, a minister convicted of sedition for espousing doctrines attributed to her. The General Court had been disfranchising, fining, and even banishing the signatories. And so now, when the court attempted to deal "with the head of all this faction," they could accuse her merely with "countenancing and incouraging" those who had been sowers of sedition. To this was added the even weaker charge that she held in her house meetings that had been condemned by the general assembly as a thing not tolerable nor comely in the sight of God nor fitting for her sex. Following these was a last and more serious indictment, that she had traduced the faithful ministers of the colony.

The ground of the first specification was that in entertaining those who had been subsequently convicted of sedition, she had broken the fifth commandment: she had dishonored the governors, who were the fathers of the commonwealth. Her nimble wit soon put her judges in a dilemma.

Mrs. H. But put the case Sir that I do fear the Lord and my parents, may not I entertain them that fear the Lord because my parents will not give me leave?

After attempting to find his way around this logical impasse, Governor Winthrop, good Puritan casuist though he was, was forced to take refuge in dogmatic assertion.

Gov. We do not mean to discourse with those of your sex but only this; you do adhere unto them and do endeavor to set forward this faction and so you do dishonour us.

The court next called upon her to justify the weekly meetings that she held at her house. In answer she quoted two passages of Scripture: Titus II, 3–5, which indicates that the elder women should instruct the younger, and Acts XVIII, 26, wherein "*Aquila* and *Priscilla* tooke upon them to instruct *Apollo*, more perfectly, yet he was a man of good parts, but they being better instructed might teach him."

COURT. See how your argument stands, *Priscilla* with her husband, tooke *Apollo* home to instruct him privately, therefore Mistris *Hutchison* without her husband may teach sixty or eighty.
HUTCH. I call them not, but if they come to me, I may instruct them.
COURT. Yet you shew us not a rule.
HUTCH. I have given you two places of Scripture.
COURT. But neither of them will sute your practise.
HUTCH. Must I shew my name written therein?

Again, after some further argument, Winthrop resorted to bare assertion, enunciating once more the Puritan theory of criminology:

. . . we see no rule of God for this, we see not that any should have authority to set up any other exercises besides what authority hath already set up and so what hurt comes of this you will be guilty of and we for suffering you.

Undaunted by the failure to prove the first two counts, the court now moved to the final and most serious accusation, that she had insulted the ministers. The basis of this charge lay in a conference held the preceding December between the ministers and Hutchinson. Even though the conference had been private, the ministers now testified that she had designated them all, except Mr. Cotton and Mr. Wheelwright, as laboring under a covenant of works. The Puritan ministers were still filled with the zeal of the Reformation, and no epithet could have been better designed to arouse their ire than the one that they now declared she had applied to them. When the court adjourned for the day, she was facing her most difficult problem.

That night she went over some notes taken at the December conference by her opponent Mr. Wilson, pastor of the Boston church. Finding that the ministers' testimonies against her were inaccurate, she demanded, when the trial reopened the following morning, that the ministers be made to give their evidence under oath. This created a great stir and only served to strengthen the hard feeling of the court against her. Finally, however, John Cotton, teacher of the Boston church and most respected theologian of the colony, was called upon to give his version of the conference. With careful diplomacy he soothed the injured pride of the other ministers and brought his speech to a dramatic close by declaring, "I must say that I did not find her saying they were under a covenant of works, nor that she said they did preach a covenant of works." And though pressed by the other ministers, he firmly stood his ground.

With this testimony the case against Hutchinson was about to collapse. The first two specifications against her had been too weakly sustained to warrant any grave condemnation, and now the revered Cotton had practically destroyed the basis of the only remaining charge. Her triumph was too much for her. Hitherto she had been on guard and had dexterously parried every rude thrust of her prosecutors. Had she been content to hold her tongue at this point, her judges might have felt obliged to dismiss the case for lack of evidence, or at best would have passed some vote of censure in order to save their faces. Instead of continuing to rely on her native wit, she proceeded to justify herself by an immediate divine revelation.

Her prosecutors could not have hoped for a better ground upon which to condemn her. The surviving descriptions of the trial make it clear that the men who were at the same time her prosecutors and her judges had determined her guilt in advance and were merely searching for sufficient evidence on which to convict her. She herself gave them that evidence. By claiming an immediate revelation, she denied the fundamental tenet upon which the Puritan state was founded: that the Will of God was expressed directly only in the Word. Now all the previous charges could be dropped and her conviction based on this alone. And so Winthrop records that

> the Court and all the rest of the Assembly (except those of her owne party) did observe a speciall providence of God, that (while shee went about to cover such offences as were laid to her charge, by putting matters upon proofe, and then quarrelling with the evidence) her owne mouth should deliver her into the power of the Court, as guilty of that which all suspected her for, but were not furnished with proofe sufficient to proceed against her. . . .
>
> The Court saw now an inevitable necessity to rid her away, except wee would bee guilty, not only of our own ruine, but also of the Gospel, so in the end the sentence of banishment was pronounced against her, and shee was committed to the Marshall, till the Court should dispose of her.

Thus ended the trial of Anne Hutchinson, a proceeding that scarcely deserves to be dignified by that name. Our indignation at its unfairness is commendable; for members of a modern state founded on self-government should be acutely conscious of the value of the forms of justice. We should remember, however, that this proceeding took place in an infant community the leaders of which looked on democracy as the worst form of government. This in no way excuses the unfairness of the trial, but it does make it easier to recognize the appropriateness of the sentence. Granted that Hutchinson proclaimed a belief in immediate revelation, it was quite impossible that she should have been retained in the Puritan commonwealth. That our natural sympathies lie with her, rather than with the rulers of the colony, is simply an indication that the Puritan experiment failed. It was because her opinions were repellent to them that the Puritans banished Anne Hutchinson, but they sincerely believed that in thus protecting themselves they were also protecting God's eternal truth. Winthrop summed up the case in characteristic fashion, with words that have the ring of genuine feeling:

Thus it pleased the Lord to heare the prayers of his afflicted people (whose soules had wept in secret, for the reproach which was cast upon the Churches of the Lord Jesus in this Countrey, by occasion of the divisions which were grown amongst us, through the vanity of some weake minds, which cannot seriously affect any thing long, except it bee offered them under some renewed shape) and by the care and indevour of the wise and faithfull Ministers of the Churches, assisted by the Civill authority, to discover this Master-piece of the old Serpent, and to break the brood by scattering the Leaders, under whose conduct hee had prepared such Ambushment, as in all reason would soon have driven Christ and Gospel out of *New England*, (though to the ruine of the instruments themselves, as well as others) and to the repossessing of Satan in his ancient Kingdom; It is the Lords work, and it is marvellous in our eyes.

—1937

CHAPTER EIGHT

The Puritan's Puritan: Michael Wigglesworth

Historians have long since discovered that the Puritans were much more human than we had once supposed. They ate and drank and fought and loved and even occasionally laughed a little. Perhaps, then, they were (like us) hearty, warmhearted creatures after all. Perhaps. When we begin to think of the Puritans this way, we sooner or later have to reckon with a man like Michael Wigglesworth. The grim pages of his *Day of Doom* have long been familiar to students of American literature. His diary is even more challenging than his verse to any liberal view of the Puritans. For the man who emerges here calls to mind those stern figures in steeple-crowned hats who represent Puritanism in popular cartoons. So closely does Michael Wigglesworth approximate the unhappy popular conception of our seventeenth-century forebears that he seems more plausible as a satirical reconstruction than as a human being. His very name, to anyone not familiar with its illustrious history, must suggest a caricature, and the suggestion is sadly borne out by the diary and supported by all that can be ascertained about him.

His biography, as we know it from other sources than the diary, is appropriate. He was one of the first settlers of New England; he attended Harvard, the Puritan college, and taught there for several years; he became a minister and spent the greater part of his life preaching Puritanism to the people of Malden, Massachusetts. He wrote a poem that his fellow Puritans bought by the thousands in order to read in vivid figures about the Day of Judgment. In keeping with the crabbed figure of the cartoon, he was a sickly man, always complaining of ill health; throughout a large part of his life he was an invalid. Yet he fathered eight children, outlived two wives, and had married a third when he died in 1705, in his seventy-fourth year.

This pattern was not an uncommon one among the first generation of New Englanders: Harvard, the ministry, the ripe and respected old age. Against this familiar backdrop his diary fills in the lines of the caricature with heavy strokes, until the Puritan emerges as his worst enemies would have him, a man with great capacity for survival—but with small reason for wanting to survive. Was the Puritan a killjoy? Wigglesworth thought that all pleasure apart from delight in God's grace was dangerous. His heart was "sunk with sorrow" when he found his students at Harvard indulging in merriment. Thus he wrote on June 25, 1653,

> I set my self again this day to wrestle with the Lord for my self and then for my pupils and the Lord did pretty much inlarge my heart in crying to him. But still I see the Lord shutting out my prayers and refusing to hear for he whom in special I pray'd for, I heard in the forenoon with ill company playing musick, though I had so solemnly warn'd him but yesterday of letting his spirit go after pleasures.

Since the students at Harvard could not fail to display a certain amount of animal spirits, this type of experience continued to sadden the teacher's heart. On one occasion he gave a delinquent student a long lecture on the dangers of pleasure, and yet "that very evening," Wigglesworth confided to the diary, "he was again at play . . . and when he saw me coming he slinked home and left his game whereby I gather that he is more afraid of me a poor sinful worm than of God and I am sorry that so solemn a warning and so efficacious for the present should have lost its power so soon." Wigglesworth had no appreciation for the humor in situations of this kind, and he suffered the most innocuous pranks of his students with a ludicrous air of mourning. When he heard some of his admonitions "with derision reiterated among the scolars," he solemnly sought comfort in his Maker. And when the students displayed a not incomprehen-

sible reluctance to study Hebrew, he saw in their intractability "A spirit of
unbridled licentiousness," and exclaimed, "Lord in mercy heal, or I know
not what wil become of New England."

If worrying would have saved New England, Wigglesworth would
have saved it. One of the most revealing passages in the diary is the one
where he records his almost ridiculously painful deliberations about a
neighbor's door swinging back and forth in the wind.

> The wise god who knoweth how to tame and take down proud and
> wanton hearts, suffereth me to be sorely buffeted with the like temp-
> tation as formerly about seeing some dores blow to and fro with the
> wind in some danger to break, as I think; I cannot tel whether it were
> my duty to giue them some hint that owe them. When I think 'tis a
> common thing, and that 'tis impossible but that the owners should
> haue oft seen them in that case, and heard them blow to and fro, and
> that it is but a trivial matter, and that I haue given a hint to one that
> dwels in the hous, and he maketh light of it; and that it would rather
> be a seeming to check others mindlesness of their own affairs, and
> lastly that there may be special reasons for it that I know not; why
> the case seemeth clear that 'tis not my duty. yet I am sorely affraid I
> should regard iniquity in my heart, and god upon this ecclypseth the
> sweet beam's of his love, he hideth his face and I am troubled.

Wigglesworth worried not only about his neighbors' doors but also, of
course, about their souls. He found his spirit "quite discouraged and soul
and body both ready to quail, because of my sorrows for what mine eyes
daly behould in others sins and mispense of their precious hours." He
resolved "to do more for christ than I haue done by reproveing lightness
and mad mirth on Sabbath Evenings and by visitings." He even became
so concerned with saving the souls of others that he found it necessary to
reprimand himself for having, as he said, "a greater desire of others finding christ than of my own."

In strange company with this solicitude went an unrestrained selfishness, which is revealed in a remarkable series of reflections on marriage.
Wigglesworth evidently believed that he was suffering from gonorrhea

and accordingly had some doubts about whether or not he should marry. His doubts arose, however, not from any concern for his bride-to-be, but from an apprehension that marriage might impair his own health. The factor that finally determined him to marry was the advice of a physician that marriage might prove beneficial, instead of detrimental. He accordingly resolved "to redeem the spring time for marrying or taking physick or both." The sad sequel is that his bride died four years after her marriage, from what cause is unknown.

His crass behavior in this episode never gave Wigglesworth any pangs of conscience, but he was by no means free from a morbid feeling of guilt for other offenses that we should probably consider entirely innocuous. Guilt, in fact, seems to have been a necessary feeling to Wigglesworth. The diary served as a kind of account book in which he rendered up the assets and liabilities of his soul, with the debit side of the ledger receiving almost all the entries. It was not that he ever behaved in a scandalous fashion outwardly; his outward behavior was doubtless exemplary. But Wigglesworth knew that man never achieves righteousness in this world. He knew that within him lay all the guilt of Adam, and he took pleasure in abasing himself for his sinful heart, for his pride, his overvaluing of creature comforts, his neglect of God. The automatic result of the daily examination of his soul was the conclusion that he was a vile worm, indeed the "chief of sinners."

The modern reader will rightly discount Wigglesworth's claim to preeminence in sin, but his frequent protestations of guilt were more than a pose. Wigglesworth was obsessed with guilt. It is perhaps significant that one of the accusations that he most frequently leveled against himself was a lack of natural affection for his father. At one point he confessed himself secretly glad at his father's death.

We should scarcely exaggerate, I think, if we described Michael Wigglesworth as a morbid, humorless, selfish busybody. In him the ugly and somewhat absurd, somewhat pathetic figure of the caricature comes to life, a Roundhead to confirm the last prejudice of the Cavalier. And yet historians have been at some pains to erase this very caricature. The popular picture of the Puritans, it has been shown, is grossly overdrawn, for Puritanism did not exclude the enjoyment of the good things of life. The

Puritans read books, wrote verses, and had their pictures painted. They were unashamedly fond of beer and wine and even of more ardent spirits. They liked to eat well and live well and made no pretensions to asceticism. They were not prudish; they made no attempt to stifle natural passions in celibacy. They were men of the world, able to deal equally well with an Indian, a Royalist, or a seidel of beer.

How, then, are we to interpret Michael Wigglesworth? Was he simply an anomaly, one of those eccentric killjoys who can be found in any society? There are surely good reasons for regarding Wigglesworth as exceptional: he never enjoyed good health, and his bodily weaknesses may have been responsible in large measure for his morbid state of mind; furthermore, his preoccupation with his father's death suggests that he may have had some psychological disorder. But to dismiss Wigglesworth as an unhealthy anomaly is to condemn him without a trial. He did, after all, teach at Harvard College; he did serve as minister to a Puritan congregation; and he did write for New England the most popular book of his time. In his own day no one accused him of heresy or eccentricity. Grant that he was exceptional, which he certainly was, did his singularity constitute a denial, or an intensification, of Puritan values? Was he exceptionally Puritan or exceptionally unpuritan? Puritanism unquestionably made rigorous demands on those who subscribed to it. The fact that Michael Wigglesworth, as revealed in the diary, does not look like the average New Englander of the seventeenth century may mean simply that he accepted the demands of Puritanism more wholeheartedly than most of his countrymen.

To affirm, then, that Wigglesworth was exceptionally and emphatically Puritan is not to cast doubt on what historians have been saying about the Puritans, but it is to suggest that the popular caricature may be closer to the central meaning of Puritanism than the friends of New England sometimes like to suppose. Although the popular view fails to do justice to the Puritan; although it neglects the strength of his conviction, the integrity of his purpose, and the breadth and subtlety of intellect with which he defended himself; although it overlooks the fact that he was, after all, a human being—nevertheless, it does emphasize the distinctive features of Puritanism as they now appear to a hedonist world. If the cartoonist could study and understand Puritanism in all its complexity, he would probably still draw the same cartoon. For the mark of the Puritan was not his human warmth but his zeal, his suspicion of pleasure, his sense of guilt; and it is these qualities that are satirized in the popular caricature. Michael Wigglesworth, who appears to be a living embodiment of the caricature, was distinctly and thoroughly a Puritan. If we measure him by the precepts of the Puritan preachers, it will be apparent, I think, that his sense of guilt, his hostility to pleasure, and even his minding of other people's business were not the anomalies of a diseased mind but simply the qualities demanded of a good Puritan.

To consider the last, most objectionable quality first, did Wigglesworth's concern with other people's sins represent merely the tedious petulance of a busybody, or was it the expression of some fundamental part of Puritan belief? In the light of the social and political theory expressed by virtually every articulate Puritan, one cannot escape the conclusion that Puritanism invited, or rather demanded, active cooperation from every member of society in the eradication of sin. It was held up as a sign of regeneration that a man should reform his friends and neighbors. The true convert, Thomas Hooker explained, was one who sought to destroy all sins. "What ever sins come within his reach, he labors the removal of them, out of the familyes where he dwels, out of the plantations where he lives, out of the companies and occasions, with whom he hath occasion to meet and meddle at any time." The obligation of the convert to reform those around him was grounded in the covenant by which God sealed the salvation of his elect. "If God make a Covenant, to be a God to thee and thine," John Cotton pointed out, "then it is thy part to see it, that thy children and servants be Gods people." And again, "when we undertake to be obedient to him [God]," we undertake not only "in our owne names, and for our owne parts, but in the behalfe of every soule that belongs to us, . . . our wives, and children, and servants, and kindred, and acquaintance, and all that are under our reach, either by way of subordination, or coordination."

In a place where every serious person was engaged in persuading himself of his own conversion such doctrine was probably sufficient in itself to create a community of busybodies. But the desire to produce evidence of one's own conversion was not the only ground of zeal for the morality of others: The Puritan believed that the outward prosperity of every social group rested upon the prevention of sin among the members. Quite apart from his individual relationship to God through the covenant of grace, every Puritan partook of a more external, social relationship with Him through the societies to which he belonged, through family, church, state, and in Wigglesworth's case, the college. Every social institution existed for the Puritan by virtue of a special covenant with God in which the members had promised obedience to the laws of God. Consequently every Puritan was bound to obey God not merely as a sanctified man (in order to prove to himself that he was saved) but as a member of every group to which he belonged. If he failed, he not only demonstrated his own damnation but brought the temporal wrath of God upon his family, upon his church, and upon his state. Thus we find Wigglesworth exclaiming over his sins, "ah Lord! I pul down evils upon others as wel as my self. Sicknesses, death of godly ones, wants, divisions have not my sins a hand in these miserys? oh Lord I am affraid of thy judgements upon my self and others." These ideas penetrated to every level of society in New England. In 1656, the year in which Wigglesworth accepted a call to preach at Malden, a miserable girl, laboring under the name of Tryal Pore, who had committed the sin of fornication, confessed to the Middlesex County Court, "By this my sinn I haue not only donn what I can to Poull doune Jugmente from the lord on my selue but allso apon the place where I liue."

In view of these beliefs Wigglesworth's zeal for correcting sin is entirely understandable and entirely in accordance with the strictest Puritan doctrine. Since the whole group had promised obedience to God, the whole group would suffer at the hands of God for the sins of any delinquent member. Manifestly every member must cooperate in avoiding such a fate. Incessant and universal vigilance was the price of prosperity. It was as if a district occupied by a military force were given notice that for any disorder the whole community—innocent and guilty alike— would be penalized. Every Christian society had received such a notice from God, and its effect upon the godly members, of whom we may account Wigglesworth one, was an extraordinary zeal for bringing others into the paths of righteousness.

A thorough selfishness was by no means inconsistent with this kind of zeal. When the Puritan sought to reform his neighbor, he had no altruistic, humanitarian goal in sight, but simply the fulfillment of his own personal promise to his Creator and the prevention of public calamities in which he himself would be involved. Even Wigglesworth's selfishness in the matter of marriage does not set him off from his contemporaries. All the evidence indicates that marriage in the seventeenth century was a business transaction to which the haggling over dowries and settlements gave more the air of an economic merger than of a psychological union. The Puritans, to be sure, regarded the relationship of husband and wife as one in which love should predominate, but the love was a duty that came after marriage, not a spontaneous passion that preceded it.

In his sense of guilt Wigglesworth likewise exhibited the frame of mind that was expected of a good Puritan. When Anne Hutchinson lost her sense of guilt and declared that God had cast her loose from the bonds of sin, the orthodox members of the Massachusetts government banished her in 1637. No one, they felt, could escape from sin in this world, not even in Massachusetts; and anyone who thought such a thing possible was either insane or in the hands of the devil or both. Thomas Hooker, sometimes considered more liberal than other Puritans, advised his readers that "we must look wisely and steddily upon our distempers, look sin in the face, and discern it to the full." The man who could take such a full view of sin could hardly be a happy human being, for according to Hooker he would be one who

hath seen what sin is, and what it hath done, how it hath made havock of his peace and comfort, ruinated and laid wast the very Principles of Reason and Nature, and Morality, and made him a terror to himself, when he hath looked over the loathsom abominations that lie in his bosom, that he is afraid to approach the presence of the Lord to bewail his sins, and to crave pardon, lest he should be confounded for them, while he is but confessing of them; afraid and ashamed lest any man living should know but the least part of that which he knows by himself, and could count it happy that himself was not, that the remembrance of those hideous evils of his might be no more.

Few persons in any time could exhibit a feeling of guilt as strong as that which Hooker here demands. That Wigglesworth did attain something like it is a sign not of eccentricity but of orthodoxy.

If we examine, finally, the sins of which Wigglesworth most often finds himself guilty, we arrive at the origin of his hostility to pleasure and at the central meaning of Puritanism as Wigglesworth exemplifies it: the belief that fallen man inevitably estimates too highly the creatures and things of this world, including himself. Pride and the overvaluing of "the creature," these are the sins of which Wigglesworth accused himself almost daily, and these are the sins involved in enjoyment of the senses. The Puritan was not exactly hostile to pleasure, but his suspicion was so close to hostility that it often amounted to the same thing. A man might enjoy the things of this world, provided that he did so in proportion to their absolute value, but since their absolute value was insignificant when placed beside the value of their Creator, the amount of pleasure that might lawfully be drawn from them was small indeed. It is not surprising, therefore, that Wigglesworth seldom recorded specific actions in which he had displayed too high a sense of his own or of the creature's value. The sin did not lie in the action itself, but in the estimate that was placed upon it, as when he found himself too happy with having one of his sermons well received. His sins were sins of attitude, sins of judgment, sins of a will that had been debilitated and corrupted by the original fall of man. They were not particular sins but the essence of sin itself. For sin to the Puritan was not simply the breach of a commandment; it was a breach of the order that God had ordained throughout all creation, an order that was inverted by sin and restored by grace. The Puritan God had created the universe to serve His own glory, but He had directed that all parts of that universe, except man, should serve him only indirectly— through serving man. As long as man remained innocent in the Garden of Eden, so long did man enjoy dominion over the creatures and direct communication with his Maker. But sin had inverted the order of things and turned the whole creation topsy-turvy. As one Puritan minister put it, "Man is dethroned, and become a servant and slave to those things that were made to serve him, and he puts those things in his heart, that God hath put under his feet." The only remedy was return to God through

Christ, a return that would be completed at the last day and that would be partially consummated here and now through the operation of saving grace. "If sin be (as it is) an aversion or turning away of the soul from God to something else besides him ... then in the work of grace there is a conversion and turning of the soul towards God again, as to the best and cheifest good of all." Again and again Puritan ministers warned their listeners that "the onely sutable adequate ultimate object of the soul of man is god himselfe," that "all true christians have Christ as the scope and End of their lives," that "no creature that is finite, can be the end of the Soul nor give satisfaction to it." Thus, in recognizing that he placed too high a value on the creatures, Wigglesworth was recognizing that in him the divine order was still inverted. No matter how often he told himself that God was the supreme good to which all else must be subordinated, no matter how loudly he called upon God to make him believe, he could not help overestimating himself and the world.

In this undeviating scrutiny of his own corruption, Wigglesworth was probably not a typical Puritan, as he was not a typical human being; but he was closer to the ideals of Puritanism than were his more warm-blooded contemporaries who indulged the flesh and enjoyed the creatures.

—*1946*

CHAPTER NINE

The Courage of Giles Cory and Mary Easty

SALEM HAS NEVER BEEN ABLE to keep the story of the witch trials to itself. For nearly three centuries the story has excited the imagination and curiosity of men and women throughout the Western world. It somehow strikes a chord that we all respond to, whether with indignation or sorrow or sympathy. It opens a window not only on Salem, not only on Puritan New England, but on the human condition.

I will not dwell on that part of the story that has been illuminated by the study of earlier social tensions within Salem Village and between Salem Village and Salem town. Without in any way diminishing the importance of those local forces in shaping the events of 1692, I want to focus on the larger tensions in New England of the time and on the wider significance of the trials for the history of Puritan New England and for later American history.

The trials occurred at a time when the people of Massachusetts were passing through very difficult times. Cotton Mather, for whom those times were particularly difficult, called them "woeful"—and with reason. In 1685 Massachusetts had lost the royal charter that had given the colony virtual independence from England for fifty-five years, an independence that had made possible the Puritan experiment, an independence that had enabled Englishmen to create institutions that departed radically from those under which they had grown up in the mother country. In 1686 a Catholic king, James II, had sent Edmund Andros, a professional soldier, with absolute authority to govern Massachusetts and all the rest of New England, and without benefit of the representative assemblies that had hitherto been the supreme power of government in every New England colony.

Fortunately the people of England liked James II no better than the people of New England liked Andros. The people of Massachusetts sent Andros packing back to England in a bloodless revolution that accompanied the Glorious Revolution of 1688 in England. And they sent Cotton Mather's distinguished father, Increase Mather, the minister of Boston's Second Church, to recover the old charter and the freedom from English control that went with it.

In London, Mather was joined by William Phips, a Bostonian who had made a fortune by the very unpuritan method of raising sunken treasure from a Spanish galleon in the West Indies. Phips was not what people at the time would have called a proper Bostonian, even though he had attained a degree of respectability by marrying the widow of the town's leading merchant. He was a rough-and-ready type, not very visibly a saint, and early in 1692 the people of Massachusetts learned that he and Mather had not succeeded in recovering the old charter. Instead, they had procured a new one, under which the king reserved to himself the appointment of the colony's governor, and the first governor he appointed was William Phips.

The colony had been limping along under a provisional government of old-time leaders who had participated in the expulsion of Andros. The old-timers had followed the old-time ways, but now there was no telling what the character of the new government would be like. Everyone felt a sense of uneasiness and insecurity. To add to this feeling, the old ways seemed to be threatened also by new religious developments. Increase Mather and his aspiring son Cotton, who were the self-proclaimed defenders of everything the founding fathers had done, seemed to others to be moving away from New England's traditional Congregationalism toward Presbyterianism; and the Reverend John Wise of Ipswich was arrayed against them on this issue, while in the West, Solomon Stoddard of Northampton was challenging them with a much more outright Presbyterianism than their own. What was troubling was not so much the substance of the challenges as the fact that the intellectual and religious leaders of the colony seemed to be at odds with one another.

At the same time the younger generation, as usual, was going to the proverbial dogs, frolicking in taverns instead of going to church. Women were wearing hoop skirts, which was shocking. Men were wearing wigs, which was equally shocking. Boston did not seem to be Boston any more. New England did not seem to be New England.

It was in this atmosphere that the Salem witch scare began.

In approaching it, we will do well to recall that New Englanders did not invent witchcraft or witch trials. In the seventeenth century virtually everyone in the Western world believed that the devil confederated with human beings and either enabled them to inflict harm by supernatural means or else did it for them. There were arguments about the extent of the powers that God allowed the devil. Some people held that the devil did not have much power beyond the ability to foresee events, so that he could get his witches to go through a lot of hocus-pocus just before, say, a big storm was coming. He could thus delude the witch—and everyone else—into thinking she had caused the storm. Others believed that both the devil and his witches could actually cause things like storms or sickness or fatal accidents. But virtually no one, whether learned or ignorant, doubted the existence of witchcraft, and very few doubted that it should be punished when detected.

How little unusual the New Englanders were in this respect can be seen from the fact that throughout the colonial period there were 32 executions for witchcraft in New England, including those at Salem, while in Europe and England during the same period the numbers ran into the thousands. For example, in Germany in the two cities of Würzburg and Bamberg there were 1,500 executions in the eleven years between 1622 and 1633. The numbers involved in proportion to total population were probably higher than in New England. For example, in the town of Oppenau, in Germany's Black Forest, with a population of 650, 50 persons were executed in less than a year and 170 more accused when the trials were stopped in June 1632. England did not have as much trouble with witches as Germany, but between 1563 and 1685 there were roughly 1,000 executions. The last execution in England was in 1685, the last in

New England in 1692. But in England and on the Continent after formal executions stopped, popular lynchings of alleged witches continued until the nineteenth century. And I might add that during the height of the trials in the sixteenth and seventeenth centuries popular demand for punishment of witches frequently outran official zeal everywhere. Even the high priests of the Inquisition in Spain often showed more compassion than the people at large.

The outbreak of a witchcraft scare in Salem in 1692 was by no means the first instance of the kind in the American colonies. There had been twelve executions before that time, the earliest at Hartford in 1646, and another at Charlestown in 1648. In 1656 Ann Hibbins, widow of William Hibbins, a former merchant and magistrate of Boston, who had himself sat as a judge in the 1648 case, was executed. In 1662 Goodman Greensmith of Hartford was executed. Witches were not always women.

None of these early cases, however, had caused any epidemic of witchcraft or any panic. And it is worth noting that in many of them, as in most of the later Salem cases, the accused persons confessed to their crimes. Some of the confessions were probably obtained under some kind of duress, either psychological or physical, but it is not unlikely that some of the persons executed actually thought that they were witches, thought that they did have supernatural powers obtained from the devil.

Witchcraft is an ancient and in some societies a relatively respectable profession. In England during the sixteenth and seventeenth centuries, witchcraft was widely used for benevolent as well as malevolent purposes. So-called white witches, sometimes called cunning women or cunning men, were to be found in nearly every community—there may have been as many of them as there were ministers—and people called upon them to cure diseases, both of human beings and of cattle, to recover lost property, to bring success in business or love, and for nearly every kind of enterprise in which normal means had proved insufficient. Such white witchcraft was frowned on by the authorities but was seldom interfered with. Indeed, white witchcraft was a part of everyday life, a way of trying to control the environment in a preindustrial, prescientific society. It was frowned on because it did constitute a kind of rival force to that of the church, but only when it turned malevolent was it likely to bring prosecution, and the persons who practiced malevolent witchcraft were usually different from the cunning men and women whom people turned to for the charms and spells that might assist them in legitimate enterprises.

There seems to be no doubt that malevolent witchcraft was occasionally practiced in England and probably in New England. It is not impossible, perhaps not even improbable, that some of the persons accused at Salem believed themselves to be possessed of diabolical powers. Certainly some of them, upon being searched, were found to be in possession of the accepted paraphernalia of witchcraft.

These paraphernalia consisted, as they still do where witchcraft continues to be practiced, of dolls that are supposed to represent the victims. When the witch strokes the doll or sticks pins in it, the person bewitched is supposed to undergo excruciating pains in the part of the body corresponding to the part of the doll the witch is touching or pricking. Many of the persons convicted at Salem were found to have dolls in their possession, a piece of circumstantial evidence that in itself was almost sufficient to convict them. But there were other ways of determining whether a person was a witch or not.

Witches were thought to have witch-marks on some part of their bodies, an area of skin that was red or blue or in some way different from the rest. Furthermore, at some time during a twenty-four-hour period, it was thought, the devil or one of his imps would visit the witch and be visible to observers. He might come in the shape of a man or a woman or a child, or a cat, dog, rat, toad—indeed, any kind of creature. The devil could take nearly any shape he chose. So the usual procedure against a person accused of witchcraft was to search his or her belongings for dolls, search his or her body for witch-marks, and then keep watch over the person in the middle of a room for twenty-four hours. God help anyone who had an old doll in his possession and in addition had some skin blemish. If there was that much evidence, it was easy enough in the middle of the night, after long hours of watching, to imagine that you saw some person or animal, perhaps a mouse, come near the witch.

But this procedure could and did result in acquittals. In England in the sixteenth and seventeenth centuries, the majority of the accused witches brought to trial were acquitted. It is interesting to notice, however, that in the English cases the attention of the court centered mainly on the question of the alleged harm done by the witch rather than on her confederation with the devil. And in England the trials were usually isolated affairs, as were the trials in New England before 1692. One trial did not generate another. The Salem trials seem to have resembled European continental witch trials more than English ones, and in several ways.

On the Continent the courts fastened their attention on the witch's alleged pact with the devil, which they made sufficient cause for execution whether the witch was believed to have done harm to anyone or not. And pacts with the devil generally involved attendance at a witches' Sabbath, where all the witches of a region gathered to perform rites prescribed by their Satanic master. Witches who confessed to their crimes accordingly were expected to name the other witches whom they saw at these gatherings. Thus the circle of the accused could widen rapidly, and a witch trial turn into a witch hunt. The same sort of thing happened at Salem. Here, too, the focus was on the pact with the devil. Here, too, the accusations multiplied with every confession. And there were other resemblances. In Salem as on the Continent, the accusers were frequently children or teenagers. On the Continent the great majority of trials resulted in convictions, and not infrequently one trial would generate another until a whole region broke out in a witch hunt like that which occurred at Salem in 1692.

The events leading up to the Salem episode are thought to have begun with the case of the Goodwin children in Boston. The four Goodwin children, the eldest of whom was thirteen, began in the fall of 1688 to show signs of being bewitched. Led by the eldest girl, they fell into fits and convulsions in which they would complain of agonizing pains, now here now there. Their tongues would hang out, and they would simulate blindness and deafness and dumbness for periods of a couple of hours. In between seizures they would behave normally. The oldest Goodwin girl accused an old Irish woman with whom she had had a quarrel of bewitching them. And the woman was accordingly brought to trial.

This pattern, incidentally, was common in witchcraft cases in England. The accused witch was usually someone with whom the accuser had had a quarrel, a quarrel in which the accuser was conscious of having in some way injured the accused. For example, a man might have turned away an old woman who came to his door begging a cup of milk. Later his cow would die, and he would accuse the old woman of having bewitched it in revenge for his failure to give her the milk. The accused person was usually poor and old, and since more women were poor and old than men, witches, at least in England, were most likely to be old and to be women.

In the Goodwin case in Boston, the accused was indeed a poor and old woman, and upon search she was found to have the proper dolls in her possession and confessed to her crime and made many dark references to the devil. She apparently believed that she actually had done the job. She was tried, found guilty, and executed, but she warned her executioners that the children's afflictions would continue, for there were others who would finish what she had begun. The children heard about this and perhaps decided that it would be a shame to give up their notoriety when the witch herself had suggested that they would continue to be attacked. Or perhaps the power of suggestion was itself sufficient to produce the seizures that they had been suffering. At any rate the convulsions continued.

It was at this point that Cotton Mather stepped into the breach. He took the oldest girl into his family in order to see whether his own superior piety would not be able to defeat the devil. For a while the girl apparently enjoyed the prestige of living with the eminent minister, and her affliction continued for a few weeks. But living in the same house with Cotton Mather must have proved in itself something of a cross to bear, perhaps too high a price to pay for notoriety. Soon Mather was able to announce his triumph over the forces of darkness. And the girl, completely cured now, was able to escape the prayers of that pompous egotist.

Mather had actually done the colony a great service, for the girl, after the execution of the Irish woman, had named a number of other persons who she said were now tormenting her. Mather kept the names of these persons secret and fought the devil, as was his wont, single-handed. When he had won his victory, however, he could not refrain from giving way to his most conspicuous weakness: he had to write a book about it. Mather would frequently rush into print on much smaller provocation than this anyhow, and now he came out with a book entitled *Memorable Providences*, in which he gave a full account of the Goodwin case and of his own spec-

tacular part in putting a stop to it. From this narrative he drew two important conclusions: first, that there definitely is such a thing as witchcraft,
for he observed it in action on the victim under his care, and, second, that
it can be defeated by the method that he followed with the Goodwin girl,
which consisted mainly of isolating the victim and praying.

In later years Robert Calef, a merchant of Boston and a personal
enemy of the Mathers, accused Cotton Mather of writing this book for
the express purpose of arousing a witchcraft scare. Calef implied that
Mather had taken a prurient interest in the girl and blamed him for the
later outbreak in Salem. The charges, which Calef did not publish until
several years after the Salem episode, were patently false, as anyone can
tell by reading Mather's book. If Mather's recommendations had been
followed, there would have been no epidemic of witchcraft at Salem. But
for some reason Calef's wild accusations have stuck, and Mather has gone
down in popular legend as one of the instigators of the Salem troubles.

The Salem episode actually began in much the same way as the
Goodwin case in Boston. Perhaps Mather's pamphlet caused discussion
of witchcraft and was a cause in that way, but there is no direct connection. Early in 1692 a group of girls between the ages of nine and nineteen
began to have symptoms resembling those of the Goodwin children. They
accused Tituba, a Caribbean Indian slave woman in the family of the local
minister, of having bewitched them. The slave was beaten into a confession and accused two old women of being her confederates. These in
turn confessed and accused others, apparently in hope of gaining lenient
treatment. The circle widened rapidly; and by the time the new governor, Sir William Phips, arrived in Boston with his commission under the
new charter, there were several dozen persons awaiting trial. The provisional government had hesitated to try the cases, because it was uncertain
of its authority. Now Phips appointed a special commission of oyer and
terminer, composed of eminent former magistrates, among them Samuel
Sewall, the diarist, and headed by William Stoughton, who proved to be a
veritable caricature of the unbending, self-righteous Puritan.

When the court proceeded to trial, he and the other judges apparently
became infected with the panic that had already seized the Salem community. The devil seemed to be at large, winning more and more adher-

ents, and the cause of God in New England, already visibly threatened in so many other ways, seemed to be at stake. The court, in the throes of this panic, began deciding cases and rendering judgments on the basis of a procedure that had long been recognized as invalid in witchcraft cases. They convicted accused persons on the ground of what was known as spectral testimony, unsupported by other evidence. Spectral testimony was testimony offered by the victim to the effect that he or she was being tormented by a specter in the shape of the accused. The assumption behind this form of evidence was that the devil could not adopt the form of an innocent person (which would thus be just about the only shape he could not take). The only human shape that the devil could take, according to this assumption, was the shape of a person who had confederated with him. If, therefore, a girl was tormented by someone who looked to her like, say, Goody Jones, then Goody Jones must have made a pact with the devil. Goody Jones, in short, must be a witch.

Now, if this sort of evidence was accepted as sufficient for conviction, it would be easy for anyone, either out of malice or because of hallucinations, to accuse and obtain the conviction of an innocent person. Even people who believed in the reality of witchcraft could see that there were great dangers in such an unregulated procedure, and it had been established for some time that spectral evidence was not to be regarded as conclusive. The Mathers and other ministers were aware of this and cautioned the members of the court privately against placing too great a reliance on this kind of evidence. For they knew it was a matter of controversy whether it should be relied on at all. There were some experts on the subject who believed that it *was* possible for the devil to adopt the shape of an innocent person, and if this was so, then of course spectral evidence had no validity whatever.

In any case, it was clear that some more objective evidence ought to be required for conviction, and the members of the court knew this perfectly well. If they had insisted on such evidence, if they had insisted that the regular, established procedures for trying witches be followed, they would have been able to prevent the Salem episode from turning into a general panic.

Unfortunately they did not insist on the regular, established procedures.

They admitted spectral evidence and convicted men and women solely on the basis of such evidence, which was offered in many cases by hysterical teenage girls who were perhaps enjoying the notoriety they had suddenly attained and who doubtless persuaded themselves, as they persuaded the court, that their fantasies were reality. The judges, like other members of the community, were alarmed at the size of the danger that appeared to face them. The devil with all his legions seemed to have invaded New England, and it was no time, they felt, to be nice about methods of dealing with him. Fight him ruthlessly with no holds barred. Better that a few individuals suffer than that the whole community be endangered.

Such a situation is all too familiar. When any group of people become sufficiently intent on attacking a particular evil, they are likely to discard as obsolete and ineffective any ground rules that society has developed for the peaceful or fair achievement of social objectives. When those on the right become exercised by the demons of anarchism, communism, or terrorism to the point where they feel themselves threatened, they call upon the government to ignore the normal procedures designed to protect the rights of individuals, or they resort to lynch law, kangaroo courts, or torture, or they persuade their legislatures to act as courts and in effect convict their enemies in wholesale fashion. Similarly, when those on the left come to feel that the duly elected officers of government have somehow betrayed them, the left also discards ordinary, orderly procedures and moves to direct action, to force, disdaining the old procedures except as they may be useful in hampering the establishment's efforts to defend itself. When any of these groups become large enough to be intoxicated by their own apparent size or power and infatuated with their own righteousness, it is the rare individual who will stand up and loudly say no.

In Salem it was not a party or faction but the whole local community that rose against the apparent legion of witches enlisted by the devil. God Himself, it seemed, surely approved of any methods used to stop them. Anyone who suggested otherwise was obviously a witch lover. Although procedures existed for trying witches, procedures that had been used in the past with seeming success, the situation appeared to call for extraordinary procedures against the devil's massive onslaught. The majority of people were either egging the court on or keeping their mouths shut.

Only after twenty persons had been executed in 1692 and hundreds more accused did a group of ministers, led by Increase Mather, have the courage to get together and point out firmly and unequivocally to Governor Phips what some of them had said privately and with reservations—namely, that the court was proceeding contrary to established practice. After they had done this, the terrible business came to an end. Phips, upon receipt of the memorial from the ministers, dissolved the special commission of oyer and terminer. The remaining cases were tried under the old, regular procedures by the newly appointed superior court. Spectral evidence was not admitted as a sufficient basis for conviction. And the result was acquittal of all but three, whom the governor promptly reprieved. So far as I know, no more trials for witchcraft were ever held again in New England, though the last trial in England was in 1712 and isolated trials and executions continued on the Continent through the eighteenth century.

The New England ministers surely deserve credit for having spoken up to stop the trials, however belatedly. But if we look at the way the trials ended by comparison with the witch hunts that had afflicted German towns during the preceding century, it becomes apparent that the Salem trials were reaching the point where the civil authorities would probably have called a halt to them within a short time anyhow. A study of German witchcraft in the sixteenth and seventeenth centuries suggests that witch hunts had a natural history that repeated itself in each of them.

At the beginning we may expect the persons accused to have been generally poor and helpless, persons whose age and poverty and manner of living placed them outside the web of human relations that initially protected other members of a community against irresponsible charges. But as the confessions of the accused widened, the circle necessarily spread beyond the immediate neighborhood. The accused, pressed for more names, probably did not know the names of ordinary people outside their immediate neighborhood. The only names they could come up with would have been those of more prominent people, people known to them not by virtue of personal acquaintance but by social standing or political position in the province at large.

As the accusations thus spread upward as well as outward, two powerful motives for doubt began to work. First, it became more and more difficult for anyone to believe that the devil had actually succeeded in confederating with such a large proportion of the population. And second, it became particularly difficult for those in power to believe accusations that touched their wives and friends and even themselves. If the trials proceeded, the whole structure of society as well as their own place in it would be threatened. Up to this point most trials would end in convictions. As doubts began to seize the members of the tribunal, acquittals would become more frequent and then suddenly become universal. Accusations and confessions would cease, and society would return to normal and lick its wounds. No one would have stopped believing in the devil or in the reality of witchcraft, but the authorities would have come to doubt the validity of their own methods of coping with it.

The Salem horror came to an end in precisely this way, which again confirms the resemblance of the Salem trials to the continental rather than the English model. The accusations were reaching way beyond Salem and were beginning to extend to men and women of some prominence in the colony. They even reached to the wife of Governor Phips himself. Huge numbers of people were under suspicion. When Phips got the signal from the ministers, it served to crystallize a conviction that must surely have come to him shortly in any case. The colony he was charged to govern would have destroyed itself if the trials had been allowed to continue much longer.

That a healthy skepticism had spread among other men in authority is evident from the way in which the Superior Court in Boston dealt out acquittals wholesale to those who were still awaiting trial when the special commission of oyer and terminer was dissolved. Not only Governor Phips but the whole colony had finally come to its senses, and the people, like those of so many German communities, could now lick their wounds. In a sense they have been doing it ever since, trying to place the blame for such horrendous events and trying to redeem them at least by learning from them.

In these efforts it has been tempting, especially since Puritanism went out of fashion, to put all the blame on the clergy and especially on Cotton Mather. In a book published in 1936 Samuel Eliot Morison did his best to dispel this too easy way of disposing of the problem, which started in 1697 with Robert Calef. Morison, with his usual salty expression, explained how Calef "who had it in for Cotton Mather, tied a tin can to him after the frenzy was over: and it has rattled and banged through the pages of superficial and popular historians." "Even today," he went on, "the generally accepted version of the Salem tragedy is that Cotton Mather worked it up, aided and abetted by his fellow parsons, in order to drive people back to church." Not so, said Morison, and demonstrated that Mather acted to stop the trials rather than promote them.

Unfortunately, however, it is pretty hard to make Cotton Mather look attractive in any situation, and in this one, innocent though he may have been of any role in stirring up the witch trials, he himself believed that he was responsible for the extraordinary activity of the devil in Massachusetts. Why, he asked himself, should the devil have chosen this particular time and place to launch so formidable a campaign against the godly inhabitants of New England? And the answer was not far to seek. It was indeed so obvious that other men, he said, had pointed it out to him. The answer was that Cotton Mather's superior godliness posed a challenge that hell itself could not ignore. And he wrote in his diary, "This assault of the evil angels upon the country was intended by Hell, as a particular defiance unto my poor endeavors to bring the souls of men unto Heaven."

Because Mather's egotism is so revolting, Morison's efforts to rescue his reputation have not been wholly successful. And Perry Miller, who considered Mather to be the most nauseous human being of his time, found particularly repulsive Mather's attempt to defend the trials after they were over. In a book called *Wonders of the Invisible World*, which Mather rushed into print immediately after the trials, he tried to smooth things over, but that meant saying a few good words for the good intentions of the judges. By implication, at least, he justified their conduct, calling upon the people of Massachusetts to renew their covenant with God now that the devil had been defeated. Perry Miller, in commenting upon this proposal, returned Mather to the unhappy position from which Morison had tried to rescue him. The passage is so eloquent and so characteristic of Miller that I cannot forbear repeating it:

Samuel Eliot Morison says that Robert Calef tied a tin can to Cotton Mather which has rattled and banged through the pages of superficial and popular historians. My account is not popular, and I strive to make it not superficial; assuredly, if by tin can is meant the charge that Mather worked up the Salem tragedy, it does not belong to him; but what Calef was actually to charge was that he prostituted a magnificent conception of New England's destiny to saving the face of a bigoted court. In that sense, the right can was tied to the proper tail, and through the pages of this volume it shall rattle and bang.

But in truth it is time to stop looking for scapegoats, even when we have ready to hand so attractive a candidate for the position as Cotton Mather. The Salem witch scare, as one reads the record today, was indeed a shameful performance, from which we would doubtless like to dissociate ourselves by putting the blame on a bunch of benighted and bigoted clergymen. But it is also necessary to look at the whole business with a greater degree of humility than was possible, say a hundred years ago, when the human race was congratulating itself on its progress toward perfection—through survival of the fittest, transcontinental railroads and flying machines, the gospel of wealth and the white man's burden—Americans found the witch trials a difficult and repulsive topic.

It was well enough to be making such wonderful progress, but a person of the early nineteenth century could actually, as a child, have known someone who, as a child, had witnessed the hanging of the Salem witches. It was a little embarrassing that there had been quite that much progress to make. Although one might grow accustomed to the existence of apes among one's distant ancestors, it was unpleasant to contemplate the presence of witch-hunters almost within the family.

In the last century, however, we have learned more familiarity with the outrageous and less contempt for the contemptible. Our own progress seems to be in the direction of an atomic holocaust, and we have also made great strides in the techniques of convicting the innocent. Salem accordingly seems a little déjà vu to us, and we can weigh with professional condescension these early experiments in the use of phony confessions, irregular procedures, and the admission of inadmissible evidence.

But if our familiarity with the outrageous brings the Salem episode uncomfortably closer, some aspects of what happened at Salem remain more novel and cannot fail to arouse a certain admiration in those of us who dislike judicial murder, murder by order of court. We can take a little comfort, for example, in the fact that the trials were brought to an end when only twenty-odd people had been hanged. The people of Massachusetts did manage to get a grip on themselves, did manage to get over their hysteria before it had carried them beyond twenty murders.

One can admire much more the courage of those who refused to confess. There was an enormous pressure on the accused to confess, for those who did so and turned state's evidence by naming accomplices were almost invariably forgiven. The Puritan code always was very lenient on those who repented. If you read the records of New England courts throughout the seventeenth century, you will find that in nine cases out of ten in which a man was convicted of a crime, he had only to humble himself and say that he was sorry for what he had done in order to have his punishment remitted to a nominal fine. After all, the motive for punishing crime was mainly to testify to God that society did not approve. If a man confessed that he had done wrong, this consideration was already taken care of. Similarly with the witches, anyone who confessed that she had conspired with the devil, but was sorry for it, was willingly forgiven. Usually, in order to convince the judges that her confession was genuine, she would describe her confederates in the conspiracy. As we have seen, it was by means of these phony confessions that the witch hunt spread.

The remarkable thing is that a number of men and women had the courage to deny the accusation at the price of their lives. They took their religion seriously enough to believe that if they confessed to a crime they had not committed, God would hold them guilty of the lie. One man, Giles Cory, was perhaps as brave a man as any in American history. Cory, accused of witchcraft, saw that he would be convicted by the unfair procedures of the court. When his case came up for trial, he simply refused to plead, that is, he refused to answer whether he was guilty or not guilty. The means prescribed by English law at that time for forcing a man to plead was that he should be placed between two wooden planks or platforms, while stones were piled on the upper one until he was ready to speak. Giles Cory was given this treatment and allowed himself to be pressed to death without saying a word. If he had pleaded guilty, confessed, and accused others, he would doubtless have been set free. If he had pleaded not guilty, he would surely have been found guilty and his property would have been forfeited to the state, for witchcraft was punished in Massachusetts not only by death but by forfeiture of property to the state, even though this was contrary to English law. By refusing to plead, Cory made it impossible for the court to convict him and thereby saved his property for his family. But he did not take the easier course of pleading guilty.

Mary Easty showed an even greater sort of courage. She pleaded not guilty, knowing what the consequences would be. She believed in the reality of witchcraft, but she knew from her own knowledge that she was innocent and the court wrong. Her dying statement was a warning to the court that deserves to be remembered for its temperance, its courage, and its wisdom. "I Petition to your honours," she wrote,

not for my own life for I know I must die and my appointed time is sett but the Lord he knowes it is that if it be possible no more Innocentt blood may be shed which undoubtidly cannot be Avoydd In the way and course you goe in I question not but your honours does to the uttmost of your Powers in the discovery and detecting of witchcraft and witches and would not be gulty of Innocent blood for the world but by my own Innocencye I know you are in the wrong way the Lord in his infinite mercye direct you in this great work if it be his blessed will that no more Innocent blood be shed I would humbly begg of you that your honors would be plesed to examine theis Aflicted Persons strictly and keepe them apart some time and Likewise to try some of these confesing wichis I being confident there is severall of them has belyed themselves and others as will appeare if not in this wor[l]d I am sure in the world to come whither I am now agoing and I Question not but youle see an alteration of thes things they say my selfe and others having made a League with the Divel we cannot confesse I know and the Lord knowes as will shortly appeare they belye me and so I Question not but they doe others the Lord

above who is the Searcher of all hearts knowes that as I shall answer
it att the Tribunall seat that I know not the least thinge of witchcraft
therfore I cannot I dare not belye my own soule.

The courage of men and women like Giles Cory and Mary Easty, who
stood up to their judges could probably be matched today. But there was
another kind of courage displayed in connection with the witchcraft trials that would be hard to find a parallel for today. Five years after the trials, in 1697, the General Court of Massachusetts decided that the trials
had sent innocent people to their deaths. January 15, 1697, was appointed
as a day of public fasting in which the people of the colony should ask
forgiveness from God for what they had done. And on that day Samuel
Sewall, one of the judges, stood up before the congregation of the church
to which he belonged, with bowed head, while the minister read a statement that Sewall had written, begging forgiveness of God and man for
the part that he had played in the witchcraft trials, asking that "the blame
and shame of it" be placed on him. On the same day the jury that had sat
in the trials published a written expression of their "deep sense of sorrow" for their decisions, "whereby we fear we have been instrumental
with others, though ignorantly and unwillingly, to bring upon ourselves
the guilt of innocent blood."

All this did not bring anyone back to life, though when the court
reversed the sentences, the survivors were able to recover some compensation for the property that the state had seized and sold. But the
remarkable thing is that a people as a whole had the courage to admit
that they had been wrong. Mind you, they had not ceased to believe in
the reality and danger of witchcraft; they had not suddenly been converted to a belief that the devil does not make compacts with human
beings. They had simply become convinced that the trials were unfair.
Can any modern people point to a similar willingness to remedy injustice, even after the event?

Consider another trial, held in Massachusetts in 1927, in the midst
of public hysteria over the red menace. Two men were convicted and
executed after a trial that was as much a travesty of justice as those held
at Salem in 1692. The men may have been guilty, just as some of the

Salem witches may have been guilty, but the trial did not prove their guilt by regularly recognized procedures. In the 1690s it took the people of Massachusetts five years to admit that they had done wrong. It took fifty years for the governor of Massachusetts to do the same in regard to Sacco and Vanzetti. And when he did, the reaction of the people of Massachusetts was rather less contrite than that of their forebears. Members of the General Court this time made indignant protests against the governor's acknowledgment that the state could ever have done anything wrong. One wonders how long it will be before the people of New England will measure up to the stature of their ancestors.

And one wonders even more whether we as Americans will ever recognize and accept our share of responsibility for transforming modern warfare from armed combat to mass murder of civilian populations. The Salem witch trials may one day look like one of the prouder episodes in our history simply because the whole society was then willing to recognize its complicity. In spite of Samuel Sewall's desire to take the blame and shame on himself, it was the whole society that fasted and prayed in acknowledgment of guilt and did not seek to shuffle off the blame on the members of their duly constituted tribunal.

The Massachusetts fast day was a fitting close to the Puritan era. Although people still believed in witches in 1697, a century later they were not so sure, as the postscript to this essay will show. But the currents were already stirring that have made our world so different from theirs. None of us, I hope, would wish to return to their superstitions, but I wonder whether we might not still have something to learn from them about the dangers of self-righteousness and the merits of contrition.

—Unpublished

CHAPTER TEN

Postscript: Philadelphia 1787

SEVENTEEN EIGHTY-SEVEN was not that long ago. What happened in Philadelphia that summer was the culminating achievement of the Enlightenment in America, if not in the world. Fifty-five men agreed on a way of government that has been more successful in almost every way than any other in a thousand years and more. Yes, the members of the Constitutional Convention all had their special interests to protect, among them the interests of slaveholders, not among them the interests of slaves. But they listened to each other. They reasoned together. And what they did was not unreasonable. It worked. It still works.

It is hard to think that those fifty-five men were much closer in time to the Salem witch trials of 1692 than they were to us. It is still harder to think that in Philadelphia that summer, in the very week when they were hammering out the most crucial provisions of the Constitution, they could have witnessed, perhaps did witness, in the streets they daily walked, an event that tied them more closely to the dark world of superstition than to the Enlightenment they cherished.

In 1787 Philadelphia was unquestionably the intellectual capital of the United States. It was not simply that Philadelphia was much larger in population than New York or Boston; it was the distinction of its citizens that made the city a magnet for foreign visitors and the obvious meeting place for men who thought, as Alexander Hamilton put it, continentally, men who could see beyond the boundaries of their town or parish or county or state. It was the city of Benjamin Franklin, the very symbol of the Enlightenment, of Benjamin Rush, America's best-known physician, of David Rittenhouse, America's leading astronomer, of Charles Willson Peale, painter and promoter, of William Bartram, the country's foremost botanist. It was the home of the American Philosophical Society, the only significant learned society on the continent. It had a flourishing theater, where, despite lingering objections from Quaker moralists, ladies and gentlemen could laugh at a farce or weep at a tragedy. It had eight newspapers and two monthly magazines (the *Columbian Magazine* and the *American Museum*). It had Peale's Museum with a display of waxworks, paintings, and scientific curiosities, the eighteenth-century prototype of the Smithsonian. It had Gray's Tavern, with the most elaborate landscape gardens in the country, complete with waterfalls, grottoes, and Chinese pagodas. Philadelphia was the place to be, the place to go.

During that summer the great Convention was not the only assemblage of notables to gather there. The Society of the Cincinnati (composed of the officers of Washington's army) and two religious denominations, Presbyterian and Baptist, held their meetings there at the same time as the Convention. Throughout the summer troops of distinguished visitors passed through, including Indian chiefs on the way to negotiate with the lame-duck Congress in New York about incursions on their lands, and enterprising land speculators making plans for more incursions. Sooner or later, it seemed, everyone came to Philadelphia.

The members of the Convention began arriving in May, the Virginians first. James Madison got there on the fifth, plans for a wholly new national government already forming in his head. George Washington rode in on the thirteenth, suffering from embarrassment that he had declined, on the pretext of his private affairs, to attend the meeting of the Cincinnati, and now was to be present in Philadelphia anyhow. Governor Randolph, with whom Madison concerted his plans, was there by the fifteenth. Benjamin Franklin, of course, was already on hand. He had just completed an addition to his house on Market Street, and on the sixteenth he entertained the new arrivals at an elegant dinner there, along with John Penn, grandson of the founder of Pennsylvania.

The other delegates trickled in at intervals. It was May 25 before enough were present for the Convention to begin. What they said to each other on the upper floor of the State House has been preserved for us by Madison, in one of the most exciting journals of American history. What they said in the evenings as clumps of them dined together at their taverns and boardinghouses can only be guessed at. What was the conversation, for example, at the Indian Queen, where Madison roomed, along with Alexander Hamilton, George Mason, Luther Martin, Charles Pinckney, John Rutledge, and Hugh Williamson?

Presumably they continued to talk, when no outsiders were present, about the things they had argued over during the day. But what did they think about the things that went on around them in the city? Were their daytime thoughts affected by the sights and sounds, the stench, the dangers, the alarms and excursions that confronted them when they stepped out of the State House? Although we cannot know the answer, we can know a little about the darker side of what they saw. Though it may not have affected the outcome of what they did, it may affect in some way our own understanding of the world they lived in and were trying to change.

The members of the Convention were concerned, we know, about law and order. The times were hard, bankruptcies looming everywhere, mortgages foreclosing, beggars conspicuous in the city. In Massachusetts there had been open defiance of government; and in several other states too, including Connecticut, Virginia, and Pennsylvania, mobs had assembled to close the courts or to retrieve property seized for debts or taxes. Law and order were threatened, and walking the streets of Philadelphia that summer one could not escape meeting up with people who made defiance of law and order a way of life.

The Philadelphia prison was right on the mall, a stone's throw from the State House, and anyone who ventured to stroll by it got a taste of what kind of people were inside. They had provided themselves with poles, attaching a little cup at the end, which they thrust out to passersby to beg for coins. To refuse was to invite a barrage of curses by expert cursers. It was well known, what the prisoners did with the coins. The jailer sold drinks in the prison's common hall, where men and women inmates cavorted together promiscuously.

It was not possible to escape the curses of prisoners simply by shunning the vicinity of the prison. A new state law had prescribed labor on the city streets as a substitute for imprisonment in many cases. Convicts with shaved heads, shackled with ball and chain and an iron collar, were to be seen everywhere at work, or allegedly at work, under the supervision of overseers. The "wheelbarrow men," as they were called, were also expert beggars and cursers. They wheedled drinks from passersby and, as the newspapers reported (three days before the Convention opened), "frequently exhibit the most horrid scenes on this side of the infernal regions—abusing the inhabitants, beating their keepers, and with drawn knives and other weapons, oblige them to fly for their lives, uttering horrid imprecations of death and destruction."

Criminals in chains were bad enough, but criminals who had not been caught were worse. In some areas of Philadelphia large numbers of houses were deserted and offered shelter to gangs of footpads. On Broad Street, south of Market, landlords even rented their aging buildings to thieves, who sallied forth to prey on unsuspecting strollers. And if poverty was a spur to crime, Philadelphia had it in large measure. During the year preceding May 14, 1787, the almshouse had admitted 196 men, 213 women, and 73 children. In addition, 19 children had been born there during the year.

For a city with a total population of 40,000, these figures bespeak a sizable underclass of the poor and the criminal, enough to make law-abiding citizens uneasy, as they were uneasy about the people in the country who were taking action against the legal collection of debts and taxes. The Convention, it was hoped, would do something to cure the larger problem, something to restore prosperity and ease the pressure that drove people to crime. But even as the Convention sat, an uglier kind of crime made its appearance in the city.

In 1787 witchcraft had long since ceased to be recognized in law. The English statute against it had been repealed in 1736, and prosecutions in both England and the colonies had ceased well before that. But belief in witchcraft could not be repealed. Fear of witchcraft continued, and so did popular methods of detecting and dealing with witches.

Trial by water remained a favorite method. A witch, bound hand and foot, when thrown in deep water, was supposed to sink if innocent, float if guilty, a procedure calculated to dispose of the victim in either case. In 1751 a woman was subjected to this test in Hertfordshire, England, where a mob dragged her back and forth through a pond and then kicked her as she lay dying on the bank. A less drastic way of dealing with a witch was to cut or scratch her, preferably on the forehead, a procedure that was supposed to counteract any evil spells she might have cast. The church and the law had long frowned on these rituals, but they survived in popular memory. And one of them, cutting on the forehead, survived in Philadelphia.

The trouble began on May 5, the day Madison rode in for the Convention. He came from the north, from New York, so he could not himself have seen the incident happen, because it took place near the New Market, on the south side of town. An old woman, known familiarly as Korbmacher, lived there. We know nothing about her except that she had formerly lived among the Germans in Spring Garden, on the north side. She had there acquired her nickname—whether she actually made baskets is not clear—and an evil reputation. She was thought to be a witch, and when things went wrong—presumably illnesses among children or cattle—she would be blamed.

On May 5, a Saturday, as the *Pennsylvania Packet* reported six days later, she was attacked "by some persons of the vicinity." The story went on,

> Upon a supposition she was a witch, she was cut in the forehead, according to antient and immemorial custom, by those persons. This old body long since laboured under suspicions of sorcery, and was viewed as the pest and nightmare of society in those parts of the town where she had hitherto lived; she was commonly called, at Spring Garden Korbmacher, by the Germans: and on that score, on the present and other occasions, unfortunately became the victim of vengeance of some individuals, who afforded her the most pointed abuse which so mislead a passion and resentment, could possibly impose and inflict.

The paper went on to say that Korbmacher, fearing for her life, had applied to the authorities for protection. Though it was not clear what kind of protection they could offer, the paper deplored "the absurd and abominable notions of witchcraft and sorcery," and hoped that they would "no more predominate in an empire like ours, that has emancipated itself from the superstitions of authority, and in fact every other species of superstition consisting in the bondage of the body or the mind." Silly fear of witches and witchcraft belonged to the old world; it must have no place "in the free and civilized parts of independent America." But after a lengthy denunciation of superstition the paper acknowledged that "prejudices, worm-eaten prejudices, as our old companions are hard to be parted with."

Such prejudices, it was feared, might threaten not only the lives of poor women like Korbmacher but also the success of the coming Convention. In another paragraph in the same issue, the *Packet* observed "that as the time approaches for opening the business of the foederal convention, it is natural that every lover of his country should experience some anxiety for the fate of an expedient so necessary, yet so precarious. Upon the event of this great council, indeed, depends every thing that can be essential to the dignity and stability of the national character."

Philadelphians could read the story of the attack on Korbmacher not only in the *Pennsylvania Packet* but in several other newspapers. One looks in vain, however, for further details. As was their custom, the other newspapers simply copied the story word for word from the one that first printed it. Even the German *Gemeinnützige Philadelphische Correspondenz* simply translated it from the *Packet*.

Springtime passed, the Convention met, and summer heat set in. The first week in July was especially hot and humid. It was a bad time for the Convention, for on the second of July the members had become deadlocked over the question of representation, and for the next two weeks, until the so-called Great Compromise was agreed to (consisting mainly of representation for all states equally in the Senate, and by population in the House of Representatives), the Convention was in danger of dissolution. The heat wave broke with a thundershower on July 9, and five days later the Convention was on course again, with the Great Compromise in place. Korbmacher did not fare so well.

Whether the weather had anything to do with it is not apparent. The south side of Philadelphia was not a salubrious place in the summer heat.

The fields in the area were a dumping ground for every kind of refuse. Dead horses and dead dogs lay amid the heaps, filling the noisome air with the stench of putrefaction. Nevertheless, nothing untoward happened while the heat wave lasted, other than the usual riotous behavior of the wheelbarrow men. But on July 10, as a cool breeze swept the city and things began to look up at the Convention, the people around the New Market broke out in rage against Korbmacher. Cutting her in the forehead had apparently not put an end to the misfortunes attributed to her. What these were is not recorded, but at least one woman blamed the death of a child on her charms. The whole story, so far as we know it, was carried in the papers in a few lines (this time the *Pennsylvania Evening Herald* was first, and the others copied from it). "We are sorry to hear," the story began,

> that the poor woman who suffered so much some time ago, under the imputation of being a *witch*, has again been attacked by an ignorant and inhuman mob. On Tuesday last she was carried through several of the streets, and was hooted and pelted as she passed along. A gentleman who interfered in her favour was greatly insulted, while those who recited the innumerable instances of her art, were listened to with curiosity and attention.

How was she carried? Perhaps in a cart? What was she pelted with? With refuse? With rocks? Who were the people who pelted her? Were they the same people who passed drink to the wheelbarrow men? Were the wheelbarrow men themselves among them? What kind of people still believed in witches in 1787? Nothing in the record tells us. But the picture is extraordinary. While America's great men sat in solemn conclave, working out the compromise that saved the union and established the form of government under which we still live, Korbmacher was carried through the streets, her tormenters reciting her supposed acts of sorcery, inviting the throng to pelt her. And the story does not end there: eight days later she was dead. The newspapers tell us what she died of:

> It must seriously affect every humane mind that in consequence of the barbarous treatment lately suffered by the poor old woman, called a

Witch, she died on Wednesday last. It is hoped that every step will be taken to bring the offenders to punishment, in justice to the wretched victim, as well as the violated laws of reason and society.

It was a pious wish, shared by "several respectable citizens" who at the time of the second attack expressed a willingness to testify in the woman's behalf, and by a "gentleman of the law" who proposed to undertake the prosecution of her tormenters. The case evidently did come to trial at the "city sessions" held by the Mayor's Court in October. The docket of that court in the City Archives is extant from 1782 to 1785 and from 1789 to 1792, but is missing for the years from 1786 to 1788. Hence once again, we know of the case only from the newspapers, which do not even record the outcome and would perhaps not have mentioned it at all, had not the judge made it the occasion for a labored exercise of tasteless wit. Here is the story, offered first in the *Pennsylvania Evening Herald* for October 27:

On Monday last [October 22] the city sessions commenced, and on Friday the business of the court was concluded. Several persons were condemned to the wheel and barrow, but the greater number of bills were for keeping disorderly houses, and committing assaults and battery—a melancholy proof of the depraved manners, and the contentious spirit of the times. One woman, who had been indicted for some violence offered to the person of the unhappy creature that was lately attacked by a mob under the imputation of being a witch, maintained the justice of that opinion, and insinuated her belief that her only child sickened and died, under the malignant influence of a *charm*. Upon which the presiding Justice made the following observation—what! that a poor wretch whose sorrows and infirmities have sunk her eyes into her head, and whose features are streaked with the wrinkles of extreme old age, should therefore become an object of terror, and be endowed with the powers of witchcraft—it is an idle and absurd superstition! If, however, some damsels that I have seen, animated with the bloom of youth, and equipped with all the grace of beauty, if such women were indicted for the offence, the charge might receive some countenance, for they are indeed calculated to *charm*

and *bewitch* us. But age and infirmity, though they deserve our compassion, have nothing in them that can alarm or facinate our nature.

So the episode closed. What did the great men make of it? What did
Washington think? What did Madison think? What did Roger Sherman
or Elbridge Gerry think, or the other New Englanders with their not so
ancient heritage of witchcraft? And what did Philadelphians, other than
newspaper correspondents and facetious judges, think? Again, the record
is silent. The attacks on Korbmacher and her death passed unnoticed in
the diaries and letters that have thus far come to light.

That fact may itself suggest something—namely, that the episode did
not seem as bizarre to people of the time as it does to us. The year 1787
was less than a century from 1692. It is worth reminding ourselves that
Benjamin Franklin once spoke with Cotton Mather. He and the other
fifty-four men who labored in the State House that summer may have
been working against greater odds than we have realized. Superstition
dies hard, and witch hunts have generally proceeded from the bottom
up. Even the Spanish Inquisition was less ardent in pursuing witches than
popular demand would have had it be. The members of the Constitutional
Convention have often been taken to task by historians for their seeming
distrust of the people. And although that distrust has been greatly exaggerated, and although it affected some members much more than others,
it was real. It shocks us a little, as we read Madison's notes of what his colleagues said, to find them at the very outset of the Convention fearful of
an "excess of democracy," worried that the people "are constantly liable
to be misled." If, however, we bear in mind the actions of this particular
mob (will anyone insist on calling it a "crowd"?) on the very doorsteps of
the Convention, we may perhaps take a more charitable view of the bias
recorded in Madison's journal. Enlightenment still had, and has, a long
way to go.

—*1983*

CHAPTER ELEVEN

The Contentious Quaker:
William Penn

CHRIST SAID THAT his kingdom was not of this world and embodied the message in his other teachings. His followers have nevertheless had to live in the world, trying in spite of his warning to bring it under his dominion or else bending his precepts almost beyond recognition in order to fit them to the ways of the world. Over the centuries Christianity has vibrated uneasily between what its founder prescribed and what the world demands. When the church becomes too fat and comfortable with the world, the contrast between the medium and the message will always prompt some prophet to summon true believers out of so unchristian an institution and into a way of life and worship that will more closely resemble Christ's. We may call them protesters, but in the course of time they become Protestants, with a capital *P*, against whom new prophets must in turn raise the flag of protest.

When William Penn was born, in 1644, England was filled with prophets, each with his own version of what the Christian life entailed. The Church of England, which had been Protestant with a capital *P* from its inception, was under challenge not only by Presbyterians and Congregationalists but by a host of more radical visionaries, many of whom thought that Christ's kingdom was shortly to commence, not by subduing the world, but by putting an end to it: Antinomians, Muggletonians, Fifth Monarchists, Anabaptists, Seekers, and so on. Penn's father and mother were none of these. They were genteel Protestants, good Church of England folk, but perhaps with some sympathy for Presbyterianism or Congregationalism. The father, also named William, certainly had no scruples about working for a government run by a Congregationalist, for he made a brilliant career in Oliver Cromwell's navy, before bringing himself to disgrace in an unsuccessful expedition against the Spanish in the Caribbean. But he also had no scruples about working for Charles II. When Charles returned to the throne in 1660, he restored Penn to his command as admiral and to a handsome living from lands in Ireland that had been confiscated from their Catholic owners. The elder Penn had reason to be content with a world that had served him well.

His son was cut from another cloth. From an early age, at least from his early teens, William Penn was preoccupied with religion to an extent that his parents found disconcerting in a young gentleman with a career in the highest places before him. They wanted him to have all the advantages that his father's position entitled him to. They saw to it that he met all the right people, that he learned all the social graces. And indeed it all came easy to him. He was lively, energetic, and quickwitted. People liked him, and he liked them, including apparently a lot of pretty girls. But he had this unseemly bent for religion and for pursuing accepted religious beliefs to unacceptable conclusions.

When he was sixteen, they packed him off to Oxford, where the learned clergymen with which the place abounded might be able to keep him on track. But he proved too hot to handle. In less than two years the learned clergy sent him back, expelled for his outspoken contempt for them and their church. In desperation his parents sent him on the grand tour of the Continent with other young gentlemen, in hopes that there he would get the spirit and the flesh sorted out into the right proportions. And though he spent some of his time in France studying theology, when he returned to London in 1664, not quite twenty, his religious zeal had momentarily abated. He was full of fashionable continental mannerisms, and he showed a proper appreciation for the sensual pleasures awaiting a young gentleman in Restoration London.

In London he attended Lincoln's Inn to learn the smattering of law appropriate to a gentleman of property; and he also attended at the King's Court, where his father was in high favor, especially with the Duke of

York, the king's brother. The duke was in charge of naval affairs, with Sir William Penn, now knighted, as his leading admiral. The elder Penn, who could not have been more pleased with the way his son had seemingly turned out, introduced him to the duke, and the two quickly became friends. In 1666 Sir William sent the boy to Ireland to look after the family estates, and young William at once made friends among the Anglo-Irish nobility. But his career as proper young gentleman was short-lived. At Cork he met up with Thomas Loe, a Quaker preacher who had entranced him as a teenager ten years before. By the end of 1667, after a brief spell in an Irish jail, he was back in London, where Samuel Pepys, a clerk in the navy office, made that classic entry in his diary: "Mr. Will Pen, who is lately come over from Ireland, is a Quaker again, or some very melancholy thing."

THE PROPHET

He was indeed a Quaker, and for his father and mother it was indeed a melancholy thing. Quakerism appeared to be another of those visionary, fringe movements that the 1640s and 1650s had continued to spawn, and of them all it may have seemed the most offensive. Its members were not content to depart from established institutions; they seemed to enjoy dramatic confrontations with authority, in which they defied not only the established church and all its ways but also the customary forms of good behavior. They wore their hats in the presence of their superiors, right up to the king himself. They refused to address people by their proper titles: they would not even vouchsafe a Mr. before the names of their betters. Some of them appeared naked at local church services. And instead of meeting in secret, where the authorities could ignore their violation of the laws against dissenting religions, they insisted on making their meetings public, in effect daring the sheriffs and constables to arrest them, a dare that was often taken.

Their beliefs were as offensive as their conduct. They claimed what amounted to direct revelation from God—the inner light they called it—of the same kind that the apostles had had from Christ himself. The Holy Scriptures, therefore, on which the whole Protestant movement rested, were no more to them than an imperfect record of past revelations of people like themselves. They denied that Christ's sacrifice was sufficient in itself to bring redemption, but they thought that all men were capable of redemption, if they followed the inner light. Thus they denied the central Christian doctrines of atonement and predestination. They rejected not only all other churches and ministers, refusing to pay their tithes to the established church, but also all sacraments and sermons. Their only preaching came from those who claimed to be enunciating messages from on high via the inner light. And they rejected original sin, too, in its usual sense, for they claimed that with the assistance of the inner light they could completely free themselves from sin in their daily lives.

In espousing such beliefs, William Penn appeared to be repudiating his heritage, repudiating the society in which he had grown, repudiating his education, repudiating his class, repudiating his parents. And there can be no doubt that he thought he was doing so. His first important tract, *No Cross No Crown*, written in 1669 while he was imprisoned in the Tower of London, had as its theme the conflict between the world and the cross, the import of its title being that no crown of eternal glory could be won without taking up the cross and undergoing the suffering and humiliation ever inflicted by the world on those who reject its ways.

There may have been something of adolescent, youthful rebellion in Penn's stance, but it persisted throughout his life in a posture of no compromise with the world. In counseling other adherents to the cause, he continually admonished them that they should "Keep out of base Bargainings or Conniving at fleshly Evasions of the Cross," that they should avoid "Reasonings with Opposers," lest the purity of their commitment be sullied.

This last piece of advice was one that Penn was never able to follow himself, for Penn, in spite of being a likable person, had a contentious streak that impelled him not only to reason with opposers but even to denounce them. Although the Quakers officially professed an aversion to controversy, Penn took it upon himself (with the blessing of other Quaker leaders) to defend them against all comers and especially against the Church of England and the more respectable dissenters of Presbyterian or Congregational persuasion. Nearly all his voluminous writings are polemical. In a three-year span alone, from 1672 to 1674, he published twenty-two tracts, several of them lengthy, in which he went on the attack with no holds barred.

When one critic disclosed in a preface that he was sixty years of age, Penn, then at the ripe age of twenty-seven, mocked the man's "decrepit" reasoning and rang the changes on the fact "that any Man should live so long, and to so little Purpose." To Richard Baxter, perhaps the foremost dissenting divine of the Restoration period, he announced, "Scurvy of the minde is thy distemper; I feare its Incurable." He was fond of proclaiming his own moderate spirit as enjoined by his faith, but even in doing so he could not resist a jab at his opponents, as when in an answer to one critic he began by saying, "I would give the Worst of Men their Due," and then added, "I justly esteem him of that Number."

In a running controversy with John Faldo, an Anglican minister, he addressed Faldo successively as Whistling Priest, Busie Priest, ungodly Priest, cavilling Priest, rude priest, ignorant priest, and told his readers,

> . . . in the Earth there is not any Thing so Fantastical, Conceited, Proud, Railing, Busie-Body, and sometimes Ignorant, as a sort of Priests to me not unknown (among whom our *Adversary* is not the least) who think their Coat will bear out their worst Expressions for Religion, and Practice an haughty Reviling for Christ, as one of the greatest Demonstrations of their Zeal; an ill-bred and Pedantick Crew, the *Bane of Reason, and Pest of the World;* the old Incendiaries to Mischief, and the best to be *spar'd of Mankind;* against whom the boiling Vengeance of an irritated God is ready to be poured out to the Destruction of such, if they repent not, *and turn from their Abominable Deceits.*

This diatribe was not mere youthful exuberance. In one of his last tracts, written when he was fifty-four, he described his opponent as a "snake-in-the-grass" and then specified what kind, a rattlesnake.

Penn coupled his unrelenting hostility to conventional Christians with an anti-intellectualism that attributed the whole apparatus of Christian theology and ecclesiastical institutions, both Catholic and Protestant, to the pursuit of forbidden knowledge that had caused the expulsion from paradise. It was one of the marks of purity in the early followers of

Christ, Penn thought, that "for the first Hundred Years, scarce an Eminent Scholar was to be found amongst the *Christians.*"

In his first publication he warned against "Extollers of Humane Learning," and throughout his life in offering advice to the godly he warned them against "that Thirsting Spirit after much Head-Knowledge," which would only clog the passages to truth that lay within them. "My Friends," he would write, "disquiet not your Selves to comprehend Divine Things, for they that do so are of the Flesh."

Those who claim direct access to divinity, whether they call it the inner light or the oversoul or by any other name, have always discounted the learning to be had from books, though they often, like Penn, couch their antibook message in books of their own (Penn's bibliography runs to over 130 titles). Penn from the time of his conversion professed to be wary of books. Solitude and silence, not books, he thought, were the way to reach the Spirit. In his final testimony of advice to his children, he cautioned them that "reading many Books is but a taking off the Mind too much from Meditation. . . . much reading is an Oppression of the Mind, and extinguishes the natural Candle; which is the Reason of so many senseless Scholars in the World."

The senseless scholars he had encountered personally in his stay at Oxford, and his impatience with human learning rose to a climax whenever he considered what went on in universities, those places of "Folly, Ignorance, and Impiety," which "infect the whole Land with Debauchery, and at best Persecution, and anti-Christian clumsy-witted Pedants, and useless pragmaticks." The universities were simply the last stop in the long line of degeneration from the simple truth of Christ and the prophets. God's message had been lost in "the obscure, unintelligible and unprofitable *Metaphysicks* of the *Heathen*, too greedily received and mischievously increased by *Fathers, Councils, School-Men* and our modern *Universities*, to the corrupting of Christian Doctrine, and disputing away the Benefit of Christian life." He was not against secular learning that devoted itself to secular things, to "Building, Improvement of Land, Medicine, Chirurgery, Traffick, Navigation, History, Government." But when brought to bear on religion, human learning was only a block to the true knowledge that came from within.

Penn's hostility to universities extended to the ministers trained there. Their objective, he claimed, was only to make a living out of religion, and their ministry was unavailing because they relied on book learning instead of the inner light. Penn thought of himself as a minister, unpaid and unordained but called, like all true ministers, directly by God. He advised others like him,

> We are not to *Study* nor speak our *own Words*. . . . We are to minister, as the *Oracles of God*; if so, then must we receive *from Christ*, God's Great Oracle, what we are to minister. And if we are to minister what we receive, then not what we Study, Collect, and beat out of our own Brains, for that is not the Mind of Christ, but our own Imaginations, and this will not profit the People.

True Christian doctrine, Penn insisted, did not have to be "prov'd by *Aristotle* and his Philosophy." The Scriptures themselves needed no interpretation. Indeed, it was ridiculous to suppose that God had made the Scriptures so obscure that they required a privileged race of scholar-priests to be explained. They were "suited to the Capacity of the Young, the Ignorant, and the Poor." And that was how Penn liked to think of the Quakers. To him they were always a "poor, despised people," poor not only in their ignorance and in the bad treatment they received, but poor in lacking the good things of the world on which false Christians prided themselves. They were, he assured himself, mostly mechanics. And he gladly assimilated their humility to himself, gladly shared their sufferings, for he was convinced that in doing so he was opening the way for the spirit, which could scarcely penetrate the antichristian world of fleshly delights and scholarly philosophy that had been his heritage.

In his professed affinity for the poor, Penn touched a dynamic element of the Christian tradition that has sparked more than one rebel against the ways of the world. There is an egalitarian leaven in Christianity, subdued by the institutions that Christianity fosters, but ever ready to breed prophets in sackcloth to denounce the churches that forget it. "Christ," Penn observed in *No Cross No Crown*, "came Poor into the World, and so lived in it." Did he call his disciples from among the learned? "I would fain know," asked Penn,

> how many *Rabbies, Greek* and *Latin Philosophers*, yielded themselves Proselytes to the Christian Religion, though they had his *Presence, Ministry, Death and Ressurection amongst them*, who was and is the Author and Master of it? If such Learning be so great a Friend to Truth, how comes it that the greatest Things have fallen to the Share of Poor and Illiterate Men; And that such have been most apt to receive, and boldest to suffer for it? Why not *Rabbies* rather than *Fishermen* . . . ?"

True Christians now as then, Penn believed, were most likely to be found among "Handicraft, Labouring, and Husband-men, Persons inexpert in the Scholastick Adages, Disputations and Opinions of the Heathenish Philosophical World." George Fox, the founder of Quakerism, whom Penn revered, had been a simple and untutored man, "not of *High Degree*," Penn recalled, "or *Elegant Speech* or *Learned* after the Way of this World." To be a Christian was to be humble, meek, of low degree. Penn never tired of citing the first epistle to the Corinthians that "not many wise men after the flesh, not many mighty, not many noble, are called." And he continued to identify the Quakers with "the *Weary* and *Heavy Laden*, the *Hungry* and *Thirsty*, the *Poor* and *Needy*, the *Mournful* and Sick."

Quaker doctrine, moreover, spelled out for him some of the egalitarian implications of Christian teaching. Quakers, as we have seen, made it a matter of principle to ignore and flatten social distinctions. Penn found refreshing their insistence on simplicity, their drab clothing, their refusal to doff their hats or to use customary forms of address. The world's addiction to these empty forms was simply another sign of its apostasy. With his usual air of defiance Penn dismissed the objections that his own sort of people made to this seeming uncouthness: if, as they claimed, it would "overthrow all Manner of Distinctions among Men," then so be it. "I can't help it," he said, "the Apostle *James* must answer for it, who has given us this Doctrine for Christian and Apostolical," and he cited the second chapter of James, where the apostle warns against respect of persons.

After joining the Quakers and assuming, however proudly, the mantle of meekness, Penn welcomed unmeek confrontations with the authorities of Restoration England, representatives of the world he had left behind. With his acid tongue and sharp wit, he was more than a match for the judges before whom he and his Friends appeared. The incarceration he nevertheless suffered at Newgate Prison and the Tower of London only gave him the leisure to grind out more books and pamphlets denouncing the ways of the world he had known and justifying the ways of the Quakers.

We have, then, a man who made his life a testimony against the world he grew up in, a world that called itself Christian and allowed, indeed enjoined, its people to study and do what Christ had taught, but which seemed to a sharp young mind to deny his teachings in all its institutions, not least in all the churches save one that claimed the name of Christ. Why, then, may we ask, have we ever heard of William Penn? The world is pretty good at sending into oblivion those who defy or deny it. The meek may inherit it later on, but they don't get far in the here and now. If we have heard of William Penn before this, it is because he was not meek. He was not humble. And being neither meek nor humble, he did not in fact reject as much of the world as he seemed to. The man who sassed his judges and filled the presses from his cell in Newgate was not content to inherit the world later on or to leave it as he found it. He wanted to change it now, and he did in fact leave his mark on it.

He left his mark because what he wanted and argued for, pleaded for, almost fought for was not quite outside the possible. He left his mark because he knew how the world worked and was prepared, in spite of his denunciations, to work within its terms.

We may find a first clue to his capacity for coming to terms with the world in his relationship to his parents. He was obviously fond of them, proud of his father's success in a career that he himself had to eschew. In recounting the sacrifices he had to make for his faith, he always dwelt on the displeasure of his parents. And his father's displeasure was real. Penn spoke of "The bitter usage" he underwent when sent down from Oxford in 1662, "whipping, beating, and turning out of Dores." And when he returned from Ireland a full-fledged Quaker in 1667, it must have gone just as badly, though by this time whipping and beating were out of the question. But the Penns, after trying to talk their son out of his queer beliefs, became reconciled to them and to him. By the time the admiral died, in 1670 (not yet forty-nine years old), he had entrusted his son with many of his business affairs and made him his principal heir and executor of his considerable estate. Indeed, according to Penn, the parents "that once disown'd me for this blessed Testimonys sake . . . have come to love me above all, thinking they could never do and leave enough for me." He showed no hesitation in accepting that share of the world which his father had accumulated, nor did he ever think of disowning his parents, as they for a time had thought of disowning him.

Admiral Penn had raised his son as a Protestant, as a gentleman, and as an Englishman. Penn was proud to be all of these. His understanding of what each entailed might differ from his father's and from many other Englishmen's, but not to the point of disavowal. Rather, he thought that if Protestants were true to their principles, they ought to become Quakers as he had. If gentlemen were true to their principles, they ought to give up the vices that he had given up. And if Englishmen were true to their principles, they ought to prevent their government from meddling in religion and threatening the liberty and property of Englishmen like him, who did not conform to the dictates of a set of bigoted priests. As a Protestant, a gentleman, and an Englishman, Penn presented his case, in terms designed to appeal to Protestants, to gentlemen, and to Englishmen.

THE PROTESTANT

Penn insisted throughout his life that he was a Protestant. In a speech before a committee of Parliament in 1678, supporting a bill for religious toleration, he told the members,

> I was bred a Protestant, and that strictly too. . . . reading, travail and observation made the Religion of my education the Religion of my judgement. . . . I do tell you again, and here solemnly declare in the presence of Almighty God, and before you all, that the Profession I now make, and the society I now adhere to, have been so far from altering that Protestant judgment I had, that I am not conscious to myself of having receded from an Iota of any one principle main-

tained by those first Protestants and Reformers in Germany, and our own Martyrs at home against the Pope or See of Rome.

Protestantism, as Penn saw it, was Christianity rescued from the apostasy that had befallen it under Roman Catholicism. And Quakerism was Protestantism rescued from the apostasy that had befallen it after the passing of the great reformers of the sixteenth century. Almost all his voluminous writings were designed to demonstrate this proposition and to defend Quakerism from denials of it by Anglicans, Presbyterians, Congregationalists, Socinians, Anabaptists, and Catholics. His first tract, in 1668, like so many seventeenth-century tracts, tried to get the whole argument on the title page: *Truth Exalted; In a Short, But Sure Testimony against all those Religions, Faiths, and Worships, That have been formed and followed in the Darkness of Apostasy: And For that Glorious Light which is now Risen, and Shines forth, in the Life and Doctrine of the Despised Quakers, as the Alone Good Old Way of Life and Salvation. Presented to Princes, Priests, and People, That they may Repent, Believe, and Obey. By William Penn, whom Divine Love constrains in an Holy Contempt, to trample on Egypt's Glory, not fearing the King's Wrath, having beheld the Majesty of Him who is Invisible.* The same intent is apparent in his other tracts, such as (without the subtitles) *Quakerism a New Nick-name for Old Christianity* and *Primitive Christianity Revived in the Faith and Practice of the People called Quakers.*

Quakerism as Protestantism required a good deal of defending, because its distinctive doctrines seemed clearly heretical, in direct defiance, as we have seen, of central Protestant Christian dogmas. Protestant heresies generally went in one of two directions: either on the one hand toward antinomianism, in which the true believer was thought to be freed from adherence to the Law by the presence of Christ within him, or on the other hand toward Arminianism, in which the believer was thought to be capable of achieving his own salvation by escaping from original sin and obeying the Law. Antinomianism entailed a belief in direct revelation, which was supposed by the orthodox to have ceased with the writing of the Bible. Arminianism amounted to a denial of justification by faith and thus a return to the repudiated Catholic doctrine of justification by works. Quakerism, it seemed, embraced not one of these heresies but both at once. In the doctrine of an inner light, Quakers claimed a direct revelation from God. At the same time they affirmed that everyone possessed this inner voice of God and could achieve salvation by obedience to it. They thus rejected predestination and affirmed or seemed to affirm justification by works.

This combination of heresies appeared to subordinate the Scriptures to some fancied inner voice, and to eliminate Christ's atonement for human sin. The recovery of the Scriptures had been central to the Reformation, which had also restored Christ as the sole savior of man, freeing the church from reliance on any kind of human merit. But the Quakers, as if to emphasize that they had no need of Christ, eliminated the sacraments that memorialized him. And to top off their heresies, they denied the conventional doctrine of resurrection of the dead at the last day.

In defending Quaker heresies as Protestant and Christian, Penn had one advantage. Protestants prided themselves on eliminating idolatry and superstition from their worship. They emphasized the Holy Spirit, which brought unmerited grace to those whom God would save. They destroyed graven images and denounced the materialism of the Roman church. Quakers, too, emphasized the spirit and explicitly affirmed God to be an infinite spirit, affirmed it far more unequivocally than orthodox Protestants did. It was thus possible for Penn to turn some accepted Protestant doctrines and institutions against his opponents in the Church of England, which still harbored many of the sensual accompaniments of worship inherited from Rome. English churches, despite the Puritans, still contained paintings and statuary, still contained some ceremonies and trappings that betrayed, in Penn's and the Quakers' view, the Protestant repudiation of graven images. It was, as Penn put it in his devastating fashion, as though "God was an *old Man*, indeed, and Christ a *little Boy*, to be treated with a kind of *Religious Mask* [i.e., drama], for so they picture him in their Temples; and too many in their Minds."

The sacraments of baptism and the Lord's Supper, in spite of the Protestant denial of transubstantiation, Penn dismissed as relics of superstition. Water baptism was only slightly less offensive than the Old Testament circumcision that it replaced, and the Lord's Supper was "a Kind of Protestant Extream Unction." Both sacraments were departures from true Christian and Protestant freedom from formalistic, external devices that encouraged sinners to think they could be saved without an inner transformation. Circumcision of the heart, baptism by fire was what Christ demanded of those who believed in him. "Where Ceremonies, or Shadowy Services [Penn's term for traditional rituals] are continued, People rest upon the Observance of them, and *Indulge* themselves in the Neglect of the *Doctrine of the Cross of our Lord Jesus Christ.*" The ceremonies by which other Protestants memorialized Christ were in fact ways of escaping the burden that he laid on his followers.

The orthodox doctrine of resurrection of the dead similarly departed from Christ's insistence on the spirit. Penn did not deny that the dead would be raised, but he regarded as grossly materialistic the notion that men would recover their earthly bodies. It betrayed a continuing sensual element in the orthodox view, as though heaven would be incomplete without a resumption of the earthly pleasures enjoyed in this world. "It makes the Soul," said Penn, "uncapable of Compleat Happiness without a Fleshly Body, as if Heaven were an Earthly Place to see, walk in, and for all our Outward Senses to be enjoyed and exercised, as in this World, though in an higher degree." This, Penn maintained, was neither Christian nor Protestant but Mohammedan. And he went on to heap scorn on the notion: if the dead were supposed to rise "so strictly . . . as they Dyed, then every Man is to rise *Married, [single], Low, High, Fat, Lean, Young, Old, Homely, Handsome,* and according to former Complexion and Sex. . . ." The idea was too ridiculous to contemplate.

The central Quaker doctrine of an inner light, the voice of God in every man, was nothing if not spiritual. To Penn it was no novelty but the essence of Christianity and especially Protestant Christianity. Nor was it difficult to find passages in the writings of Christians from Saint Paul onward that could be interpreted to support it, a task to which Penn gladly devoted himself. Almost all explanations of saving grace, of God's calling of his saints to salvation, could be read as expositions of the Quaker doctrine. Orthodox divines, to be sure, took pains to indicate that saving grace did not involve direct revelation; but the line between the two had always been difficult to maintain, and Quakers relieved themselves of the difficulty by erasing it. The inner light and saving grace, Penn maintained, were one and the same. They were the voice of Christ, who was God within man, enabling man to sin no more, to be made pure and thus acceptable to God.

In answer to the charge that Quakers denied Christ's atonement for sin, Penn developed a distinction made by other Quakers, between past and present sin. Christ's sacrifice, he maintained, was necessary to atone for the sins that every man committed before he submitted to the inner light. Christ justified man before God for these past sins, but this did not excuse future sins. And it was sacrilege to suggest that God would welcome to his bosom men who continued to sin. The inner light, Christ within man, enabled believers to stop sinning. Christ not only atoned for past sins but prevented future ones, and he did so for all men and women who heeded his voice within them. Such a view precluded predestination and robbed original sin of its power. And Penn went on the offensive against both these dogmas. Predestination he derided as the work of narrow, pinched-up souls who made "the Eternal God, as partial as themselves, like some Ancients, That because they could not Resemble God, they would make such Gods as might Resemble them."

But it was unnecessary to waste much argument on predestination, for it was out of favor in the Church of England anyhow. Penn reserved his greatest scorn for the doctrine of original sin as something that debilitated men and prevented them while in the flesh from ever fully complying with the will of God. Penn dubbed this a "lazy" doctrine for "sin-pleasing times." It was simply, in his view, an excuse for sinning, and he mocked the orthodox ministers who preached it. "Methinks," he wrote,

> these Hireling Ministers are like some Mercenary Souldiers . . . that cannot bear to think of the Enemy's being totally routed, lest their War end, and their Pay with it. . . . They had rather the Devil were unsubdued, than they disbanded, that his being unconquered might be a Pretence for keeping such Mercenaries always on foot.

For all his wit, Penn was hard pressed to defend as Protestant a doctrine that resembled so closely the Catholic one of justification by works, but he could cite a good many Protestant divines, as well as Scripture, to show that the presence of saving faith was normally evidenced by good works. And he argued that making good works necessary to salvation was not the same as making them merit salvation. Good works, he said, were

> not strictly meritorious; only they have an inducing, procuring, and obtaining Power and Virtue in them. That is Merit where there is an Equality betwixt the Work and Wages; but all those Temporary [i.e., temporal] Acts of Righteousness, can never equal Everlasting Life, Joy, and Happiness (being of Grace, and not of Debt) and therefore strictly no Merit.

This may seem a distinction without much difference, but Penn was convinced that "Preferring Opinion before Piety hath filled the World with *Perplexing Controversies*," and this was one of them. The Puritan's tendency to separate saving grace from morality seemed to him monstrous. Indeed, "This Distinction betwixt moral and Christian," he thought, was "*a deadly Poyson these latter Ages have been infected with* to the Destruction of Godly Living, and *Apostatizing* of those Churches [Presbyterian and Congregational] in whom there might once have been begotten some *Earnest, Living Thirst* after the Inward Life of Righteousness." It was God who had joined grace and virtue, and it was human "stinginess of spirit," not Protestantism, that separated them.

In demonstrating the Christian and Protestant character of Quakerism, Penn knew that he had to meet other Protestants on their own ground. They would not listen to an argument that defended the inner light and other Quaker doctrines by means of the inner light itself. Erudition was what it would take, and in spite of his hostility to learning, Penn was prepared to supply erudition, probably better equipped to do so than any other Quaker. He knew Latin. He knew French. He knew enough Greek to discuss Greek texts of the New Testament. He could even put on a display of linguistic pyrotechnics (discussing the ninth chapter of First John) that included translations into French, Italian, German, Dutch, Anglo-Saxon, Hebrew, Syriac, and Chaldee (though it is clear that he did not know all these). Although he was no theologian and thought that theologians were in large measure responsible for the apostasy of Christianity from its primitive purity, he had studied the church fathers and the scholastic and Protestant divines enough to mine their writings for arguments. Similarly, although he held fast to the Quaker insistence that the inner light was a more direct and reliable avenue to God's will than the Scriptures, he knew the Scriptures backward and forward and could always summon up appropriate passages to serve his cause.

Penn's usual method of attack was to refute his opponents by appeals to reason and to Scripture and then to offer voluminous passages from past authorities. For example, in arguing that the inner light was present and recognized in all men before Christ's appearance as well as after, he quoted, among others, passages from Orpheus, Hesiod, Thales, Sybilla, Pythagoras, Heraclitus, Anaxagoras, Socrates, Timaeus Locrus, Antisthenes, Plato, Parmenides Magnus, Zeno, Chrysippus, Antipater, Hieron, Sophocles, Menander, Philo, Cleanthes, Plutarch, Epictetus, Seneca, Diogenes, Xenocrates, Virgil, Justin Martyr, Clemens Alexandrinus, Tertullian, Origen, Lactantius, Athanasius, Chrysostom, and Augustine. In defending the Quaker refusal to take oaths, he dredged up no fewer than 122 authorities from ancient times to the seventeenth century.

When Penn was not occupied in defending the Quaker movement, he was often busy keeping it defensible. He recognized how vulnerable it was to the charge that reliance on the inner light could be used to justify any kind of conduct, say, "Murder, Adultery, Treason, Theft, *or any such like Wickedness*." In answer he could only say, in effect, that it did not, that "God's Spirit makes People free from Sin, and *not to commit Sin*." Which was to say that Quaker morality was for the most part conventional Protestant morality: the inner light did not call Quakers to immoral actions. But Quakers had broken with convention at several points: in their mode of address, in refusing to take oaths, in wearing their hats before their betters. Penn was aware that some members, having broken convention at one point, might throw it to the winds. Such had been the case with another group, the so-called Ranters, antinomians who defined their actions, whatever they might be, as righteous by attributing them to the spirit of Christ within them. This was dangerously close to Quaker doctrine, and if Quakers were to gain the acceptance Penn thought they deserved, it was necessary to keep the movement free from such anarchistic tendencies.

Accordingly Penn took a strong stand, along with George Fox, in support of a church discipline that could restrain eccentricity and eccentrics. There was, for example, the case of William Mucklow, who carried his attachment to his hat to a stage that violated the whole purpose of Quaker practice. Quakers refused to take off their hats to human superiors in order to testify against worldly honors, and they could thereby distinguish their reverence for God by taking off their hats in worship. But Mucklow insisted on wearing his hat in prayer. When admonished for it, he fell back on the inner light and denied the right of the church to command his conscience. Others took up the same cry, challenging the right of the weekly, monthly, or yearly meetings of Quakers to supervise the conduct of members, including the right that the meetings had begun to exercise, of determining the appropriateness of members' marriages.

In these controversies Penn was always on the side of authority, affirming the right of the church to rid itself of "Wrong Spirits under never such right Appearances." His commitment was not simply to the doctrines of Quakerism but to the movement. He was ready to use arguments that he would have scorned in a Church of England man, maintaining that the majority in a church were more likely to be right than any individual, and advising anyone who dissented to "wait upon God in Silence and Patience ... and as thou abidest in the *Simplicity of the* TRUTH, thou wilt receive an Understanding with the rest of thy Brethren." And if this failed, "since the Spirit of the Lord is one in all, it ought to be obey'd through another, as well as in one's self." If anyone persisted in mistaking his own idiosyncrasies for the Spirit of the Lord, the only recourse was to expel him from the movement.

With Penn's assistance, though it required adjusting principles a little, the Quakers avoided the errors of the Ranters. Though Quakers remained at the outer edge of Protestantism, they became, thanks in no small measure to Penn, a recognized church, a force in the world, unlike the ephemeral groups around them. And Penn, fervently a Quaker, could continue to think of himself as a Protestant.

THE GENTLEMAN

That Penn was a gentleman and remained a gentleman is apparent both in his behavior and in his beliefs. His social position gave him an access

to power that no other Quaker enjoyed. At the same time, his gentil-
ity affected his understanding of Quakerism's most controversial doctrine
and helped to shape that doctrine in ways that presented a special challenge to men of his class.

The most radical departure of Quakerism from orthodox Protestantism was its insistence on the possibility of perfection in this world, the
possibility of living entirely as God would have us live, pure and sinless.
When Penn called on Christians to take up Christ's cross in opposition
to the ways of the world, he did not think he was asking the impossible.
True Christians could imitate Christ, for Christ would enable them to
make the imitation, to become pure and sinless. But what did purity and
sinlessness require?

Since Penn continually emphasized the affinity of Christ for the poor
and humble and of the poor and humble for Christ, it would be plausible to suppose that he thought the imitation of Christ required poverty,
that those of his own class who gave up the ways of the world had to give
up the privileges and perquisites that went with wealth and rank. And
the Quaker refusal to recognize worldly honors in forms of address and
behavior would seem to support such a supposition. But Penn took pains
to assure everyone that this was not his meaning.

We get our first hint of his position in *No Cross No Crown*, immediately after his defiant statement that if Quaker doctrine will overthrow all
distinctions among men, so be it, the apostle James must bear the blame,
not the Quakers. This ringing declaration is followed by a statement that
sounds odd to modern ears, beginning with a derision of worldly honors and closing with an affirmation of the obligations that Christianity
imposes on the different ranks of men: "The World's Respect," he says,
"is an Empty Ceremony, no Soul or Substance in it. The Christian's is
a solid Thing, whether by Obedience to Superiors, Love to Equals, or
Help and *Countenance* to Inferiors." Superiors, inferiors, equals—to an age
that associates human progress with equality, Christian perfection would
seem to have little to do with the duties of inferiors toward superiors or of
superiors toward inferiors.

What this passage tells us is that Penn's world was not ours. It was
a world that, for all its faults, still bore the mark of its Creator. Most of

the people who lived in it violated the Creator's intention in many ways but not in the orderly, hierarchical structure of their societies. That kind of order, for Penn (and for virtually everyone else at the time) was part of the original plan. "Divine Right," Penn believed, "runs through more Things of the World, and Acts of our Lives, than we are aware of; and Sacrilege may be committed against more than the Church." It could be committed, one gathers, by ignoring social order as much as by following the empty ceremonies that proffered unfelt or exaggerated honor. "Envy none," Penn told his children, for "it is God that maketh Rich and Poor, Great and Small, High and Low."

In taking up a strange religious belief, Penn seemed to many of his contemporaries to be himself committing a kind of sacrilege against the divine right embedded in the social order: gentlemen ought not to depart from the religion established by law and thus set a bad example for lesser folk. When his Quakerism got him in trouble again on a visit to Ireland in 1670, an Irish friend, Lord O'Brien, thought it sheer stubbornness for Penn to persevere in so strange a religious belief when it would have been perfectly easy for him to stick to the standard Anglican one. Penn, he said, was rejecting "not what you cant but what you wont believe, . . . it is certainly possible for you to believe our faith, for it is reasonable." Nevertheless, Lord O'Brien and Penn's other noble friends in Ireland were clear that queer and stubborn religious beliefs were not sufficient in themselves to deprive a gentleman of his rank. His friends intervened for him against the mayor of Cork, because as one of them said, wrong religious opinions "certainly cannot make any man degenerate from being a Gentleman who was borne so."

Penn's priorities differed from his friends'. If religion and social position were at odds, religion had to prevail. But Penn saw no good reason why they should be at odds. Although he thought religion demanded of gentlemen a standard of virtue that few attained or even attempted, it did not follow that a man's religious beliefs, whether strict or loose, should affect his place or power in society. That his friends should pull rank to help one of their own kind was perfectly proper, and he in turn used his own rank and influence to help himself and his Quaker friends in their encounters with authority.

Penn's knowledge of the law, gained during his brief period of studies at Lincoln's Inn, may have been superficial, but he had learned enough to be a troublesome defendant. When brought before the courts, he assumed not merely the defiant stance of the self-righteous but also the assurance of the cultivated gentleman in dealing with officials whom he evidently regarded as not quite his equals either socially or intellectually. When arrested for preaching at a Quaker meeting in 1670, he lectured the judges on the law and taunted them into statements that left the jury totally committed to him. He demanded to know what law he had broken, and when he was told it was the common law, he asked what that was, as if he didn't know. There then followed this exchange:

COURT: You must not think that I am able to run up so many Years, and over so many adjudged Cases, which we call Common-Law to answer your Curiosity.

PENN: This answer I am sure is very short of my Question; for if it be Common, it should not be so hard to produce.

This evoked an apoplectic response and more exchanges, in which Penn seemed to be interrogating the court instead of vice versa. When the judge told him, "If I should suffer you to ask Questions till to Morrow-Morning, you would be never the wiser," Penn could not resist the opening thus given him, and replied that whether he was wiser or not would depend on the answers he got.

The jury, in spite of browbeating by the bench, refused to convict this Quaker who talked back to his judges with such aplomb. A few months later the constables caught Penn preaching again and hailed him before the court, this time for violating the so-called five-mile act, which required no jury trial. Even without a jury to play up to, Penn maintained his posture of superiority and contempt. Asked at the outset of the hearing if his name was Penn, he answered, "Dost thou not know me? Hast thou forgotten me?" to which the judge replied, "I don't know you, I don't desire to know such as you are."

"If not," said Penn, "why dost thou send for me hither?"

"Is that your Name Sir?"

"Yes, yes, my Name is Penn, thou knowst it is, I am not ashamed of my name."

After he had reduced the court to fury with a number of diatribes, the judges called for a corporal with musketeers to escort him to Newgate Prison, to which Penn gave his final sneer: "No, no send thy Lacky, I know the Way to Newgate."

Although he served his terms in Newgate and the Tower of London, as other gentlemen had done before, Penn was able to retain or recover the place at the king's court that his father had won for him, and he was able to do it without sacrificing his religious convictions. In 1681 he got the king to give him Pennsylvania as a refuge for Quakers, presumably in payment of a debt owed his father. After the Duke of York came to the throne as James II in 1685, Penn enjoyed even greater opportunities for influence, and he took them. His father, on his deathbed, had adjured the duke to help young Penn out of the difficulties that his religion would surely get him into, and the duke honored the request as king. From 1685 until revolution ousted James from the throne in 1688, Penn was in daily and effective attendance at Whitehall, pulling strings for better treatment of Quakers and of other religious dissenters.

Penn's rejection of the world, then, was not a rejection of the existing social order or of the allocation of power within it. "I would not be thought," he said, "to set the Churl upon the present Gentleman's Shoulder." And at every opportunity he advertised the submission and obedience of Quakers to civil authority, excepting always when civil authority required a violation of their special beliefs.

In keeping with this acceptance of the existing social order, Penn's appeals for the Quaker cause were directed upward, to those in power, not downward to the mass of mechanics and laborers whom he liked to think the cause embraced. The direction of his efforts is apparent even in the record of his extended missionary tour, along with other leading Quakers, through the Rhineland and the low countries in 1677. His journal of the tour is studded with the names of potentates and of highly placed merchants and gentlemen and gentlewomen whom he sought to convert, if not to the cause, at least to toleration of it. Wherever he and his friends arrived, their first inquiry was to find out who were the most "worthy" local people, and it quickly becomes apparent that by "worthy" he meant the people who were worth something in wealth and power. He spent hours and days with Elizabeth, the Princess Palatine of the Rhine, and with her companion, the Countess van Hoorn, and later urged them to the faith in lengthy, almost passionate letters. The faith did not require, he was careful to assure them, that they give up their power and possessions. "I speak not," he said, "of deserting or flinging away all outward substance."

If Penn did not think the imitation of Christ required flinging away all outward substance, we may fairly ask what he did think it required. If perfect obedience to God was possible in this world and it did not mean a change in the social or political order, what precisely did it mean? Penn gives us the answer in numerous admonitions, denunciations, and apostrophes. Here is one written in 1677 and intended, he says, for "all Ranks and Qualities, from the Highest to the Lowest, that walk not after the Spirit, but after the Flesh":

> Arise, O God, for thy Name's Sake! O what tremendous Oaths and Lyes! What Revenge and Murders, with Drunkenness and Gluttony! What Pride and Luxury! What Chamberings and Wantonness! What Fornications, Rapes, and Adulteries! What Masks and Revels! What Lustful Ornaments, and Enchanting Attires! What Proud Customs, and Vain Complements! What Sports and Pleasures! Again, what Falseness and Treachery! What Avarice and Oppression! What Flattery and Hypocrisie! What Malice and Slander! What Contention and Law-Suits! What Wars and Bloodshed! What Plunders, Fires and Desolations!

These are supposedly the sins of the age, and a number of them like lying and swearing and fornication were available to all classes, but hardly anyone outside the higher ranks of society and outside the corridors of power would have had the resources to indulge in most of them. Similarly, *No Cross No Crown*, Penn's longest diatribe against self-indulgence, was aimed primarily at men and women who took pleasure in "curious Trims, Rich and changeable Apparel, Nicety of Dress, Invention and Imitation of Fashions, Costly Attire, Mincing Gates, Wanton Looks, Romances, Plays,

Treats, Balls, Feasts, and the like. . . ." In yet another catalog of the five great crying sins of the time, in 1679, Penn included: first, drunkenness; second, whoredom and fornication; third, luxury; fourth, gaming; and fifth, oaths, cursing, blasphemy, and profaneness. All but luxury would presumably be possible for the general run of people, but in discussing the prevalence of these sins Penn showed that he had in mind the people of his own class. Drunkenness was exemplified by having several different wines at one meal, whoredom and fornication resulted from following French fashions, gaming was bad because it resulted in the careless loss of great estates, cursing was most reprehensible in persons of quality, and so on.

In other words, Penn identified sin with the failings of his own class. He had been brought up among the gentry and nobility and reached his young manhood at a time when gentlemen were cutting loose from the restrictions of Puritan England. He was just sixteen when Charles II returned to the throne and set an example of licentiousness that had been missing in England for two decades. For a time Penn followed the example. He knew the vices of the gentry at first hand, as he often reminded his readers, and it was these vices he had in mind in his denunciations of the ways of the world; they were the ways of his world. His insistence that perfect obedience to God was possible for Christians meant that it was possible to do without the vices of gentlemen, the vices that he had learned at the court of the king and on the grand tour in France. Perfection was a matter of not doing what he had formerly done, and taking satisfaction instead in the pleasures of the spirit.

Thus the sinless perfection that Penn called for consisted largely in giving up those extravagant pleasures that only the few could afford anyhow. He sometimes defended this kind of abstention as socially beneficial. If gentlemen would deny themselves extravagant food, drink, and other fleshly pleasures, they could give more to the poor. He even recommended forming a public stock for the purpose, derived from "the Money which is expended in every Parish in such vain Fashions, as wearing of Laces, Jewels, Embroideries, Unnecessary Ribbons, Trimming, Costly Furniture and Attendance, together with what is commonly consumed in Taverns, Feasts, Gaming etc." The funds could be used to provide "Work-Houses for the Able, and Alms Houses for the Aged and Impotent." He never doubted that there would always be a supply of poor both able and impotent, to be thus relieved, as there would always be a supply of gentlemen to deny themselves in order to relieve the poor.

But relief of the poor was not the main objective of self-denial. Self-denial was an end in itself, pleasing to God, the essence of virtue. By suppressing the self, men not only avoided sin but opened the way to spiritual communion with the part of God that lay within them, the inner light. For some Quakers the inner light demanded specific actions. And it was standard Quaker doctrine, which Penn defended at length, that the inner light rather than Scripture was the guide by which to determine the rightness or wrongness of any particular action. Penn also, as we have seen, thought that ministers should be no more than mouthpieces for the inner light, passing on to their hearers what the inner light revealed to them. Yet Penn seems to have thought of the highest communion with the spirit as something that could not be put into words, as a feeling unconnected with the thoughts that words conveyed. Indeed, thoughts were to be banished from the mind, lest they get in its way. Not words, not speech, not even works, but silence, solitude, passivity were its usual accompaniment: "wait in the Stilness upon the God of all Families of the Earth, and then shall you have a true *Feeling* of him."

Nowhere did Penn argue that this feeling, this silent, wordless, thoughtless reception of the spirit must eventuate in positive actions. He continually insisted on the good works that Christ would enable the believer to perform and that would justify him in the sight of God. But precisely what these works had to be, apart from avoidance of the sins he cataloged, remained nebulous. It was good to give to the poor, and especially to widows and orphans, but the objective to be sought in self-denial seems to have consisted mainly in the feeling of bliss that came to the soul when it was freed from the distractions of earthly pleasures.

What Penn demanded of Christians, then, was not beyond their reach: self-denial and passive reception of the spirit. It was no wonder that Christians were to be found most often among the humble, for the humble could reach these goals with less effort than the mighty. Penn directed his appeals upward, because it was the high and mighty who most needed them, and even for them the goals were not impossible. In order to make way for the spirit, his noble friends need only do out of choice what the humble did out of necessity. If it seemed to them like a pretty dull life to do without their accustomed pleasures of the flesh, Penn asked them to consider how they expected to amuse themselves throughout eternity. Better begin learning to appreciate spiritual joys now!

Few of the gentry and nobility to whom Penn addressed his demand were ready to comply with it, and his own austerity, he tells us, brought him a good deal of derision from his former boon companions. But if self-denial was not in fashion among the gentlemen of Restoration England, the demand for it was not something to disgrace a gentleman. Indeed, it was part of the traditional ideal of what a gentleman was supposed to be.

Penn did not compile a list of authorities to prove that gentlemen should be Quakers, as he did to prove that Protestants should be, but it would not have been impossible for him to do so. In handbooks that told seventeenth-century Englishmen how to behave, there are passages strikingly similar to the injunctions that Penn urged on them. The most popular handbook, Richard Brathwait's *The English Gentleman*, could almost have been written as an introduction to *No Cross No Crown*. Brathwait argued, as did Penn, that virtue, not wealth, was what conferred nobility, and that the essence of virtue lay in self-restraint. Brathwait even urged something like the Quaker simplicity of dress. "Gorgeous attire," he said, "is to be especially restrained, because it makes us dote upon a vessell of corruption, strutting upon earth, as if we had our eternall mansion on earth." Virtue was something internal: "she seeketh nothing that is without her." And Brathwait went on to praise the Levites who "were to have no possessions: *for the Lord was their inheritance*." Brathwait can scarcely have expected English gentlemen to follow that example literally, but neither did Penn. And like Penn, Brathwait believed "there is no *Patterne* which we ought sooner to imitate than Christ himself." Penn could even have found in Brathwait a rationale for directing his efforts so exclusively to those at the top. Self-restraint, temperance, was particularly important for gentlemen, Brathwait told them, because "You are the *Moulds* wherein meaner men are casten; labour then by your example to stampe impressions of vertue in others, but principally *Temperance*, seeing *no* vertue can subsist without it."

In urging temperance, Brathwait probably did not have in mind quite the degree of restraint that Penn required. But Penn, in comparing such admonitions with the conduct of his noble friends on the one hand and of the Quakers on the other, could easily conclude that the Quakers were closer to the ideal of what a gentleman should be. As to be a Quaker meant, for him, to be truly a Protestant, to be a Quaker could also mean to be truly a gentleman.

THE ENGLISHMAN

Penn grew up in England at a time when it was not altogether clear what an Englishman was supposed to be, as the country swung from monarchy to republic and back to monarchy, from the Church of England to Presbyterianism, Congregationalism, and back to the Church of England. In spite of these transformations, perhaps because of them, most Englishmen who thought about the matter tried to locate themselves in relation to a more distant past. The national identity of any people generally rests, if not on their history as it actually happened, at least on a shared popular opinion about that history. Since the sixteenth century, Englishmen had seen themselves at the end of two great chains of past events: those comprised in the rise, fall, and recovery of the Christian church and those that gave their country its special form of civil government. In the minds of Englishmen the two were intertwined at many points, and there was a tendency for every group to identify itself and its own time as the proper culmination of developments inherent in both.

It was agreed by all except Catholics that the Christian church, beginning in purity, had quickly fallen prey to evil and worldly ways, indeed had fallen into the hands of Antichrist in Rome. John Foxe, in his *Book of Martyrs,* had shown how the spark of true faith had been kept alive in England, had been blown into flame by Wycliffe and the Lollards in the fourteenth century, who spread it to Hus in Bohemia, who spread it to Martin Luther. England had thus been the spearhead of the Reformation. The English were an elect nation, replacing the Jews as God's chosen people, and the English had therefore to lead the way in recovering primitive Christianity. There were many variations on this theme in the seventeenth century, as Englishmen disagreed over what primitive Christianity might be, what it required of true believers, and what the organization of England's exemplary churches should be. By the time Penn came of age, a certain weariness had set in, as the high expectations of the preceding decades faded.

There was no weariness among the Quakers. They took a somewhat less provincial view of church history than other Englishmen, but they saw themselves nevertheless as the culmination of the Reformation. Penn believed that the apostasy of Christians "began immediately after the Death of the Apostles" with the development of ceremonial worship. It continued with the conversion of kings and emperors, who tried to enforce Christianity on all and thus change the kingdom of Christ into a kingdom of this world, "and so they became *Worldly*, and not true Christians."

Penn dwelt less on the rise of the papacy than on the general degeneration of Christians, and he saw the beginnings of recovery in the French Waldensians and Albigensians of the twelfth and thirteenth centuries. But he also gave more immediate credit to the English martyrs of the sixteenth century and to the Presbyterians and Congregationalists of his father's day. The difficulty was that the Presbyterians and Congregationalists, too, had succumbed to worldliness, and by his own time he thought they were no better than the Church of England, especially in the Presbyterians' continuing wish to force their own way on the whole nation. Quakers, he said, honored all true worshippers, especially the Waldensians and Albigensians, but it was the Quakers themselves who represented the highest point of the recovery that began with the Reformation. "We do confess," he said, "it is our Faith, that so glorious a Vision, since the Primitive Days, has not happened to any, as to us in this our Day." Not all England, but a small group of Englishmen at least, remained at the forefront of the history of redemption, making their way, not through force, not through any kind of coercion, but by their words and their example. In their own way, Christ's way, they might eventually bring the whole country, nay the whole world, back to primitive Christianity and forward into the kingdom of God.

In thus placing the Quakers within a position that Englishmen had long assigned to themselves, Penn was following the path that might have been expected of any English spokesman for a holy cause. But Penn was also concerned, probably more than any other leading Quaker, to place the Quakers in the center of the English political tradition, at the end of the other chain of past events by which Englishmen identified themselves.

That chain of events, like the sacred one, had begun to take shape in the minds of Englishmen during the sixteenth century and had been fully articulated in the ferment of the contest between king and Parliament in the seventeenth century. It rested on the assumption that the people of a country are the ultimate source of the powers exercised by their government and the determiners of the form their government should take, the doctrine that has come to be known as popular sovereignty. The people of England, as Saxons, were supposed to have begun the exercise of these powers in the forests of Germany. When they migrated to England, it was held, they established a constitution of government to which they had adhered ever since and which their chosen governors could not rightfully alter. That constitution provided for a mixed government in which a hereditary king was limited by an assembly of his subjects. True, England had been invaded more than once by conquering hosts, most notably by William the Conqueror in 1066. But the conquests were not, in this view, truly conquests, for the conquerors had agreed to abide by the ancient constitution of the Saxons and had obtained the consent of the people to their authority only on that condition.

The kings and queens of England over the centuries had occasionally defied the ancient constitution and attempted to rule the land by arbitrary power, but the people had each time brought them back to the mark and obliged them to recognize the limits that the constitution set on them. The result was a set of landmarks in which the details of the constitution and of the rights of Englishmen had been set down in black and white, most notably in Magna Carta in 1215 and in the Petition of Right in 1628. The years since 1628 had seen more varied assaults on the constitution, first by Charles I attempting to rule without Parliament, then by Parliament attempting to rule without the king, and finally by Oliver Cromwell establishing a government without a king. But the English people, after suffering these usurpations had restored the ancient constitution and the monarch in 1660.

What the contest between Charles I and Parliament had demonstrated most significantly for Penn was that not only kings but Parliaments, too, could violate the constitution. The Long Parliament, which began in 1640, had attempted to perpetuate itself without recourse to the people who chose it. It had tried to alter the form of government, thus destroying its own foundation. Hitherto it had been Parliament that repaired breaches made in the constitution by the king. But how to repair breaches made by Parliament itself, by the very persons whom the people chose to protect their constitution? Englishmen had thought long and hard about this question without finding a satisfactory answer, though Oliver Cromwell had effected an unsatisfactory one. Yet one thing was clear: the representatives of the people in Parliament ought not to have powers that their constituents did not vest in them.

Such was the political tradition into which Penn was born, such was the history of England into which he had to fit the Quaker cause. Penn was no more successful than other Englishmen in finding a solution to the problem of how the people could prevent their own representatives from exceeding their powers, but he was squarely in the center of the tradition, as the recent past had shaped that tradition, in affirming that those representatives could not rightly alter the ancient constitution on which their very existence rested. There were two kinds of law, as Penn saw it. First, there were fundamental laws that obtained their authority from the direct consent of the people. Such was the constitution itself, the structure of the government inherited from the immemorial past, which neither king nor Parliament could legally change. Second, there were superficial laws, made for convenience. These were the proper business of Parliament, which could alter them or make new ones whenever circumstances demanded. For Parliament to meddle with fundamental laws was to betray its trust: "The Fundamental makes the People Free, this Free People makes a Representative; Can this Creature unqualify it's Creator? What Spring ever rose higher than it's Head?"

From this premise, for which he cited a multitude of authorities, especially Chief Justice Edward Coke, Penn argued that Parliament had no business at all to meddle with religion. Quakers did not ask that their religion be supported by government. Their political ideal was to have no religion supported by government. And this, Penn maintained, was precisely what fundamental law required, because the ancient constitution, the most fundamental of fundamental laws, gave Parliament no authority to prescribe religion. "Religion," he insisted, had been "no Part of the Old *English* Government." Indeed, how could the ancient constitution have made adherence to the Church of England a requirement for the enjoyment of the rights of Englishmen when the Church of England did not even exist at the time when the constitution was formed: "Our Claim to these *English* privileges, rising higher than the Date of Protestancy, can never justly be invalidated for Non-Conformity to any Form of it." Yet the Restoration Parliament did require conformity to the Church of England, required everyone to pay tithes to support the church, virtually forbade other religions to exist at all, and thus deprived Englishmen of their fundamental rights in direct violation of Magna Carta. That great charter, Penn said, "considers us not, as of this or that perswasion in matters of Religion, in order to the obtaining of our antient Rights and Priviledges, but as English men." And being English did not mean being of the Church of England: "A Man may be a very good *Englishman*, and yet a very indifferent *Churchman*."

Penn's position, that the English government was purely secular, was not a novel one. It had been adumbrated by radical religious groups in the 1640s and 1650s. But Penn was able to attach his argument to English political tradition in a variety of ways designed to win support even from the most ardent conservatives of his day. Given the propensity of men in all ages to justify revolution or rebellion on religious grounds, there is an inherent paradoxical conservatism in denying government any religious function or sanction. Penn, like Roger Williams before him, could denounce the monarchomachs, whether Catholic or Protestant, who called for the overthrow of kings whom they thought heretical. The Puritans who persecuted Quakers in Massachusetts were of a piece with the Puritans who brought Charles I to the block in England. Both, in Penn's view, were enemies to civil peace and freedom. And he never lost an opportunity to denounce the arch-Puritan and monarchomach, Oliver Cromwell, and the "Oppression & Persecution which Reign'd during his Usurpation"—a position well designed to win the approval of the restored monarchy.

Although the new monarch himself was unwilling to forgo his position as head of the Church of England, Penn continually suggested to him that in attaching his regimen to any church, he was actually subjecting himself to ecclesiastical control, allowing "the *State* . . . to be Rid by the *Church*." Charles II was content to be rid by the Church of England if that was the price of his throne, but he probably did not enjoy it. Penn's good relations with him and his brother and Penn's influence at court may have been owing in part, at least, to the fact that Penn did not regard the king's religion as having any proper connection with his authority. Charles and James were both Catholics, Charles secretly, James openly; their subjects were not, and ultimately they ousted James from the throne because of his Catholicism, but not with any help from Penn.

Although Penn's close ties with James resulted in accusations that he was himself a Catholic, accusations that jeopardized his campaign to prove that Quakers were Protestants, he considered his position to be the ultimate and true Protestant one. Religion, he maintained, was something that did not affect authority. The allegiance of subjects to their king was based on the fulfillment of his civil and political duties; his religion was his own business.

By the same token, according to Penn (though not according to Charles or James), a subject's religion was his own business, not the king's. It was probably on this ground that Penn and his father had finally become reconciled. Penn gives us at least a hint that his father shared his feelings about mixing religion and politics. At the beginning of the war with the Dutch in 1665, Charles asked the elder Penn for a list of the ablest naval officers to serve in the war. The admiral, according to his son,

> pickt them by their Ability, not their [religious] Opinions; and he was in the Right; for that was the best Way of doing the King's Business. And of my own Knowledge, *Conformity robb'd the King at that Time of Ten Men, whose greater Knowledge and Valour* . . . [would] *have saved a Battel, or perfected a Victory.*

Father and son agreed at least in making religious opinion irrelevant to the functions of government; and if Admiral Penn felt that way, probably a good many other Englishmen did.

But Penn's strongest appeal against government interference in religion rested on the threat it posed, not to the monarch's power but to the subject's property. In the apostrophes that Englishmen regularly addressed to the ancient constitution, the protection it offered to property had always been paramount. Penn pointed out to them that bringing religion into the picture could impair this fundamental protection. The "plain *English* of publick Severity for *Nonconformity*," he said, could be reduced to a simple maxim: "no Property out of the Church." This was not only unconstitutional; it was a ridiculous intrusion of the church into a sphere where religion had no place, an attempt to make the security of property depend on religious opinion. Accordingly when Penn proposed to Parliament in 1678 two bills for toleration of religious dissent, he entitled the first one "An Act for the Preserving of the Subjects Properties, and for the repealing of Several penal Laws, by which the lives and properties of the subjects were subject to be forfeited for things not in their power to be avoyded." The second one he called "An other Form of bill for the better Preserving, and maintaining English Property, being the true Fundation of English Government." In the preambles to both bills, Penn recited the evils that the penal laws (against noncomformity in religion) had brought upon England, especially in inducing sober and industrious men to leave the country and in preventing others from coming there.

Penn did not get either of his bills passed, and three years after they failed, he took the step that made him famous, in establishing a refuge where sober and industrious people could enjoy the security of property that England continued to deny to people of his persuasion. Pennsylvania was designed not as an alternative to the ancient constitution of England but as the fulfillment of it in an age that had betrayed it.

If his colony had turned out as he wished, it would have been appropriate to call William Penn finally a Pennsylvanian. He had great plans for his colony when he arrived there to supervise its founding in 1682, but he left after two years, frustrated by the unruliness of the people who joined him, an unruliness continued by their successors until his death in England in 1718. In his dreams for his colony, he had envisioned "a blessed government, and a vertuous ingenious and industrious society, so as people may Live well and have more time to serve the Lord, then in this Crowded land." In Pennsylvania, Penn expected Quakers to set an example of Christian, Protestant virtue. Quaker gentlemen would prove to be truly gentlemen, and with the willing consent of the people their paternal government would revive the ancient constitution of England, free from domineering prelates. Penn even rose to millennial hopes for his colony. "God," he wrote, "will plant Americha and it shall have its day: the 5th kingdom or Gloryous day of [Jesus?] Christ . . . may have the last parte of the world, the setting of the son or western world to shine in."

The prospect of a millennial kingdom in the New World brought out the prophet in Penn. While he was engaged in defending the Protestantism of Quakers and the rights of Englishmen, while he had George Fox by his side, fighting to keep the Quaker movement from splintering, Penn was dealing with a world where he knew his limits, a world in which one contended with hostile authority to achieve whatever approximation of right one could. In a new world, where he himself would hold the reins of authority, there seemed no limits to what might be achieved. If men were capable of perfection, Pennsylvania was the place where they could begin to show it, unhampered by the corruption that had overtaken England. Unfortunately Pennsylvania and the Pennsylvanians proved less than perfect.

And so did Penn. In escaping from the restraints of the world that had hitherto bound him, he expected too much both of himself and of those whom he persuaded to settle in his colony. If perfection meant self-denial, he was not ready to deny himself privileges and rights that he thought his position as founder of the colony entitled him to. And his colonists seemed unwilling to deny themselves anything.

Penn's unfounded optimism became apparent even before the founding, as he planned and replanned a constitution for the colony. He had had some experience at planning already as one of the proprietors of West New Jersey, where he and his colleagues proposed in 1676 a government in which virtually all power was placed in a representative assembly of the colony's freemen. In his initial plans for Pennsylvania, Penn again envisaged a government close to the people, with power centered in their representatives, who would be unable to act at all except under the instruction of their constituents. Though he provided for a bicameral legislature, the upper house was to be chosen by the representative lower house, which would have the initiative in proposing legislation (approved in advance by constituents). In assigning so much power to the people and their immediate representatives, Penn seems to have assumed that the settlers of Pennsylvania would align themselves willingly with his wishes for them or that they would spontaneously want for themselves what he wanted for them. It was symptomatic of his thinking about the colony that he did not specify his own power, except to place limits on it by providing for meetings of the assembly without summons from a governor and by providing for laws to take effect automatically if not assented to by the governor within fourteen days. He simply took for granted that there would be a governor—either himself or his substitute—and that the governor would normally give his assent to legislation.

As Penn thought about this scheme and discussed it with others, he evidently became concerned that the settlers might include some of the wrong sort of people and that the government should therefore be placed more firmly in the hands of the right sort, of which he had to be one. In his final "Frame of Government," he provided for an upper house of the legislature, to be elected from "Persons of most Note for their Wisdom, Virtue and Ability" ("ability" in the seventeenth century carried the connotation of wealth) and for a governor who should sit with this "Council" and have a treble vote in its proceedings. He now assigned to the council virtually all governmental powers, with the sole authority to initiate legislation, which the representative assembly, no longer bound by instruction of their constituents, was empowered only to accept or reject without amendment. Again Penn left unspecified most of his own powers as governor (beyond the treble vote in the council), but provided that laws should be enacted "by the Governour, with the Assent and Approbation of the Freemen in Provincial Council and General Assembly." He may have intended this to mean that laws would now require his assent. And he implied that his powers (whatever they might be) were to descend to his children, for in one clause he referred to "the Governour, his Heirs or Assigns," and he made provision for a commission to serve in case the governor should be a minor.

What Penn wanted was a popular government in which a grateful people would gladly accept the measures that he and other men of "Wisdom, Virtue and Ability" devised for them. He disclosed his manner of thinking when he sent an agent to West New Jersey to take charge of the town of Salem there, which he had acquired as one of the proprietors. He had bought the title, but he wanted the people to sign some sort of agreement (the text is now lost) asking him to assume government over them. The agent went to Salem and reported the reaction: "some said if the Government belonged to thee, thou might assume it without our petitioning thee thereto, I replied, thou wouldst rather have it by Consent of the people also; for William called the Conqueror acknowledged, he was chosen King, by the consent of the people."

That was perhaps how Penn saw himself, a Quaker king by consent, William the First of Pennsylvania. Besides deciding on a proper government for Pennsylvania, he decided on a set of laws for the people of the colony to consent to at the outset. Here again he revealed his high hopes—and wishful thinking—for a society that was not to be troubled by the self-indulgent gentlemen, misguided statesmen, and corrupt prelates whom he contended against in England. Pennsylvania would be a place where his laws favored the industrious and penalized the idle (all children would be taught a skilled trade), where he would make all persons free to worship God as they chose, where he would allow no one to engage in "Stage-Plays, Cards, Dice, May-Games, Gamesters, Masques, Revels, Bull-baitings, Cock-fightings, Bear-baitings and the like, which excite the People to Rudeness, Cruelty, Looseness and Irreligion," and where he would restrain the litigious by requiring every litigant to declare in court, before beginning a suit, "That he believes in his Conscience, his Cause is Just."

IN HIS PLANS for Pennsylvania, Penn showed none of the realism that marked his dealings with the English world. Instead of consulting his own past experience, he studied the scheme of government that James Harrington had concocted for an imaginary England in *Oceana* (1656). This was the source of his notion of a representative assembly whose supine members would be content with saying "yea" or "nay" to laws proposed by their superiors. Anyone who thought twice about the behavior of England's actual House of Commons should have known better. Quaker representatives might practice self-denial, but they were no more ready than other Englishmen for this kind of self-denial.

To be sure, some of Penn's troubles with his colony came from the presence there and nearby of non-Quakers. After learning a little of the geography of Pennsylvania, he thought that he must have, in addition to his original grant, the area now comprised in the state of Delaware. Otherwise his settlers would not have proper access to the sea. He succeeded, through his friend the Duke of York, in wresting this area from Lord Baltimore, who claimed it as part of Maryland. But it was already inhabited by Swedish, Finnish, Dutch, and English settlers who showed no sympathy with Quaker principles. And Baltimore, though frustrated here, entered into a lengthy dispute with Penn over Pennsylvania's southern boundary, a dispute that kept Penn in England, after a brief stay in his colony (1682–84), during most of the rest of his life.

But it was neither Baltimore in England nor the outsiders on the Delaware who turned the early history of Pennsylvania into a contest between Penn and his settlers. The settlers at first accepted most of the Frame of Government he devised for them and elected leading Quakers, men of "ability" if not of wisdom and virtue, to the powerful Council. They even accepted, however grudgingly, the gubernatorial veto power over legislation that Penn made explicit once the colony was founded. But they saw Pennsylvania as their colony, and Penn saw it as his. In moving from England to the New World, both Penn and his settlers thought of themselves as moving from a position of opposition to a position of control. In England, Penn was their spokesman and defender against a hostile government—and he continued to fill that role in England before and after the overthrow of his friend James II—but within Pennsylvania the settlers did not need him. Within Pennsylvania he became the authority against which they would themselves contend, assisted by new homegrown leaders: the very men of ability who sat on the Council.

What they contended about mostly was property and the power that accompanied property. Penn, as proprietor of the colony, felt that it should bring him some revenue. He had never thought of it as a way of flinging away all outward substance. Though he had sold and continued to sell large amounts of Pennsylvania land, he had spent more than he gained in getting the colony started, and he expected some return on his investment, at the very least a small quitrent, such as the king collected in royal colonies, on lands in private hands. Moreover, the political power he claimed as governor seemed to him small indeed for one who still owned most of the colony. But the settlers did not see it that way. They had invested their savings and committed their lives in an enterprise that was supposed to make them free as they had never before been free, free not only in their religion but in their property and government. They wanted to pay no quitrents, and they wanted no directions from Penn or from the governors and agents he sent to represent him.

The settlers won. Though they were divided among themselves, they united in resisting Penn in almost every measure he proposed. The story is familiar and need not be repeated here. Penn's settlers, led by large Quaker landowners and merchants, paid him no quitrents, or none to speak of; they defied his governors; they ignored his messages. In the end, though he retained his formal veto power, it was of little use. He continued to plead for his rights, both against the settlers and against attempts by the English government to bring the colony under royal control, but the settlers were less willing than the king to recognize his rights (though for two years, 1692–94, King William assumed control of the government). In Pennsylvania, it seemed, everyone's rights were secure except Penn's. After two decades of strife the colony wound up with a popularly elected unicameral legislative assembly that dominated the government and continued throughout the colonial period to quarrel with Penn and his heirs.

And yet Pennsylvania must be counted a success, a success not for Penn himself but for the principles he fought for all his life. He had contended that Quakers were Protestants, in the mainstream of Christianity and not wild enthusiasts who threatened the social order. In Pennsylvania, despite internal quarrels, they proved it. Though the settlers defied Penn, they established on a small scale the same sort of social order that prevailed in England, with small men deferring to those who had made their way in the world. And in Pennsylvania enterprising men made their way very rapidly indeed. Penn had contended that religion should be no concern of government, that making it so was a threat to the security of property and the rights of Englishmen. In Pennsylvania, although Penn compromised his principles by limiting public office to Christians (of whatever persuasion), all religions were tolerated, and the colony flourished economically beyond any other. The rapid growth of Philadelphia, outpacing all other colonial cities, the ships loading and unloading at its docks, the lush farms of the interior, all testified to the viability of a society where government was not entangled with the church.

Penn was not part of it. While his colony flourished, he languished in an English debtor's prison (an institution he had tried to eliminate in Pennsylvania). But Pennsylvania could not have happened without him. There, in spite of himself, he left his mark on the world. If it was not as deep a mark as he might have wished, that was because, when it came to Pennsylvania, he wished for too much. But a prophet may be forgiven for sometimes asking more of himself and others than they can give. Without Penn's prophetic vision, his colony would not have offered to the world the example that it did of religious freedom coupled with economic prosperity. And without his acceptance of so much of the world, he would not have had the opportunity to found a colony at all. Though he never became a Pennsylvanian, Pennsylvania became the testimony of William Penn—his mark on the world and at the same time a mark of his accommodation with the world.

—1983

CHAPTER TWELVE

Ezra Stiles and Timothy Dwight

In the eighteenth century college presidents exerted a large influence on their students by doing most of the teaching. This is a story about the influence of two presidents of Yale in the 1790s, when Yale figured more conspicuously on the national scene than it probably ever has since then. Historians of American religion have awarded the two presidents an even larger role in those years than they deserve. How that came about is part of the story. But first a word about who the two men were.

Ezra Stiles was president of Yale from 1778 to 1795. He was a man of strong likes and dislikes. He liked Newport, Rhode Island, Yale College, and men of learning everywhere. He disliked Baptists, Quakers, Anglicans, and Timothy Dwight.

Timothy Dwight was president of Yale from 1795 to 1817. He was a man of strong likes and dislikes. He liked Greenfield, Connecticut, Yale College, and everyone who liked him. He disliked deists, democrats, and—apparently—Ezra Stiles.

The judgment of historians, often reiterated, is that Timothy Dwight rescued Yale from a condition of infidelity and decay in which his predecessor, Ezra Stiles, had left it. When Stiles died, in 1795, one gathers from the historians, Yale was in pretty bad shape: student morale was low, discipline archaic and ineffective, and teaching uninspired; worst of all, religious infidelity was rampant among the students. Timothy Dwight changed all this. Dwight was the great opponent of infidelity. He argued and inspired and disciplined the students into a glowing body of zealous, though not fanatical, Christians. Student morale went up; learning went up; and deism went down.

The Yale episode has assumed a more than local significance in American religious history as an epitome of what shortly took place on the national scene. Christianity was at a low ebb in the 1790s, but about the turn of the century it took on new life. Led by Dwight and men like him, the revival of 1800 broke the back of deism and ushered in a half century of evangelical Christianity.

Such, I believe, is the accepted view, and historians have offered much testimony to support it. Their first witness, who sets the tone for those that follow, is a very lively, likable, and talkative old man named Lyman Beecher, who was a freshman and sophomore at Yale under Stiles and a junior and senior under Dwight. He knew both men and was therefore qualified to compare them. One day in the 1850s he did so, while sitting in the comfortable house of his daughter Harriet Beecher Stowe. He was dictating his autobiography, a rambling series of reminiscences, and his children had gathered in Harriet's house to listen and write it down. After he died, in 1863, they published it; and when scholars began to write the history of American religion, they discovered it with sheer joy. The old man had spoken, as he lived, with gusto; and his words enlivened the drab story of controversies that had lost their point for a later generation. The historians quoted him freely and effectively, and one of the passages they quoted to greatest effect was his description of his undergraduate years at Yale:

> In my Sophomore year (September, 1794–'5) I did comparatively little.... In May of this year Dr. Stiles died, and Dr. Dwight became President at the next Commencement. He had the greatest agency in developing my mind.
>
> Before he came college was in a most ungodly state. The college church was almost extinct. Most of the students were skeptical, and rowdies were plenty. Wine and liquors were kept in many rooms; intemperance, profanity, gambling, and licentiousness were common. I hardly know how I escaped....

That was the day of the infidelity of the Tom Paine school. Boys that dressed flax in the barn, as I used to, read Tom Paine and believed him; I read, and fought him all the way. Never had any propensity to infidelity. But most of the class before me were infidels, and called each other Voltaire, Rousseau, D'Alembert, etc. etc.

They thought the Faculty were afraid of free discussion. But when they handed Dr. Dwight a list of subjects for class disputation, to their surprise he selected this: "Is the Bible the word of God?" and told them to do their best.

He heard all they had to say, answered them, and there was an end. He preached incessantly for six months on the subject, and all infidelity skulked and hid its head.

The impression given here of the unhappy and ungodly condition at Yale under Ezra Stiles and its rescue by Timothy Dwight was heightened by other passages describing the college's decrepit philosophical apparatus and the inability of Stiles to make the students behave.

Few historians of American religion have overlooked these passages, and those interested particularly in the history of Yale and Connecticut have found other evidence to confirm what Beecher said. Matthew R. Dutton, who had been a tutor for four years under Dwight, was even more decided in his opinion than Beecher. In a brief biography written after Dwight's death, he wrote,

The College, when he came to its presidency, was in a dreadful state of disorder, impiety and wickedness. Infidelity was so common, and so generally thought to be an indication of genius and spirit, that an aspiring, ambitious youth hardly dared avow his belief in the Christian religion. Neither was this spirit confined to the walls of college. It prevailed alarmingly in the state and perhaps through the union. . . . Doctor Dwight, with his constitutional ardour and intrepidity threw himself into the gap, and stayed the progress of this overflowing scourge. . . . The effect of this part of his labours in college, is evident from one fact. For many years before his death, no person dared openly express the sentiments of infidelity in that semi-

nary, lest he should be despised by his comrades, for stupidity, ignorance and depravity.

His labours were not less effectual, to purify the morals of the
institution over which he watched with the affection and anxiety of
a father. Several cases of exemplary punishment, at first, and a regular course of unwavering discipline afterwards, accompanied by the
influence of moral persuasion and divine truth, changed that college,
through the blessing of God, from a sink of moral and spiritual pollu-
tion into a residence not only of science and literature, but of morality and religion, a nursery of piety and virtue, a fountain, whence has
issued streams to make glad the city of our God.

The Reverend Gardiner Spring, in a funeral oration on Dwight, made
the same point. "It is a fact not to be denied," he said, "that at the time
Dr. Dwight entered upon this official charge, the College was in a state of
lamentable declension. Its funds were low, its policy not the most happy,
its numbers small, and its morals corrupt."

Even more impressive than the reminiscences of old men are the letters of students written on the scene at the very time when Dwight took
over from Stiles. The most striking of those that have survived is from
Timothy Bishop (class of 1796) to Thomas Robbins, a classmate who
transferred to Williams in his senior year:

You will easily suppose that since Dr. Dwight, a person so different from his predecessor, has been elected by the united voice of the
electors, to the supreme authority, affairs have taken a quite different situation from what they were under Dr. Stiles, the government
of college at present possessing more energy and claiming greater
respect which however was not owing altogether to the neglect of Dr.
Stiles but to his great age.

The character of Dr. Dwight is remarkable, he is the most fitted and the best qualified both for the instruction and government of
this college that could be obtained. . . . We now see the advantages of
having an able director at the head of affairs one whose commands
are energetic, respected and obeyed; for if the tree is corrupt so also

will be the branches. It is surprising to see what a difference there is in the behaviour of the students since last year; at present there is no card playing, at least very little of it, no nightly revellings, breaking tutors windows, breaking glass bottles etc., but all is order and quietness, more so I believe than was ever known for any length of time in this college.

The senior year formerly you know was but of very little use to the students, except only for reading the studies being of small importance having but only one recitation a day but in consequence of the new regulations it has become of as much importance as any of the four years. We have two recitations a day read disputes as was usual junior year; and four compositions a week, and six speak weekly.

Other classmates wrote to Robbins in much the same terms during the first year of Dwight's presidency. Henry Belden chided Robbins for leaving and told him that Dwight was "just such a man as every one would wish himself to be." Charles Denison thought that "college has not, since I have been a member of it, been in so good a situation as it has during this term. . . . All college are perfectly pleased with the President. Our class has two recitations each day. . . . The Pulpit is at present supplied by Dr. Dwight, which you may be sure is not displeasing to the students." Benjamin Silliman, also of the class of 1796, and later to become Yale's professor of chemistry and natural history, likewise expressed great satisfaction with the new administration. "The President," he wrote his mother, "gives universal satisfaction; college is in fine order; commons are decent; the weather is fine; and we have every opportunity for improvement which we can wish."

Historians, reading such letters, have found in them ample support for the story told by Beecher, and indeed the case appears to be an obvious one: Stiles, though a learned man, must have been unsuccessful as a college president, and Dwight, in that respect at least, his superior. The evidence, to all appearances, is overwhelming. But appearances in this case are deceiving.

We might begin our examination of the evidence by noticing that Lyman Beecher's memory was faulty in some details: it can be demonstrated, for example, that the philosophical apparatus that he made so much fun of was relatively new. But we all know that memories are tricky and subject to error in much less than fifty years' time. The surprising thing is that Beecher was probably right about two important matters: the college church *was* near to extinction when Ezra Stiles died, and Timothy Dwight probably *did* allow the students to discuss the question whether the Bible was the word of God. Where Beecher erred, and where historians have erred more grievously in following him, was in the significance attached to these two facts. By placing them in their context, we may perceive that the situation at Yale in the 1790s was not quite what Beecher supposed when he recalled it fifty years later.

When Beecher said that the college church was almost extinct, he presumably meant that very few students were members of it in his day. The records of the church bear him out: although Yale students were obliged to attend the college church, few became members. Only three new members were admitted in 1792, only one in 1793, and only two in 1794. These figures, however, can be understood only in conjunction with a good many more.

The Yale College church, like many New England churches of the eighteenth century, had its beginnings in controversy, the controversy that followed the Great Awakening of 1741–42. The awakening divided New England into two hostile camps—the New Lights, who supported it, and the Old Lights, who opposed it. Thomas Clap, Yale's rector from 1740 to 1745 and president from 1745 to 1766, had been one of the staunchest Old Lights. He had stood firmly for the Reverend Joseph Noyes, minister of New Haven's First Church, when itinerant New Light preachers denounced Noyes and split his church. Yale students, Clap saw to it, did not go wandering after strange gods; every Sunday morning, whether they liked it or not, they sat in the First Church and listened to Joseph Noyes. But by 1753 Clap himself, to the consternation of his friends, became a New Light. In order to remove Yale students from an influence that he suddenly saw as undesirable, he announced the astonishing doctrine that a college constituted a church in itself. Clap was probably the most forceful personality ever to sit in the president's chair at Yale, and in spite of the fact that Noyes was himself a member of the corporation, he carried his point. In 1757 the college church was gathered, with a professor of divinity, the Reverend Naphtali Daggett, to minister to it. It has existed ever since.

Several factors must be considered in judging the health of the Yale College church in the eighteenth century. The first is the size of membership in other New England churches of that time. One of the characteristics of the New Light churches (of which the college church, in the beginning at least, must be accounted one) was a strict standard of admission. Though there were wide variations on this point, New Light ministers generally wished to see a return to the Congregational practice of the seventeenth century, when a religious experience conveying assurance of salvation was a prerequisite of membership. Other ministers took a more liberal view, urging all persons who hoped for salvation to join. But even where the minister was liberal, congregations, whether Old Light or New, seem to have been less so; and the numbers who joined a church in full communion remained surprisingly small throughout the eighteenth century.

A small church membership did not necessarily mean an indifference or hostility to religion or to Congregationalism. New Englanders attended church in large numbers, and paid for the support of the minister, even in Rhode Island, where no law obliged them to. But few became members. The number of members in a given church was usually no more than half, sometimes much less than half, the number of families served by the church. In other words, about half of the families attending a particular church normally contained no member. The average New Englander in the eighteenth century was a churchgoer but not a church member. The number of members to be expected, therefore, in a church composed entirely of college students and faculty (the president, a professor or two, and three or four tutors) may be expected to run well below the size of the total student body.

In the case of the college church it must also be remembered that, apart from the faculty, members could remain so for only four years at the most. And even among the faculty the post of tutor was a temporary one, seldom held for more than three or four years. The only permanent members of the church had to be drawn from the presidents and professors and their families, and during most of Stiles's presidency there was only one professor. The church was thus constantly facing the threat of extinction by graduation. Commencement day was an annual disaster.

The threat was heightened by the fact that already in the eighteenth century New England churches relied on religious revivals to bring in new members. Such revivals occurred at irregular intervals, separated by periods of quiescence when only occasional members were added. The college church, like other churches, enjoyed revivals, but the effect of them on membership totally disappeared within four years' time.

Still another factor tending to depress the number of members in the college church may be found in the age of the college students. If we examine the age of church members at the time of joining in other churches, it will be found that only a minority joined before the age at which most students graduated. The urge to join a church usually came to eighteenth-century New Englanders, if it came at all, between the ages of twenty-two and forty. For a boy to join while still in his teens was very unusual, and most college students were in their teens. Moreover, if a boy did have the urge to join, he might very well join the church in his own town and never transfer his membership to the college church.

A final factor affecting church membership is one that almost eliminated the very possibility of a college church. The most surprising fact of New England religious behavior in the eighteenth century is that women members of churches usually outnumbered men by about two to one and sometimes by as much as three to one. The figures vary from place to place, but the New Haven First Church may serve as an example. Of 164 members admitted in the twenty years from 1768 to 1787, 115 were women and only 49 were men. There were, of course, no women students at Yale.

From these facts it will be apparent that the college church was bound to be a small and perishing body. Its shifting membership, however, serves as a rough barometer of the condition of religion at Yale from year to year. The number of admissions under Stiles as compared with those before and after will give some clue to the merit of Beecher's judgment of Stiles and Dwight.

The records of admissions are pretty complete from the time of the church's formation in 1757 to about 1774 and again from 1780 to about 1810. What they show is an average of about three admissions a year during the first eighteen years of the church's existence (1757–74). Under Stiles the average was about six admissions a year, double what it had been under his predecessors, and incidentally more than double the rate of admissions of men to the New Haven First Church during this period. During the first fifteen years under Dwight, the average was still higher, almost ten a year. The increase corresponds roughly to the increase in college enrollment during the years concerned.

The average figures are somewhat deceptive, because of the periodic revivals. The first revival in the college church occurred under Stiles in 1784, when twenty-four students joined the church. Under Dwight revivals occurred in 1802, 1808, and 1812. In the 1790s, however, there was no revival under either Stiles or Dwight. In the last four and a half years of Stiles's administration, a total of fifteen students were admitted; in the first four and a half years of Dwight's administration, fourteen. Thus during the years when Lyman Beecher was at Yale, the membership of the college church remained about even. It was nearly extinct when he entered under Stiles, and it was even more nearly extinct when he graduated under Dwight. Near-extinction was, in fact, its normal condition, in which it remained during the early years of Dwight's presidency.

It was not until 1800 that admissions showed a rise, and not until 1802 that a revival can be detected. This was long *after* other Connecticut churches had begun to experience the great revival of that period. The movement that has been called the second Great Awakening struck Connecticut heavily in 1799. Though historians, led perhaps by Beecher's reminiscences, have sometimes given Dwight credit for helping to start it, the fact is that the revival spread from other churches to the college and not vice versa. Religion at Yale, as measured by membership in the college church, did not show any improvement as a result of the change from Stiles to Dwight.

There can be no doubt that infidelity existed at Yale in the 1790s. It existed also in the 1780s and to a lesser degree in earlier and later decades. Adolescence is generally a time for questioning the principles of one's elders, and doubtless many Yale students went through a period of skepticism about Christianity. Ezra Stiles himself did so in the 1740s, and so have many other Yale students before and since; but that Yale was more infidel than the rest of the nation in the eighteenth century is very unlikely. It is true that the 1780s and 1790s saw the rise of deism in Connecticut and in the country at large to a degree never before known. But there is no contemporary evidence to suggest that Yale was a center of this sentiment. On the contrary, the principal criticism leveled against the college until the reform of its charter in 1792 was the fact that it was governed by clergymen, and no one suggested that the clergymen were leading the students toward deism. One might add that the proportion of those students who became ministers was larger under Stiles than under Dwight.

But statistics are cold and tricky. They may fail to reveal the spirit that pervades a place. What about the strikingly different way that Stiles and Dwight handled infidelity? Under Stiles, Beecher tells us, the students "thought the Faculty were afraid of free discussion," while Dwight dumbfounded them by letting them discuss the question "Is the Bible the word of God?"

That Dwight presided over such a discussion is highly probable, for reasons that will become apparent. That this discussion surprised the students is highly improbable.

The episode Beecher described was a formal disputation, and he did not mean, I am sure, to imply that disputations were novel. They had been in use since the Middle Ages and were still a regular and important part of the curriculum throughout the eighteenth century. In their junior and senior years students at Yale (as in other American colleges) were required to apply their learning to the defense of various assigned propositions. Half the class took the negative, half the affirmative, and the tutor (for the juniors) or the president (for the seniors) presided, awarding the decision to the side that marshaled its arguments the more skillfully. This was a weekly exercise, in which Stiles had participated as a student in the 1740s and Dwight in the 1760s.

The disputations were of two kinds, forensic and syllogistic. The latter were in Latin, intended as exercises in formal logic; the forensic disputations were in English and designed to develop rhetorical abilities as well as to train the student in clear thinking. Before Stiles's time the propositions for both types of debate tended to be universal questions of philosophy or religion: whether the mind always thinks, whether polygamy is lawful, whether virtue would be eligible if there were no life hereafter, whether miracles in themselves prove a divine revelation, whether human laws bind the conscience, whether deception is ever lawful. Propositions such as these were debated year in and year out. When Stiles became president, he continued to assign them as syllogistic topics and occasionally as forensic ones, but he generally reserved forensic debates for subjects of more immediate and compelling public interest.

Since public events continually suggested new issues, the subjects of forensic debates under Stiles frequently changed from year to year. He recorded many of them in his diaries. Unfortunately he failed to do so in the last years of his life, while Beecher was a student, but the notebook of Thomas Robbins, a junior, containing forensic topics for 1794–95, has survived. It reveals how fearful the faculty may have been during Stiles's last year of allowing students to discuss controversial issues. The propositions debated forensically by the junior class, from December 1, 1794, to April 21, 1795, were as follows:

Ought a man to be punished for a crime committed when in a state of intoxication.

Whether a man ought to be imprisoned for debt.

Ought a man to be put to death for any crime except murder.

Whether Democratic societies are beneficial.

Would foreknowledge encrease our happiness.

Whether physical knowledge is favourable to morality.

Ought property to be a necessary qualification for publick office.

Whether the interest of money ought to be regulated by law.

Would it be just and politick for the United States to emancipate all their slaves at once.

Whether raising money by lotteries is politic.

Whether representatives ought to be directed by their constituents.

Whether it was right to confiscate the estates of the refugees, last war.

Can universal salvation be proved from scripture.

Whether theatres are beneficial.

Is a republican preferable to a monarchical government.

Is the observation of the Sabbath a temporal benefit.

Whether the Indian War is just on the part of the United States.

Whether those who have suffered by the western insurrection ought to have restitution made by government.

Is our method of electing members of Congress and our Upper House preferable to that of other states.

Whether the Clergy ought to be exempt from taxation.

Can the various complections of the human species be accounted for from natural causes.

Whether it would be best for the United States to adapt their spelling to their pronunciation.

Whether the discovery of the mines in South America have been advantageous.

Whether sumptuary laws are beneficial.

Whether the principles of the French Revolution are just.

Whether a destitution of property ought to exclude a man from voting.

Whether an insurrection of a minority against a majority can ever be justified.

Whether a discovery of a mine would be beneficial to the United States.

Whether self-love is the sole incitement of action.

Whether a time ought to be fixed when a person shall act for himself.

Ought the study of the dead languages to make a part of a liberal education.

Whether representation ought to be according to population.

Are commercial towns in danger of being too populous for the good of community.

Whether a publick is preferable to a private education.

Whether the Senate and Congress have sufficient reason for holding their debates in private.

Ought persons to be allowed to set up trades without serving an apprenticeship.

Would it be politic for this state to diminish their number of representatives in the assembly.

Whether corporations of mechanics ought to be encouraged.

Would it be politic for this state to turn out the Upper House of our Assembly.

Whether divorces ought ever to be granted.

The particular proposition that is supposed to have astounded the class half a year later under Dwight is not here; but that proposition, in one form or another, had actually been debated at Yale for at least forty-five years. It was one of the old, standard topics, and is in one of the first student notebooks of disputations at Yale that I have been able to discover, that of Eleazar May in the class of 1752. May debated it on December 31, 1750; and as it happened, the instructor who presided over the argument was young Ezra Stiles, then serving as a college tutor. Ammi Robbins, father of the boy who recorded the topics listed above for 1794–95, debated the proposition in 1758. Stiles noted it in his diary as a subject for the seniors in 1778, 1780, 1781, 1787, and 1788. Eli Whitney debated it in 1790 and 1791 and Thomas Robbins's notebooks show it as the subject of an English composition for the juniors on April 19, 1795, less than a month before Stiles's death. When Dwight selected it as a topic for disputation by the same class some six months later, the students could scarcely have been surprised, except perhaps at being allowed to worry that same old topic once again.

Thus Beecher's recollections on these two matters, the state of the college church and the subject of the seniors' first disputation under Dwight, though probably correct as to facts, are wholly misleading about the significance of the facts. How, then, does it happen that Beecher's general impression was supported by so many other witnesses?

The strongest corroborative testimony is that of the students' letters written in 1795 and 1796. These are inescapable, contemporary sources, and they speak so highly of Dwight that they inevitably cast his predecessor in the shade. At least one deliberately contrasts the two men, much to the detriment of Stiles. Was Beecher right, after all, in his general impression? Though the letters actually say nothing and imply nothing about infidelity under Stiles, they do give a glowing picture of the improved student morale, not to say morals, under Dwight.

Before deciding that Beecher was right in general if wrong in particular, one should consider the fact that Beecher, like the authors of the contemporary letters, formed his impressions as a student. Fifty years later he remembered how he felt as a student, and there can be no doubt that the students at Yale gave Dwight an enthusiastic reception. Historians, most of whom teach in colleges and universities, know something at first hand of student fashions and student enthusiasms. Students as a class are surely fickle. Few historians, I believe, would be ready to turn over the choice of a college president, or even of a faculty member, to their students.

Unhappily when historians read the letters of an eighteenth-century student, they do not always employ the same perspective. The expiring condition of the college church and a debate on the divinity of the Scriptures assume a different significance when placed in the context of what came before and what came after. By examining a larger number of student letters, we may gain a similar perspective on them. It is not even necessary to read very far in order to observe the rapidity with which student feeling vibrated from enthusiasm to discontent and back again.

The most enthusiastic letter about the improved morale of the college under Timothy Dwight was written by Timothy Bishop to Thomas Robbins on January 11, 1796. Within three months Bishop had begun to cool off. When he wrote to Robbins again on April 14, 1796, he said that things were still, on the whole, going well, "but there are some individuals in the class who are very negligent in their studies and likewise in their attendance upon the exercises of College more so I believe than they ever have hitherto been. Day after day and week after week will pass away when these persons will scarcely look into a book or attend once upon the exercises of college." Benjamin Silliman, who had written his mother so happily in December 1795, had a different story on July 4, 1796:

The students are making a great rout, about commons—petitions, remonstrances, and resolves, have been sent into the corporation (which were yesterday sitting). I believe they have at least been saved the mortification of a refusal, and I believe nothing more. A large number of our stout-hearts have given out, that if they cannot obtain leave from the corporation to live out, they will take it from themselves.

Similar alternations of sentiment could be cited from almost any student correspondence. Mills Day on July 12, 1802, writes his brother Jeremiah of the great religious revival at Yale and of his own thoughts of joining the church; but by December 24, 1802, he says,

> The students in the lower classes have become rather unruly. Mr. Knight was rusticated for 2 months for rolling a barrel down stairs against the tutors door and afterwards denying it before the Authority. About the same time the bell rope was cut, the Bible and Psalm book concealed and a dead duck put under the cushion in the desk. Soon after Tutor Stuart had 5 or 6 of his window glass broken; and last evening a piece of gammon hung on his door and over it a paper on which was written "Turkeys for sale, 3 pence per pound." I have not yet been detected in any of these tricks nor do I know that they even mistrust me.

By this time both the students and the faculty seem to have lost the zeal for study that prevailed in the first months under Dwight. In the same letter Mills Day writes, "We recite lessons but four or five times in a week. The rest of our time is spent in writing, attending the other collegiate exercises, or in such other employment as we chose to be engaged in. Altho' we have no less than five professors appointed to instruct us in the various branches of science we enjoy the benefit of none of them at present."

Twenty years earlier or twenty years later, student correspondence tells much the same story. Jedidiah Morse wrote his parents from Yale on August 21, 1781, "since I have been a member of College prospects were never more promising, pleasant, and agreeable; a laudable ambition prevails; Virtue and Piety flourish; and Literature is in its Meridian splendor." On January 6, 1782, however, "Religion in this otherwise

flourishing society is at a low ebb—I wish it was in my power to inform
you otherwise. . . ." By the following August 1782, college had been dis-
turbed by the revelation of student debauchery too shocking for Morse
to describe, but on June 20, 1783, a "Seriousness considerable prevails in
College—one we hope is happily converted. God only knows how far it
may spread." This was the beginning of the religious revival of that year.

College authorities learned to take these sudden shifts in their stride.
Ezra Stiles was not unaware in 1795 of the low student morale that
Beecher remembered, nor was he complacent about it. But Stiles knew
what Beecher did not, that this kind of thing was part of any college president's life. On February 12, 1795, three months before his death, Stiles
wrote to Professor Eliphalet Pearson of Harvard in saner words than
Beecher or any other student could have used: "Our college has been in
a Tumult, nor is yet calm, altho' I hope we are quieting. The abolition of
the Winter vacation by the Corporation last fall, has occasioned it. But
we shall get along. I hope matters are tranquil at Harvard."

The fact is that neither student recollections nor student letters can
furnish an accurate guide to the condition of a college. Lyman Beecher
remembered that student morale was bad at the time that Stiles died and
that it improved when Dwight took over. His memory played tricks on
him in providing details to substantiate the impression, but the impression itself was correct. What Beecher could not have understood was that
morale would probably have picked up under the continued ministrations
of Ezra Stiles as readily as it did under those of Dwight.

There remains the testimony of Matthew Dutton and Gardiner
Spring, but these men may be quickly dismissed. Both were writing eulo-
gies of Dwight after his death in 1817, and though they knew Dwight in
his later years, they did not know Stiles. Dutton had been only twelve
years old and a resident of Watertown, Connecticut, at the time when
Stiles died and Dwight became president in 1795. Dutton did not enter
Yale until he was twenty-three, in 1806. Gardiner Spring was ten years old
in 1795 and a resident of Newburyport, Massachusetts. He did not enter
Yale until 1800. Both Spring and Dutton therefore spoke from hearsay.
Neither knew at first hand what he was talking about.

But is it not remarkable that two men speaking from hearsay (Dutton and Spring) and one (Beecher) speaking from memory, perhaps over-laid with hearsay, should have recorded the same impression, that Ezra Stiles was incompetent, especially as an opponent of infidelity, and that Dwight was competent and inspiring? Where did this unanimous impression come from? Could it have arisen entirely from the faulty perspective of students?

No final answer is possible here. But having seen more substantial evidence dissolve under scrutiny, we may perhaps be permitted to speculate about this. We know that there was no love lost between Stiles and Dwight. The details of the feud are hard to get at because the crucial documents have been lost or destroyed, but we know that they disliked each other. We know also that a change took place in the religious atmosphere of New England during the years when Dwight was president of Yale. Whether or not Dwight had anything to do with it, there was a great revival of religion about the turn of the century. We know that Dwight fancied himself as a crusader against infidelity. He would hardly have been averse to taking credit for the awakening.

We know also that from an early date Dwight opposed the French Revolution, while Stiles went to his grave in 1795 still confident that the French had ushered in a new era of freedom. We know that Dwight, like most of the New England clergy, became an ardent Federalist, while Stiles gave every sign of gravitating toward the Jeffersonians. We know that Dwight looked on all supporters of Jefferson and all supporters of the French Revolution as infidels; he even propagated the rumor, which was utterly false, that a secret society of deists, linked with the French Jacobins, was seeking the overthrow of government in the United States.

Under these circumstances is it not likely that Dwight thought Stiles was soft on deism, indeed soft in every way? Is it not likely that in discussing Stiles with friends and protégés Dwight conveyed precisely the impression that prevailed with Dutton, Spring, and Beecher? Even if he did not, would it be surprising if these men remembered the change that took place in New England around 1800 and associated it with the change from Stiles to Dwight? Memory has played stranger tricks.

What, then, have we proved? Not that Ezra Stiles was a great man and a great Christian, or that Timothy Dwight was not—merely that the most positive evidence will sometimes take on a different meaning when placed in its proper context. We may also have shown that a man who values his historical reputation had better outlive his enemies. It is time, I think, to reopen the case of Stiles vs. Dwight and to judge the two men, not by what students thought of them at a particular time, not by what they thought of each other, and not by what old men remembered of them, but by their actual achievements. We may in the end decide that Dwight was the bigger man, but if so it will not be because Stiles plunged Yale into a chaos of infidelity from which Dwight rescued it. Whatever Timothy Dwight's achievements—and they were many—no good evidence has yet been offered to show that this was one of them.

—1958

Part Three

REVOLUTIONARY
LEADERS

CHAPTER THIRTEEN

———

The Power of Negative Thinking: Benjamin Franklin and George Washington

FOR THE PAST SEVERAL YEARS, while reading the papers of Benjamin Franklin, I have found myself continually comparing him to George Washington. Superficially the two did not resemble each other at all. We remember Washington as a commanding presence, massively dignified, preoccupied with his awesome responsibilities, not given to small talk, with agreeable manners but formal in his graciousness, not someone you would feel quite comfortable to spend an evening with at home. Nor, you sense, would *he* have felt quite comfortable with you. Franklin, on the other hand, we picture as a bit casual in appearance, easygoing, always ready with a joke, clubbable, someone you *would* feel comfortable with, making small talk and serious talk as well, over a convivial bottle or punch bowl.

There is no record that the two of them ever spent a social evening together, and it is unlikely that they did, though they did meet on more than one occasion. But without much personal contact they maintained an extraordinary admiration and respect for each other, evident in their correspondence, which was mostly official, occasioned by the offices they held. One of the few examples of a purely personal letter was Washington's last letter to Franklin, the year before Franklin died. "If," Washington wrote, "to be venerated for benevolence: If to be admired for talents: If to be esteemed for patriotism: if to be beloved for philanthropy, can gratify the human mind, you must have the pleasing consolation to know that you have not lived in vain" (September 23, 1789). At the time Franklin received this letter, he had just written in his will, "My fine crab-tree walking stick, with a gold head curiously wrought in the form of a cap of liberty, I give to my friend, and the friend of mankind, General Washington. If it were a Sceptre, he has merited it, and would become it."

But a scepter, even with a liberty cap on it, was not what either man would have wanted for himself or his country. Despite their different personalities, they were united in their dedication to keeping scepters out of the hands of power. How Franklin arrived at his rejection of monarchy is easier to understand than Washington's. Franklin spent sixteen years in London, trying in vain to make a monarchical government recognize its own best interests in its dealings with its colonies. By the time he returned to America in 1775, he had lost all patience with monarchy. Washington in Virginia had not had such intimate contact with the ways of kings. Nor can we say that he was guided like Thomas Jefferson by reading books. He was not much influenced by abstract thinkers about political philosophy, nor was he much given to egalitarian sentiments about the lower classes, whether slave or free. His personal opposition to British rule, by his own account written in 1774, began from "an innate spirit of freedom" that rejected British measures toward America as "repugnant to every principle of natural justice." How the mind of this Virginia aristocrat traveled from outrage over British policies toward the American colonies to a positive belief in independent republican government is not plain from his surviving writings. But travel it did.

For him as for Franklin, the American Revolution became more than a matter of righteous resistance against violations of natural justice. That was how it began. Then it became a war for independence. And the war for independence itself became much more than that. For both men independence came to mean a demonstration that a people could govern itself without submission to a king, a demonstration that republican government could prosper in a world that scorned it. Hitherto republics had been thought suitable only for small countries, not worth the trouble of annexation by a monarchy, but ineffectual in government because the people could never agree on anything important, least of all on waging war. For some Americans independence meant simply the creation of thirteen small republics, improbably associated for the purpose of defeating their former monarch. But for Washington and Franklin, as for many other leaders of the Revolution, the people who joined in declaring independence were one people. They were creating something new in the world: a great republic, a republic on a continental scale. Washington led an American army, a continental army. He took his orders from a Continental Congress. Franklin led an American diplomatic mission and took his orders from the same Continental Congress. While Washington remained a Virginian and Franklin a Pennsylvanian, both were first of all Americans, engaged in establishing an American republic. In a phrase later used by Alexander Hamilton, both men "thought continentally."

Unfortunately they were both a little ahead of their time. Not all Americans could think continentally, except in short intervals. Many retained a greater allegiance to their miniature republics than to the great republic. Washington and Franklin in their respective positions had to marshal the forces of a continental republic against the powers of their former monarch. In doing so, however, they had to contend at the same time with people who thought provincially, the petty politicians ensconced in the governments of thirteen republics, and with the tunnel vision of the representatives whom those little republics too often sent to a supposedly Continental Congress. Washington had to win the war with men who were ill fed, ill clothed, ill armed, and ill housed because the states barred Congress from levying taxes and then failed to levy enough themselves. These state governments wanted to wage war on the cheap. They did not have the nerve to ask their people to pay as you go for the war they were conducting. To feed, clothe, and arm Washington's army, Franklin had to borrow from the French in amounts far in excess of what he and Washington believed that their countrymen could have paid from their own pockets. On top of that, the states borrowed for themselves, sending envoys to Europe to compete for the loans that Franklin was seeking for the United States. "I cannot but observe," Franklin complained from Paris, "that the Agents from our different States running all over Europe begging to borrow Money at high Interest, has given such an Idea of our Poverty and Distress, as has excedingly hurt the general Credit, and made the Loan for the United States almost impracticable."

Washington faced a similar competition from the separate states in recruiting for the Continental army. Just as the states offered higher interest for loans than they would authorize the Continental Congress to pay, many of them offered higher bounties for enlistment in their militias than they would authorize Congress to grant for the Continental army. In 1776, as the terms of enlistment ran out, Washington, desperately trying to hold his army together, was faced with persuading men to reenlist who knew, he acknowledged, "that their Townsmen and Companions are receiving 20, 30, and more Dollars, for a few months Service" in their state militias. Remaining loyal to Washington meant longer service for less pay. And while Franklin was bargaining to buy ships for a United States navy, South Carolina elevated a sleazy politician to the office of state commodore and sent him to France to outbid Franklin for an autonomous South Carolina fleet. Washington and Franklin had reason to say with a later American president, "I can deal with my enemies, but my friends, my goddamn friends!"

The two men nevertheless succeeded. If it can be said that any two men made the American republic, they conspicuously did. Not so conspicuous is a talent that these two very different men shared, a talent that enabled them to accomplish what they did where others might have failed.

It was the talent for getting things done by not doing the obvious, a talent for recognizing when *not* doing something was better than doing it, even when doing it was what everyone else wanted. It was a talent easily mistaken for laziness, indecision, irresponsibility, or even cowardice. Franklin's exercise of it struck John Adams as mere laziness and irresponsibility. When Adams belatedly joined the legation in Paris, Franklin's easygoing ways had already won formal recognition of American independence in a treaty of amity and commerce, while he was talking the French into loan after loan and gift after gift of money and supplies. Adams took a quick look and saw only chaos. "I found," he wrote, "that the Business of our Commission would never be done unless I did it. The life of Dr. Franklin was a Scene of continual Discipation." And Adams proceeded to *do* things that antagonized the French, nearly spoiling Franklin's carefully crafted inactivity. At home Washington's similar inactivity called forth charges of incompetence and timidity as a general because he did not start battles he could not win, while waiting and watching for those he could. An impatient Congress was full of detractors who wanted him replaced, as there were also proposals that Franklin be recalled in favor of more energetic men.

Both men knew the risks they took in not doing what others wanted them to do. It was not that they did not care what others thought of them. Quite the opposite. Both men cared enormously about their reputations, about their honor. Their deliberate refusals to do things, employed to great advantage in serving their country, originated in a personal ambition to gain honor and reputation of a higher order than most people aspired to. Several historians in studies of Washington have emphasized his eagerness to project the best possible image of himself. One book, by Paul Longmore, is entitled *The Invention of George Washington*, the inventor being Washington himself. Washington was highly conscious of how his actions and inactions would color his reputation.

The same was true of Franklin. As a young man in Philadelphia, he found it easier to get things done by seeming not to do them. Whenever he wanted to propose some civic scheme, like a public library, he contrived to keep himself in the background, giving credit to a number of anonymous friends. His *Autobiography* advised others to adopt the same self-effacing method. "The present little Sacrifice of your Vanity will afterwards be amply repaid," he counseled. "If it remains a while uncertain to whom the Merit belongs, some one more vain than yourself will be encourag'd to claim it, & then even Envy will be dispos'd to do you Justice, by plucking those assum'd Feathers, & restoring them to their right Owner." By the same reasoning Franklin never issued a public defense of his theories of electricity derived from his experiments. When would-be scientists challenged them, he was content to let his discoveries make their own way, as they quickly did. He became a world-famous scientist, in part at least, because he would *not* defend his breakthroughs as the personal achievements that they actually were.

What Franklin and Washington understood was the distinction between fame and vanity. They both wanted fame but knew that they would not get it by doing things that showed how much they craved it. They counted instead on really deserving it, and that meant *not* taking attractive shortcuts to it. On one level it was simply a matter of personal style. Franklin did not cut a good figure at the podium and never made a single significant or memorable public speech. He did *not* have a commanding presence and had a positive genius for working behind the scenes.

Washington shared Franklin's aversion to ostentation and officiousness, but Washington did have an aura of command and could not avoid commanding, either as a general of the army or as president of the United States. Nor did he underestimate the importance of looks. Franklin could afford to dress negligently (how the French doted on his "Quaker" garb and coonskin cap) and keep in the background. Washington had to remain in the foreground and had to look the part of a born commander. His uniforms were gorgeous, and he was always splendidly mounted. I believe he was sincere in his often expressed wish to live as a private gentleman at Mount Vernon. But that was not an option for him. He had continually to be in public and in command. The position of command in a republic, and particularly in a republic as large as the United States, required a keen sensitivity to what needed doing and what must not be done.

It was much more difficult for Washington than for Franklin. Franklin in France was a beggar, albeit a well-connected one. Washington in America was in charge, surrounded by supplicants. If he had held a scepter, if he had been a monarch or a tyrant, the decision whether or not to do things would have been simpler, but in a republic the people were the ultimate source of law and power as well as reputation. A commander had to decide what was in the people's best interests, and weigh the demands that were not. At the same time, when the demands were made by their formally elected representatives, he was bound by them, even when the government was as weak, hapless, and shortsighted as the Continental Congress.

Washington had to face the problem most painfully in the war for independence. The army Washington was up against not only had superiority in soldiers and guns; it also had generals who could make strategic and tactical decisions in the field without having to worry about the popularity of what they did. The people who might criticize them were three thousand miles away. Washington had to make strategic and tactical decisions that would outwit the enemy but at the same time satisfy popular demand and popular expectations. To ignore what the people expected of him would have been to give up the whole enterprise to which he had committed himself. He had to walk a thin line between doing what was necessary to win the war and doing what the people's representatives kept asking him to do. When he could comply without seriously jeopardizing his plans, he did, but the ultimate success of the republic depended on his knowing when to say no. He knew what the country needed: an army enlisted for long enough to turn out soldiers and have them ready to strike against the enemy when opportunities arose. Instead, he had for the first years of the war to command a half-formed soldiery that was always disappearing as the terms of enlistment expired. He could ask Congress for what he wanted, but he could not demand it.

He faced the problem even in the deployment of his troops. With a much smaller force in the field than the British, Washington wanted to keep it as concentrated and as mobile as possible. The Congress and the several states were continually asking him to detach troops to defend or fortify towns or regions threatened by the redcoats. Washington had again and again to say no. As he explained to one state governor who begged for help against British raids, "A few hundred Continental Troops, quiet the minds and give satisfaction to the people of the Country; but considered in the true light, they rather do more harm than good. They draw the attention of the Enemy, and not being able to resist them, are obliged to fly and leave the Country at the Mercy of the foe."

In 1775, with the British holding both New York and Philadelphia, and Washington with his army in between in New Jersey, there were clamors for him to attack either one city or the other. But his troops, many of them raw recruits, needed training. They also, as Elizabeth Fenn has shown in her remarkable book *Pox Americana*, needed inoculation against smallpox. The British had already been inoculated or retained immunity from previous bouts with the disease, but most of Washington's troops were vulnerable to the epidemic then raging. Withdrawing to winter quarters, he took the opportunity to have them inoculated, making possible their future health and mobility when the time came for a decisive move. While acknowledging that "popular expectations should always be complied with where injury in the execution is not too apparent; especially in such a contest as the one we are engaged in, where the Spirit, & willingness of the People must, in a great measure, take [the] place of coercion," he nevertheless did *not* attack New York or Philadelphia.

The failure of Congress to supply him with adequate troops on long service required him to fight a defensive war. But he was often obliged to risk some kind of minor action in order to mollify popular opinion. One example was the attack on Stony Point in 1779. As he explained to Congress, he authorized the action because of "the necessity of doing something to satisfy the expectations of the people and reconcile them to the defensive plan we are obliged to pursue, and to the apparent inactivity, which our situation imposes upon us."

He had to say no not only to popular demands but also to misguided proposals by his own subordinates. In 1777 when Brigadier General Thomas Nelson in the southern department wanted to station troops on the York peninsula to watch for a British move by sea there, Washington sent a quick no. Nelson's troops could easily have been cut off from the rear and forced to surrender, a scenario that did not occur to Lord Cornwallis four years later when he encamped at Yorktown. When to say no to a Canadian expedition was another example. At the outset of the war it would have been a great advantage to bring the Canadians in on the American side, and Washington sent a detachment of troops there under General Montgomery. He had not yet had them inoculated against smallpox, and the expedition was sorely defeated. More of them fell victim to smallpox than to shot and shell. After sending Benjamin Franklin to assess the situation, Washington ordered them back and gave up on Canada. The next year, with the Marquis de Lafayette on hand and keen to lead a French force on the same mission, Washington had to give another no. He recognized that Lafayette, as a Frenchman, might succeed where Montgomery had failed. But for that very reason he did not want it. If French troops took possession of Canada, they might never give it up.

When Cornwallis did what Washington had told Nelson not to do and the war ended, Washington was faced with the problem of preserving the great republic he had brought into being, and he had to begin with a resounding no to the officers of the army who had served him so loyally. Not all shared his vision of that great republic. They had thought and fought continentally, but they wanted a truly continental government more than they wanted a republican government. As the Continental Congress had shown itself to be uncontinental, Washington's officers thought a monarchy or dictatorship was the only solution. There was only one man who could be at the top. Now he had to utter a most emphatic no. A yes could have resulted in the army's putting him on a throne, as Oliver Cromwell's army had in effect done for him in England in 1653. Washington gave an icy and vehement no. He told one officer who carried the proposal, "You could not have found a person to whom your schemes are more disagreeable. . . ." The general had not fought a war for republican government in order to destroy it himself.

On the other hand he knew, perhaps better than anyone else, the danger that the republic would destroy itself and, with it, the honor he had earned in bringing it into existence. He had watched the enthusiasm of 1775 and 1776 fade into the fecklessness of 1783 and 1784. The timidity of the Continental Congress in governing the national republic had threatened the dissolution of his Continental army throughout the war. With the coming of peace and international recognition of the United States, the great republic he had fought for was inexorably dissolving into thirteen insignificant republics. People who believed in a great republic recognized the danger as he did. As they prepared to do something about it in the Constitutional Convention of 1787, they knew that success would hinge on his participation. It went without saying that he would be invited to attend and preside over the Convention to rescue the republic. But it was not Washington's way to insert himself into the process. He understood the need for the Convention, but he was not sure it could succeed. He had had a bellyful of the narrow provincialism of the state politicians who might dominate it. If he had taken the lead in bringing it about, he might be seen as the king-in-waiting his officers had wanted to make of him. His judgment told him to stay in the background. He debated with himself whether he should even attend the Convention. People everywhere saw Washington as the symbol of continental America. He must use the strength which that position gave him and use it to the best effect.

So he attended the Convention, betting that it would succeed, and he presided over it but took no part in its deliberations. We all know that the members divided over many crucial issues, particularly over the so-called New Jersey plan empowering the separate states and the more nationalistic Virginia plan. Washington gave no indication where he stood on either. His only speech came at the end, after the disagreements had been worked out, when he suggested that the ratio of popular representation in Congress specified in the document be made more democratic. The Convention immediately changed the ratio from one representative for every forty thousand people to one for every thirty thousand. By not participating in the earlier debates, Washington avoided the appearance of favoring any side in any division. It was simply his presence, and indeed Benjamin Franklin's presence, that mattered. Neither man had much to do with the terms of the Constitution that emerged from the Convention. It was their being there that mattered and mattered crucially. By standing aloof from the debates, Washington maintained his prestige as a national figure and could place it behind the creation of a national government to end the fragmentation of his beloved republic.

In the campaign for ratification, Washington again kept himself above the fray. Virginia's acceptance would be crucial, but Washington did not campaign for it in his home state or anywhere else. To close friends he intimated his strong approval of the new Constitution and his contempt for the small minds who opposed it. If the Constitution was adopted, he would be elected the first president of the new government. He must have known that. If he did not, there were plenty of people telling him. But to strive for its ratification could be seen as politicking. If he was to use his popular strength on behalf of the United States, he could not dilute it by publicly taking sides.

When the new government was finally in place, it was time for Washington to enlist his prestige behind it. Once again he was in a position of command. He believed, as did most Americans, that the future of republican government in the world rested in his hands. The great doubt so long entertained about the inherent weakness of republics had to be dispelled by an executive who could act forcefully when action was needed. He would have no trouble showing his capacity for acting decisively in situations that required it. But in his early days in office much would depend on his daily behavior. As in the war, he had to draw a line between what would be good for the country and what people expected of their democratically chosen leader. Until governmental action was called for, he had to mind appearances, to give to his office a distinction, a character, to match the authority attached to it. His way of doing it was another instance of his knowing what not to do.

As with Franklin in France, John Adams offers us the contrast between a man who wanted to do too much and a man who knew when to stand still. When it came time for the new United States Senate to address the president, Adams was eager to dignify the office he would one day hold by something resembling the extravagant phrases enjoyed by royalty, such as "your highness" or "your benign highness," or "your majesty." Washington made it plain that he would have none of this: dignity, yes, fulsomeness, no. He was the president of the United States. That was the title by which he and every subsequent president would be addressed and announced. Washington's personal authority endowed it with a dignity that florid honorifics would have impaired.

In conducting his new office, Washington knew that he was sailing an uncharted sea. What guided him still was his vision of a great republic. He had hopes that the new Constitution would embody that vision for all his countrymen. He believed in republican government, in government by the people. That meant that the people must make their own decisions, that he must not decide for them in making laws. He must not even try to influence the way they voted for their representatives. In 1792 when a candidate for Congress in the coming November election spread the rumor that he had Washington's backing, Washington rebuked the man publicly and privately. To have expressed a preference for any candidate, he declared, "would have been incompatible with the rule I had prescrib'd to myself, and which I had invariably observed, of not interfering directly or indirectly with the suffrages of the people, in the choice of their representatives." On the same principle Washington was loath to veto bills of which he did not approve. As he confided to his friend Edmund Pendleton, "I give my Signature to many bills with which my Judgment is at variance." It was Washington's misfortune to find the people and their representatives frequently at odds with his own views. His response was to blame party leaders for misleading and misinforming the people. To the end he believed that they would do the right thing if only they were fully informed. In the year he died, 1799, when the people seemed to be doing everything wrong, he reiterated his confidence in republican government. "I am persuaded," he wrote, "the great mass of our Citizens require only to understand matters rightly, to form right decisions."

That Washington could retain such a view after the trials he endured in his presidency is a measure not only of his confidence in democracy but also of the deep humanity that lay behind his sense of when to say no. Underlying Washington's aloofness, his refusal to do what people wanted him to, was a fundamental respect for mankind. It is not always apparent in the pressures of the moment when he had to say no to seemingly reasonable requests. This is most clearly visible, I think, in his conduct of foreign relations. The neutrality he preserved in the international conflicts that followed the French Revolution may have looked like indifference, simply a way of doing nothing. But its sources lay in an unwillingness to take advantage of other people's misfortunes to gain favors for his own country. He explained it best in a letter to Gouverneur Morris in 1791, when the distress of Europe offered opportunities for the United States to gain benefits in treaties with countries needing assistance. Here is what he told Morris:

> Should a treaty be formed with a Nation whose circumstances may not at this moment be very bright much delicacy would be necessary in order to shew that no undue advantages were taken on that account. For unless treaties are mutually beneficial to the Parties, it is in vain to hope for a continuance of them beyond the moment when the one which conceives itself to be over-reached is in a situation to break off the connexion. And I believe it is among nations as with individuals, the party taking advantage of the distresses of another will lose infinitely more in the opinion of mankind and in subsequent events than he will gain by the stroke of the moment. (July 28, 1791)

That was what republican government was all about. You had to say no to "strokes of the moment." Washington had to say it often, but he still enjoys the good opinion of mankind that he won by saying it.

—Unpublished

CHAPTER FOURTEEN

The End of Franklin's Pragmatism

"PRAGMATISM" IS THE WORD most commonly used to describe Franklin's way of dealing with the world. We don't mean by it an adherence to the philosophy of Charles Sanders Peirce or William James, from which the modern word probably derived (it was not in Franklin's vocabulary). We mean, I think, simply a willingness to compromise in pursuit of some goal, a willingness not to insist on some abstract principle in transactions with other people, a willingness to make concessions. A prime example would be Franklin's best-known contribution to the proceedings of the 1787 Convention that created the federal Constitution, the so-called Great Compromise, which he proposed as a way to break the deadlock over representation between the small states and the large. The states would be represented equally in the Senate and in proportion to their populations in the House of Representatives.

This compromise went against Franklin's own beliefs. He would have preferred a single national representative assembly based strictly on population or, failing that, a bicameral legislature in which the members of both houses were apportioned that way. From the time when the states first joined in the Continental Congress, Franklin had objected to their voting by state: he thought it ridiculous for a state the size of Rhode Island or Delaware to have the same share in making decisions as Virginia or Pennsylvania. He did not prevail in the Continental Congress or in the Constitutional Convention, but he and those who thought like him at least got half of what they wanted—or, rather, more than half. They got the union, first of the colonies, then of the states. Like Abraham Lincoln after them, they put the union first, ahead of goals that could not in any case have been reached without it. Franklin's pragmatism meant putting first things first, accepting half a loaf if he could not get the whole, and ungrudgingly accepting nothing at all if that was the price of carrying on an enterprise he believed in.

Franklin learned his pragmatism in Philadelphia before he ever had need or opportunity to apply it on a continental or global scale. Putting first things first in his printing business doubtless contributed to the success that enabled him to retire at the age of forty-two, but his retirement is only one sign that he already had goals that he put ahead of making money. As he told his mother in 1750, "I would rather have it said, *he lived usefully*, than, *He died rich*." It will be admitted that he succeeded in that goal, and his success was the result of a personal philosophy in which putting first things first often meant putting himself last. He organized a whole array of societies for improving life in Philadelphia: a fire company, insurance company, library, hospital, university. In these initiatives, guided by the insights into human psychology that he put in the mouth of "Poor Richard," he learned to lead from the rear. As the instigator of so many projects for public benefit, he found it most effective to present them as coming from other people. He employed the same technique on a larger scale when his colony's government failed to arm Pennsylvania against the threatened wartime invasion by the French in 1747. He organized a militia and raised money for fortifications while making it all seem the spontaneous work of other leading citizens. In his militia he served as a common soldier, declining any position of command. Pragmatism was not just a willingness to compromise; it was an art.

By the end of his pragmatism I intend both the common meanings of the word "end"—a goal or purpose, and the place where something stops. Where did his pragmatism end, stop? For what goals was Franklin willing to compromise, and where did he draw a line and say no compromise or no further compromise? The answer is not easy, for there were many goals, many principles, he believed in but did not pursue or struggle to attain. He believed in free trade among nations. He believed that there should be an international law embodied in treaties to forbid privateering and also to forbid nations at war from interfering with the peaceful activities of farmers, sailors, and merchants. These were beliefs he did not hold lightly; as the principal United States negotiator in the treaty that ended the War for Independence, he made an effort to secure their recognition. But he was pragmatic. He did not draw a line and say no treaty without them. In early life Franklin had a plan for an international party of virtue, whose members would further goals like these. He was going to write a book on the art of virtue, which would be a kind of manifesto for an international movement. He was still thinking about it in the 1780s, but he never did write it. I think it is fair to say that Franklin recognized that his major goals for the good of mankind in general were unattainable, that even small steps toward them would be too small to be worth fighting for. He was not Don Quixote, and he would not waste his time breaking lances with the guardians of the status quo in contests he could not win.

But there were occasions when he dug in his heels and refused to make concessions, occasions when his goal was nonnegotiable, when defeat was preferable to compromise, when his pragmatism came to an end, a stop. One of these was in his campaign to substitute royal government for proprietary government in Pennsylvania. The campaign had begun in the Pennsylvania Assembly's attempt to tax the tax-exempt lands of the Penn family. Frustrated by the veto of the Penns' appointed governor (the Penns themselves remained in England), the Assembly sent Franklin to England in 1757 to get the British government to require the Penns to allow the taxation. Franklin failed in this mission or, rather, won a very limited right to tax a portion of the Penn lands. He returned to Pennsylvania in 1764, determined to secure what he and his political allies may have had in mind from the beginning, a revocation of the Penn family's authority over the colony in favor of direct royal control. Franklin and his allies dominated the Pennsylvania Assembly, and the Assembly sent him back to England with his desired petition for royal government. But it was not a popular move in Pennsylvania and unlikely to succeed in England. It did not succeed, and it was unrealistic to imagine it ever could have. In this case I think Franklin had already achieved a pragmatic halfway measure in making some of the Penn lands taxable. His new goal, the destruction of the Penns' authority, could not be reached pragmatically. It was nonnegotiable.

We have to ask why he thought it was a good idea anyhow. We cannot rule out the role of personal feelings. By the time he began his campaign, Franklin had developed a bitter hatred of the principal proprietor, Thomas Penn (son of William), and Penn returned the favor. Penn had seen Franklin's organization of a militia to protect the colony as a threat to his authority, a "Military Common Wealth." He wished that Franklin would take his role as tribune of the people somewhere else. When the two finally met in England, Franklin came away with "a more cordial and thorough Contempt for him than [he] ever before felt for any Man living." Personal feelings may have raised the stakes in the contest, but Franklin's eagerness to bring down the Penns had deeper roots, as will become evident if we consider another case in which his pragmatism ended.

The two are closely linked, though they may seem at odds with each other. During the colonists' quarrel with the mother country, which was just beginning when Franklin returned to England with his petition for royal government, he became the unofficial spokesman for the colonists in their protests against the British Parliament's attempt to tax them. As will be seen, he came to view Parliament's exercise of authority in America in the same way that he viewed the Penn family's, as an unacceptable interposition of other Englishmen between the king and his American subjects. As he developed this view, his pragmatism was at first very much in evidence. He did not himself believe in the natural rights that the colonists kept affirming, and he hoped to work out a compromise, as in effect he did for a time. Largely through his efforts Parliament repealed the Stamp Act in 1766, while at the same time asserting in the Declaratory Act that it had a right to pass such an act.

The Declaratory Act was not Franklin's idea, but he was content to have Parliament claim the right, provided it was not exercised. In succeeding years, as Parliament again exercised it in the Townshend Acts of 1767 and the Tea Act of 1773, he did his best to excuse and defend the colonists' declarations and manifestos and to minimize the violence that accompanied them. At the same time in letters home, he urged the colonists to calm down, to avoid the confrontations that were giving them a bad name in England, to be patient until the mother country changed its policies, as he was urging it to do at every opportunity. His hope was that the British would recognize the need to adjust their policies to the reality of colonial opposition before the opposition hardened to the point of no return, to the point of withdrawing from the empire in independence.

His hopes were frustrated, of course, though only because the British proved blind to the realities of the situation. Again, his frustration may have been aggravated by personal feelings about the people he had to deal with. Lord Hillsborough, secretary of state for the colonies from 1768 to 1772, he described as "proud, supercilious, extreamly conceited, . . . fond of every one that can stoop to flatter him, and inimical to all that dare tell him disagreeable Truths." Lord Dartmouth, who succeeded Hillsborough, was effusive in expressions of good will but no more capable than the other great lords of comprehending what was going on in North America. The men governing Great Britain and the empire, Franklin concluded at last, had "scarce Discretion enough to govern a Herd of Swine."

By the time he left England, late in 1774, his pragmatic efforts to save the empire had reached an end. From that time forward he knew that independence was the only way Americans could gain the rights they claimed and would never give up. He waited for other Americans to catch up, as the Continental Congress made pragmatic efforts to save the empire in petitions to the king that he knew were useless. But in July 1776, in the document he helped to draft, independence became nonnegotiable. After his colleagues in Congress sent him as their envoy to France, he gave a frosty answer to all British overtures to win the colonies back. There was now no room for pragmatism, no room for concessions, no halfway house on the road to independence. But what had been the end, in the sense of purpose, of his pragmatic efforts to smooth relations between Britain and the colonies before they reached the point of no return?

Franklin has been called a reluctant revolutionary, and so he was, reluctant to break up the empire. But that label is a little misleading, for he was never a reluctant American. Throughout his public career, whether he was making compromises or stubbornly refusing to, the end, the goal, of his pragmatism was a vision that others only gradually learned to share and none ever fully shared. Franklin's vision, his ultimate goal, first began to take shape in an essay he wrote in 1751, but did not publish until 1755, entitled "Observations concerning the Increase of Mankind, Peopling of Countries &c." The immediate occasion of it may have been the British Iron Act of 1750, limiting iron manufacturing in the colonies. Most Americans at that time, and right through their quarrel with the British Parliament over taxation, had taken care not to object to the restrictions imposed by Parliament on American manufacturing. There was no public outcry against the Iron Act when it was passed. Even the Declaration of Independence, in its catalog of tyrannical British actions, made no mention of the limitations placed on colonial trade and manufactures. Franklin objected to them in 1751 because they would inhibit a growth that he saw as the most significant development in modern history.

The growth that he foresaw in the immediate future was not a growth of manufacturing iron or anything else that would compete with British products. It was a growth in the number of Americans, who would actually, for the foreseeable future, become customers for those products. British policy, he argued, should take account of something that the policy makers had not noticed—namely, the increase of population in America from causes unique to new countries. To understand the impact of Franklin's argument and its implications both for him and for the American future, it has to be seen in the context of a continuing discussion in print among writers of the time on British economic policy.

It was a basic premise of the discussion that a country's prosperity and strength were to be measured by the size of its population. Anything that increased population was good; anything that decreased it was bad. Immigration was good; emigration was bad. Another premise was that the population within a settled country could be increased only by adding manufacturing enterprises and the laborers engaged in them—at the lowest possible wage that would keep them alive. Colonies in this formula were by nature bad, because any number of people emigrating to them weakened the mother country by that much. But it could be argued, and was, that if the colonists could be required to buy all their manufactures from the mother country, their trade would make up for the loss in numbers at home by expanding the number of laborers needed to supply them. Colonies could be, in effect, foreign countries whose economies you could control, as England had been doing all along with the American colonies, in the Navigation Acts of the seventeenth century and in the acts forbidding or penalizing colonial manufactures: the Woollen Act of 1699, the Hat Act of 1732, and the Iron Act just passed.

Some writers, but by no means all, were convinced by this reasoning. Many continued to regard colonies as more of a burden than a benefit to England's population. Franklin entered the discussion with a new slant on the sources of population increase. The argument of his essay was that population in new countries, that is, America, did not depend on the same forces that governed population in old, urbanized countries like England. Americans occupied a continent originally peopled by natives who could maintain only the numbers that a life of hunting and gathering could support (a misconception about Indian economies but not about their post-Columbian numbers). The English settlers, by farming the land, could grow in numbers as fast as they could marry and have children, which they did at an early age in large families. Sustained only by farming the abundant land, they doubled their numbers every twenty-five years. It was foolish and needless for the English (and irritating to the Americans, or at least to Franklin) to limit manufacturing in America, because Americans were too busy farming to spend their time on any but the crudest manufactures. They bought English goods in quantities that grew with their numbers and would continue to do so as they continued to grow, and thus would enable the English manufacturing population to grow. It was also foolish to allow immigration to English colonies from other countries, foolish to admit the Germans who were swarming to Pennsylvania and the Africans who were dragged forcibly to the southern colonies. America should be an extension of England, peopled by the prolific American Englishmen already there.

This was an argument, on the surface, against restricting American manufactures. But it seemed to make the restriction more needless than harmful. At the same time it advertised a fact that could make uneasy the writers and policy makers who measured a country's wealth and greatness by the size of its population. Some eighty thousand Englishmen, Franklin estimated, had peopled the colonies in the seventeenth century. They were now more than a million. "This Million doubling, suppose but once in 25 Years, will in another Century be more than the People of England, and the greatest Number of Englishmen will be on this Side the Water." And he went on to rhapsodize about the great accession of power to the British Empire, including the ominous fact that the number of American privateers in the war with France just concluded (the War of the Austrian Succession), exceeded in both men and guns the entire British navy in Queen Elizabeth's day, the navy, he did not need to say, that defeated the Spanish Armada.

Franklin was undoubtedly sincere in his exultation over the new power that American Englishmen were bringing to England, not to mention the new customers they were bringing to English merchants and manufacturers. This was more than a mathematical calculation. It was an expression of the pride in his country's future that sustained him in his pragmatic efforts to guide the British to a peaceful acceptance of that future. He could not have been unaware of the implications of his prediction that in another century there would be more Englishmen in America than in England. Modern readers are a little shocked by the ethnocentrism of his appeal against Africans and Germans. But contemporary readers must have noticed that this was based on his identification of Americans as Englishmen. The American colonies were not a foreign country that you could control. They were Englishmen and would soon outnumber their brothers and sisters in England.

He reprinted the essay at the end of his famous "Canada Pamphlet" of 1760, in which he argued for the retention of Canada rather than the French West Indies in the peace that would conclude the Seven Years' War (the French and Indian War). The conquest and retention of Canada would open a vast new territory to be peopled, not by a needless immigration from England, but by American Englishmen as they proliferated and spread over the continent. They would bring to "the British name and nation a stability and permanency that no man acquainted with history durst have hoped for, 'till our American possessions opened the pleasing prospect."

Note that he says "name and nation." Franklin was developing a vision of the empire in which North America, with its immense territory and limitless natural resources, would be the center of "the greatest Political Structure Human Wisdom ever yet erected." As he said to his Scottish friend Lord Kames in 1760, after finishing the Canada Pamphlet, "I have long been of Opinion, that the Foundations of the future Grandeur and Stability of the British Empire, lie in America." He did not say, then or later, that he had plans for transferring the government of the empire to the center of its power and population. But when his "Observations concerning the Increase of Mankind" landed among the writers who had been discussing population as the measure of a country's strength, they were not slow to draw the inference that Franklin's objective was to bring the government where the people were. Josiah Tucker, dean of Gloucester, had been an ardent proponent of laws to encourage foreign immigration to England as a means of increasing population. In the reverse of Franklin's argument against allowing the non-English to people America, Tucker argued for laws to make naturalization easier for foreign immigrants to England. He viewed colonies as a burden and a dangerous burden at that. They were a drain on the population of the mother country. They were not a foreign country under your control but one you could not control, one that might in the end control you. Franklin, he believed, was the man who meant to bring that about. In 1767 in a conversation with Lord Shelburne about a paper Shelburne had written anonymously, advocating settlements in the Ohio Valley, Tucker remarked "that he was sure that paper was drawn up by Dr. Franklin, he saw him in every paragraph; adding that Dr. Franklin wanted to remove the seat of government to America; that, says he, is his constant plan."

It was not, in fact, Franklin's plan, but it could very well have been his unspoken prediction. In pressing the colonists' case against Parliamentary taxation in the 1760s and 1770s, Franklin was arguing simply for their recognition as Englishmen, the full equals of Englishmen in England, united with them in allegiance to the same king. His campaign against the Penns can be seen as the first application in practical politics of the view of the British Empire that he had adumbrated in his essay on population growth. It was an empire of Englishmen, divided into many kingdoms: England, Scotland, Ireland, Pennsylvania, Virginia, Massachusetts, and so on. The king's government in each of his kingdoms was conducted by representative assemblies of the people under the direction of royal appointees. Pennsylvania (along with Maryland) was an anomaly, where the king's authority had been mistakenly entrusted to the family of one of his private subjects, a kind of imperium in imperio. That needed correcting. No subject should stand between the king and his other subjects anywhere, as the Penn family did in Pennsylvania. Much worse was the interposition of the British Parliament between him and his other subjects in all the American colonies. The campaign for removing the authority of the Penns in Pennsylvania was a dress rehearsal for removing the authority of Parliament anywhere outside of Great Britain.

The Penns, Franklin and his allies contended, were "private subjects" like everyone else in Pennsylvania and should be required to obey the same laws and pay the same taxes as everyone else. More importantly, they should not be given powers that properly belonged only to the king, powers that placed them between the king and other subjects. After the king's privy council finally rejected Franklin's petition for royal government in 1766, an ally in Pennsylvania, Joseph Galloway, warned Franklin that his countrymen would never "be easy under a Government which Admits of the Intervention of a Private Subject between their Sovereign and them." By this time Franklin, a little ahead of other Americans, had decided that the authority of Parliament extended only to Great Britain: the colonies had their own parliaments and were joined to one another and to Great Britain only by allegiance to the king. Other Americans may have reached that position from a belief in natural and constitutional rights. For Franklin it was a matter of colonists' being Englishmen united in equality before the king.

Franklin's stubborn and fruitless demand for royal government in Pennsylvania did not arise from oppression by the proprietary government, which actually gave more power to the colony's representative assembly than was the case in existing royal colonies like Massachusetts and Virginia. What Franklin objected to was placing the Pennsylvania colonists on a different footing from other Englishmen. Similarly what he objected to in Parliamentary taxation was not the burden, which in the attempted statutes would have been small, but Parliament's usurpation of the king's authority over his subjects in America. The expressed devotion to the king was scarcely a prostration before the throne. It was a way of displacing Parliament from its already anachronistic place at the top of an empire that would soon be, properly speaking, American. And the equality of subjects meant more, at least for Franklin, than an equality of rights. It meant an equality that would deflate the air of condescension he had to suffer in the officials he had to deal with, all of them his intellectual inferiors, who could treat him and his constituents as supplicants.

As early as 1754 Franklin had confided to a friend in London, Peter Collinson, his opinion that "Britain and her Colonies should be considered as one Whole, and not as different States with separate Interests." As the colonies' quarrel over taxation developed, Franklin dreamt of a consolidation of the empire under a new, written constitution that would treat Americans the same as Englishmen in England. At first he thought of simply admitting American representatives to Parliament. When he realized that this was not practicable, he was willing to settle for making American legislative assemblies equal to Parliament. He would still have preferred a general reorganization of the empire, a union of Great Britain and the colonies on the equal terms that the word "union" implied. In 1767 he confided his hopes to Lord Kames, with whom he could be more open than in public statements. Such a union, he explained, would actually benefit Britain more than America by preserving for Britain an equal place in an empire that must soon be principally American. America had resources far outweighing what the British Isles possessed. It was bound to "become a great Country, populous and mighty; and will in a less time than is generally conceiv'd be able to shake off any Shackles that may be impos'd on her, and perhaps place them on the Imposers. In the mean Time, every act of Oppression will sour their Tempers . . . and hasten their final Revolt."

Franklin continued to hope that British statesmen would recognize the opportunity they had for preserving their empire by ceasing to treat the colonies as a foreign country they could control. The only alternative if they continued on their course was for America to become a foreign country indeed and one beyond their control. More and more as he viewed at first hand the way the British ran their empire, the more he despaired of his attempts to save it for them. In Pennsylvania his friend Galloway, without Franklin's firsthand experience, worked on a plan for the union they had both wanted. When the Continental Congress met in 1774 and Galloway presented them with his plan, the Congress rejected it, and so, when he learned of it, did Franklin. America, treated as a foreign country, had become one, and Franklin did not wish to see its future inhibited any longer by connection with a people so blind to America's future importance. "When I consider," he wrote Galloway from London, "the extream Corruption prevalent among all Orders of Men in this old rotten State, . . . I cannot but apprehend more Mischief than Benefit from a closer Union."

The vision that had guided Franklin's pragmatism continued to guide him in the years ahead. He still had many good friends in England, but they had no more power than he did to lift the blinders from the king's ministers. He regretted, as he told them, that his hopes for allowing England to remain a part of the great American future had been destroyed "by the mangling hands of a few blundering ministers." But America's growth to greatness, he assured his friends, could not be stopped: "God will protect and prosper it: You will only exclude yourselves from any share in it."

The greatness that Franklin envisioned for America embraced the whole continent but was not to be measured merely by the huge population he predicted. It was to be found in "the greatest Political Structure Human Wisdom ever yet erected." Independence had become a necessary step toward that goal. The peace treaty that ended the Revolutionary War, with boundaries short of Canada, Louisiana, and Florida, was another step. The Constitution of 1787 was another step. Each step had been worth taking, worth whatever compromises and concessions it had required. But they all stopped well short of the great political structure he predicted. His vision of that structure had itself grown. He had long since found reason to repent his expressed wish to exclude the German immigrants from a share in it, if only because they had become a force to be reckoned with in Pennsylvania politics. And at some time after he returned to Philadelphia, he joined his friends there in a wish to give Africans a share. There had never been a chance that the Constitutional

Convention of 1787 would abolish slavery. In one of the last acts of his public career, he put his name on a petition to the new Congress for a national abolition of slavery; and just before he died he penned one of his most effective satirical pieces, mocking the reasons offered in Congress for rejecting the petition.

It may be worth asking, then, how the great political structure of his vision would have differed from what Americans actually got and now have in place. Franklin never set out a plan for his ideal state, as he never got around to writing his treatise on the art of virtue. But we know that his model for the United States, besides abolishing slavery, would have given the separate states no power as states in the national government. There would have been no president with the powers that office now carries. Even with slavery still established in the South, southern states would not have had the extra power that the three-fifths clause of the Constitution gave them, and the people of the small states today would not have the extra power that the Senate and the electoral college give them.

From a few letters to friends we know that Franklin would have given far fewer privileges to private property and especially to large accumulations of property than the Constitution and the courts have accorded them. He regarded property as "the Creature of publick Convention" and believed that the public should therefore, through its governing bodies, have the power "of limiting the Quantity and the Uses of it." This was a long-standing belief with him. As early as 1750 he had given his opinion "that what we have above what we can use, is not properly *ours*, tho' we possess it." He was probably the author of a provision of the Pennsylvania constitution of 1776 limiting the accumulation of property, a provision that did not survive in the final document, as his proposals for the United States Constitution did not survive discussion in the Convention. His great political structure would have embodied a much more egalitarian society than the United States has ever seen. But Franklin did get as much as was pragmatically possible. The result has prevailed through many challenges. His vision remains unfulfilled, itself a challenge to Americans who still search for a better world.

—2005

CHAPTER FIFTEEN

The Founding Fathers' Problem: Representation

Nothing is more surprising to those, who consider human affairs with a philosophical eye, than to see the easiness with which the many are governed by the few; and to observe the implicit submission with which men resign their own sentiments and passions to those of their rulers. When we enquire by what means this wonder is brought about, we shall find, that as Force is always on the side of the governed, the governors have nothing to support them but opinion. 'Tis therefore, on opinion only that government is founded; and this maxim extends to the most despotic and most military governments, as well as to the most free and most popular.

— DAVID HUME, "Of the First Principles of Government"

I

W E MAY PERHAPS question today whether force is *always* on the side of the governed—or even whether it always has been—but by and large Hume's observation commands assent. All government rests on the consent, however obtained, of the governed. And over the long run mere force, even when it is entirely at the disposal of the governing few, is not a sufficient basis for inducing consent. Human beings have to be persuaded, if only to maintain a semblance of self-respect. They have to have opinions to sustain their consent.

The few who govern take care to nourish those opinions; and that is no easy task, for the opinions needed to make the many submit to the few are often at variance with observable fact. The success of government thus requires the acceptance of fictions, requires the willing suspension of disbelief, requires us to believe that the emperor is clothed even though we can see that he is not. And, to reorder Hume's dictum, the maxim extends to the most free and most popular governments as well as to the most despotic and most military. The popular governments of England and the United States rest on fictions as much as do the governments of Russia and China.

Government requires make-believe. Make believe that the king is divine or that he can do no wrong, make believe that the voice of the people is the voice of God. Make believe that the people *have* a voice or that the representatives of the people *are* the people. Make believe that governors are the servants of the people. Make believe that all men are equal, or make believe that they are not.

The political world of make-believe mingles with the real world in strange ways, for the make-believe world often molds the real one. In order to serve its purpose, whatever that purpose may be, a fiction must bear some resemblance to fact. If it strays too far from fact, the willing suspension of disbelief collapses. And because fictions are necessary, because we cannot live without them, we often take pains to prevent their collapse by moving the facts to fit them, by making our world conform more closely to what we want it to be. When the fiction takes command and reshapes reality, we are apt to call it, quite appropriately, reform or reformation.

Although fictions enable the few to govern the many, it is not only the many who are constrained by them. In the strange commingling of political make-believe and reality, the governing few, no less than the governed many, may find themselves limited—we may even say reformed—by the fictions on which their authority depends.

It would be possible to illustrate this point from the history of almost any people at any time. I think one could show, for example, that the exaltation of kingship in the fiction of the divine right of kings—and I presume it will be admitted that this was a fiction—could be used as a means of popular control over the king's government. Anyone reading the parliamentary debates of the early Stuart period will find the members of the

House of Commons seemingly beside themselves with enthusiasm for the claim of James I to be God's lieutenant. In speech after speech they would outdo one another in expounding the wisdom, perfection, and omnipotence of that pretentious monarch, abasing themselves so abjectly that one begins to wonder what they were up to. What they were up to, it quickly becomes apparent, was attributing to the king a godlike character that they could then ask him to live up to. They did not say, "The king is wise and good; therefore let us do what he wants." Instead, they said, "The king is wise and good; therefore it stands to reason that he must want what we want." The king's perfection and divinity became a lever by which his subjects could direct and control him.

In popular governments—governments wherein authority derives from the people rather than from God—the fictions that enable the few to govern the many exalt, not the governors, but the people governed. And just as the exaltation of the king could be a means of controlling him, so the exaltation of the people can be a means of controlling *them*. Popular government is a much more complicated matter than kingly government and requires more complex fictions to sustain it. It requires us to believe, or act as if we believe, that the people, as a people, can make decisions and perform actions apart from their government, that they can authorize individuals to act in their name and can also limit, instruct, or otherwise control those individuals. To endow the people with these fictional powers was a delicate matter for those who first undertook it, because it had to be done without encouraging the simpleminded to mistake fiction for fact. A too plausible, too persuasive argument for popular authority might result in what was always deplored as "confusion"—that is, for the people (or rather some fraction of them) to take direct action in matters that were best left to their superiors. The men who first promoted popular government did not think they were striving for a government by the many over the many. They had strong ideas about who should govern, and they did not, to begin with at least, propose to meddle with the structure of the societies in which they themselves commanded positions near the top. In locating the source of authority in the people, they thought to locate its exercise in themselves. They intended to speak for a sovereign but silent people, as the king had hitherto spoken for a sovereign but silent God.

Their opponents—royalists and loyalists—were quick to point out the probable consequences of deriving authority from the people, namely, that men in the lowest ranks of society might break silence and accept the invitation that seemed to be extended to them. The loyalists and royalists turned out to be right; as time went on, more and more of the advocates of popular sovereignty faced the fact and actually came to welcome and even to seek the extension of popular participation in governmental processes. The history of popular government is a history of the successive efforts of different generations to bring the facts into closer conformity with the fiction, efforts that have transformed the very structure of society. But in the early stages of popular government the problem was to gain credence for the fiction without upsetting the patterns of deference, without upsetting the settled opinions of rank and degree that gave stability to society and that enabled the few to command the many not merely in acts of government but in all the transactions of daily life. This is the problem we can observe in the establishment of popular government in eighteenth-century England and America, the problem of reconciling the fictional sovereignty of the people with an actual hierarchical social order.

It is doubtless stretching things a little—indulging in a historical fiction, perhaps—to give the name "popular" to the government either of England or of its colonies in the eighteenth century. But both had a popular element, or one at least that claimed to represent the people and that already played a dominant role in government: the House of Commons in England and the representative assemblies in the colonies. After 1776, when all government in America was presumed to rest on the people, the change from royal to popular authority came about, in effect, as it later did in England (and had done briefly in the 1640s), by representative assemblies taking full command. Popular government in both England and America has been representative government, and representation is the principal fiction by which the larger fiction of popular sovereignty has been itself sustained.

II

Representation began in England as a mode of ensuring consent to the king's government. The king summoned representatives from counties and boroughs to come to his Parliament armed with powers of attorney to bind their constituents to whatever taxes or laws they agreed to. The power of attorney had to be complete, a blank check, so that the representative could not plead that he had to go back and consult his constituents. His consent, given in Parliament, had to be as much theirs as if they had come in person. "As if." Representation from the beginning was a fiction. If the representative consented, his constituents had to make believe that they had done so.

The way in which any group of subjects was first persuaded to pretend that one of them could substitute for all of them is not altogether clear. It is possible that originally a representative could consent only in the name of individuals who specifically empowered him and that those who did not, even though in the same community, were not bound by his actions. We can observe such a situation in the first representative assemblies gathered in the colony of Maryland in the 1630s. The royal charter to Lord Baltimore gave him power to govern Maryland as he saw fit, including the power to make laws, but it also required him to obtain the consent of the free men (*liberorum hominorum*) to whatever laws he made. Baltimore delegated his authority to a governor, and in the first year after the arrival of the settlers the governor apparently summoned the free men to get their consent, as prescribed, to a number of laws. We have no records for this assembly or of how many persons attended it. But for the next assembly, in 1638, the records show that some free men attended in person while others delegated representatives, each of whom was entitled to his own vote and also to all the votes of those who had selected him as their representative. He did not represent anyone who had not specifically and individually empowered him; and a man could even change his mind, revoke the assignment of his vote, and attend in person. Thus we find in the records on the second day of the meeting: "Came John Langford of the Ile of Kent gentleman . . . who had given a voice in the choice of Robert Philpott, gentleman, to be one of the Burgesses for the freemen of that Iland; and desired to revoke his voice and to be personally present in the Assembly; and was admitted." One could also transfer one's proxy, as it was called, from one man to another after the session began. Thus "Richard Lusthead desired to revoke his proxie [given to Richard Gannett] and was admitted and made Robert Clark his proxie." The records imply that elections of representatives were held in particular neighborhoods, but those who voted against the winner were not bound to recognize him as their representative. Thus Cuthbert Fenwick came to the assembly and "claimed a voice as not assenting to the election of St. Mary's burgesses and was admitted."

The result was a politically bizarre situation: within the assembly some men had only their own vote, while others had the votes of all their proxies in addition to their own. On one occasion an aspiring politician named Giles Brent had enough proxies to constitute a majority of the assembly all by himself. In the 1640s the assembly was gradually reduced to a strictly representative body, with each community in the colony choosing, by majority rule, a representative who would stand for the whole community, including the minority of free men who had voted against him. And he would cast a single vote in the assembly, regardless of the size of the community he represented.

It is not certain that the original development of the fiction of representation in England followed this pattern. What seems clear is that when representatives ceased to be mere proxies for individuals, whether in England or in America, they represented distinct, geographically defined communities. In England they represented counties or boroughs. In Maryland and Virginia they represented plantations or hundreds or counties, in New England they represented towns, in the Carolinas parishes. It was possible to stretch the fiction of one man standing for another or for several others to the point where he stood for a whole local community. But, in England and America at least, the community was always geographically defined. It was the Isle of Kent or the borough of St. Mary's; it was Shropshire or Staffordshire, Norwich or Bristol; it was never the worshipful company of grocers or cordwainers, never the tobacco farmers' union or the association of shipowners. In the eighteenth and nineteenth centuries the fiction of representation was sometimes explained and defended as a means by which all the different economic or social "interests" in a country had a voice in its government, but representation in England and America has never in fact been based on anything but geographically defined communities.

This local geographical definition seems to have been essential to the credibility of the fiction. Once again the early history of an American colony illustrates the point. The colony of Massachusetts was founded by a trading company, the Massachusetts Bay Company, in which the stockholders, designated as "freemen," were empowered to meet four times a year in a "General Court," to make laws for the company and for its colony, and to elect the officials of the company, i.e., a governor and eighteen "assistants." The company was given power, like Lord Baltimore in Maryland, to govern the colony as it saw fit, but was not required to obtain the consent of the free men of the colony for its laws. The majority of the company, gathered in England, determined in 1629 to transfer the meeting place of the company to the colony itself, and once there the small number of freemen (stockholders) who had made the voyage opened their ranks to all orthodox male Puritan church members. They accompanied this move, however, with a transfer of legislative authority to the elected governor and assistants.

Now, the charter did not authorize such a delegation of the freemen's legislative power. Neither did it offer to ordinary settlers who were not freemen, that is, who were not company members, any right to be consulted about the laws that the company might make. But in 1632, when the assistants, acting in their newly assigned legislative capacity, levied a tax, the people in Watertown refused to pay it, on the ground that the government did not have authority "to make laws or raise taxations without the people." Governor John Winthrop explained to them that the assistants were like a parliament, that they were elected by the freemen and therefore could do the things that Parliament did in England.

This seems to have satisfied the people of Watertown for the moment, but in truth the assistants were not like a parliament, for they were elected at large and did not represent particular districts or towns. Apparently this fact was quickly recognized, for two months later Winthrop recorded, "Every town chose two men to be at the next court, to advise with the governour and assistants about the raising of a public stock, so as what they should agree upon should bind all." Two years later the freemen of the towns revoked the legislative power of the assistants and insisted that all laws be made in the General Court, which was now to include representatives ("deputies") elected by the freemen of each town. Non-freemen still did not share in the election, just as the majority of Englishmen were excluded from voting for members of Parliament, but this defect seems not to have affected the viability of the fiction. What was needed was not that every man, woman, and child share in the choice of a representative but that the choice be perceived as that of a geographical community. A representative had to represent the people of a particular place; he ceased to represent when he lost his local identification. A representative assembly had to be *assembled*. It had to be composed from the parts of the whole. The fiction would collapse if it was stretched to have all representatives chosen by all voters, even in so small a society as Massachusetts Bay in the 1630s. The local character of representation was present at the beginning in England as well as in England's colonies, and it has remained to this day essential to the credibility of the fiction.

Closely linked to the requirement that the representative be attached to a locality was a need that he be perceived as a subject of government. In order to represent other subjects he had to be himself a subject. The Massachusetts assistants, though annually elected and bound by the laws they enforced, were perceived as rulers, not ruled, just as the king and his appointed council, though bounded by law, were rulers, not ruled. King and council, governor and assistants, were there to exercise authority over the whole society, representatives were there to give the consent of their particular counties or towns or districts to what the rulers did. As we shall see, the distinction began to blur very early, but it remained an essential ingredient in the fiction of representation and in the way people thought about government. In Massachusetts the Reverend John Cotton, who was by no means simpleminded, thought that a political system that confounded rulers and ruled—that is, a democracy—was a contradiction in terms. "If the people be governors," he asked, "who shall be governed?" And in his view and John Winthrop's the representatives of the people, the deputies whom the various towns sent to the Massachusetts General Court after 1634, were subjects, mere substitutes for the people who chose them. Like the first representatives whom the king summoned to Parliament, they assembled in order to bind their local constituents to obey the laws and pay the taxes agreed upon at the center. The very act of consent identified them as subjects, and the consent they gave was the consent of the particular localities that they represented.

If representatives had been, or had remained, mere subjects—if they had been merely the agents of their constituents, empowered only to consent for other subjects to measures propounded by the authority of a government of which they were not strictly speaking a part—then the fiction of representation would have been a much simpler and more plausible matter than it has ever in fact been. It is possible that in England the House of Commons continued for some time after its inauguration to be considered in the way that its members so often pretended to consider it, as a gathering of mere subjects, representing various communities of subjects throughout the land. But the representatives very quickly began to act like something more than mere subjects. Not content to give or withhold consent to measures presented to them by the king and his council, they concocted measures of their own, presenting them as petitions to the king, but nevertheless in effect making governmental policy, making laws. Already by 1530 laws were regularly enacted "by authority" of Parliament.

The representatives who sat in the Commons in the seventeenth century, still protesting that they were mere subjects, for a time in the 1640s assumed all powers of government to themselves. And after the restoration of the monarchy in 1660 there was no longer even the pretense that representatives were mere subjects. They were subjects, yes, but not mere subjects. If there was any doubt, the Revolution of 1688 resolved it.

Similarly, in the colonies, representative assemblies took the initiative in government almost from the beginning. In Maryland the free men and their proxies, even before representation was fully developed, did not wait for Lord Baltimore or his governor to present them with laws for passage: they made their own and presented them to him. In Massachusetts, once the General Court resumed legislative authority in 1634, there was no doubt that the representatives would share in that authority. But they went further. The General Court was the supreme judicial authority of the colony. Winthrop insisted that the deputies sent by the towns not share in this authority, because they were mere subjects; but the deputies demanded the right to sit in judgment on judicial matters, and they got their way. In Virginia the authority to make laws lay in the Virginia Company, resident in London, but the company called a representative assembly in the colony in 1619, and that assembly presented the company with a series of laws, which, with the company's approval, became the first laws enacted by a representative assembly in America.

As soon as representatives began to make laws and policy for the larger society to which their communities belonged, they did not cease to be subjects but they ceased to be *mere* subjects. By the same token, though they did not cease to be the agents of local communities, they ceased to be merely that. The laws they made were to bind not only their own communities but the whole realm, the whole nation, the whole society. In making policy for the larger body, they had to think in different terms from the needs and desires of their localities; sharing regal authority, they had to think regally, to think for the nation rather than the neighborhood. The well-being of the whole society might be different from that of any one part or even from that of the sum of all the parts. Insofar as they assumed authority and directed their attention to whatever they perceived as the welfare of the whole, representatives necessarily lost something of their character as subjects and as local agents and took on the trappings of a national aristocracy or ruling class.

Logically this meant a transformation in the meaning of representation, but chronologically, historically, it was not so much a transformation as a paradox or conflict present in representation from the beginning or almost from the beginning. It is quite likely that the persons selected by a community to represent it in Parliament were from the outset those who could command the assent of that community by virtue of their own local power and prestige. It is not impossible that the first representatives to the House of Commons were self-selected, without benefit of an election, as in effect a large percentage of members came to be or still were in the eighteenth century. And the local character of borough representatives in the Commons was already vitiated by the fourteenth century when nonresident country gentry began to buy and bully their way into possession of borough seats, elbowing out local but lesser dignitaries. A statute of 1413 required that a representative be a resident of the borough that chose him, but the lawyers in the House of Commons quickly interpreted this to mean that he need not be a resident of the borough that chose him.

As representatives assumed the mantle of authority, they stretched the fiction of representation to justify the attenuation of their ties to local constituencies. It may be counted as a step in this direction when they began, as early as the fourteenth century, to argue that they collectively represented the whole realm and could give the consent of every Englishman to what they did in Parliament. The English Parliament had never contained representatives from every town or village community. Though every county sent representatives, only selected boroughs were required or allowed to do so. But Sir Thomas Smith was able to state as a truism in 1583 that "everie Englishman is entended to bee there [in Parliament] present. . . . And the consent of the Parliament is taken for everie mans consent."

From this premise it was possible to argue, though it might require an unusual logic, that each representative could and must speak and act, not for the local community that chose him, but for all the people of the realm. Sir Edward Coke, who was good at this kind of logic, may have been the first to state the idea in so many words. "Though one be chosen for one particular County or Borough," he said, "yet when he is returned and set in Parliament, he serveth for the whole Realm, for the end of his coming thither, as in the writ of his election appeareth, is generall." From the fiction that one man may stand in the place of a whole community and bind that community by his actions, Coke had extrapolated the more extended fiction that one man may stand for the entire people of a country, most of whom have had no hand in designating him for that purpose. The classic statement of this notion was to come in the next century, when Edmund Burke explained to the electors of Bristol why he owed them nothing but the courtesy of listening to their wishes before acting as he thought best for the whole country. But already in Coke's formulation we are very close to the point where representation becomes representative government. At the time when Coke wrote, whatever authority representatives could claim over other subjects presumably came from the king. But it was only a short step from representing the whole people to deriving authority from them.

When Englishmen took that step in the 1640s, they did not affirm the sovereignty of each county or borough. It did not even occur to them to think that way. They were replacing the authority of the king, and the king had been ruler of all England. It was not a question of particular counties or boroughs declaring their independence from his rule any more than it was particular towns or counties in his American colonies that declared independence in 1776. There would have been no logical barrier to thinking of the people of every village as a sovereign body, but that is not what happened. The people whose sovereignty was proclaimed were the whole people of the country or colony, far too numerous a group to deliberate or act as a body. It was their representatives who claimed for them the authority that only a representative body could exercise. The sovereignty of the people was not said to reside in the particular constituencies that chose the representatives, it resided in the people at large and reached the representatives without the people at large doing anything to confer it. Again, there would have been no logical barrier to having the people confer authority by a nationwide election at large of any number of men to serve as rulers, but that is not what happened. What happened is that representatives elected by particular counties and towns assumed powers of government over a whole country and claimed that their powers came from the sovereign people as a whole.

It would perhaps not be too much to say that representatives invented the sovereignty of the people in order to claim it for themselves, in order to justify not the resistance of their constituents but their *own* resistance to a formerly sovereign king. The sovereignty of the people was an instrument by which representatives raised themselves to the maximum distance above the particular set of people who chose them. In the name of the people they became all-powerful in government, shedding as much as possible the local, subject character that made them representatives.

As much as possible. The English Revolution actually went awry when the Long Parliament (1640–49) became too long, when the representatives declined to return to their constituents for reelection or rejection. The representative's national authority cannot be magnified to the point of eliminating his identity as a local subject without at the same time destroying the fiction of representation and putting an end to representative government. The conflict cannot be eliminated; it has to be muted and contained. One element may be emphasized over the other at different times and places, and the history of representative government may be read as a dialectical process in which one element rises or falls at the expense of the other. But if either is wholly missing, representative government either ceases to be government or ceases to be representative. When the local, subject character of the representative is emphasized too much, it becomes difficult to perceive him as a proper repository of the national authority with which the sovereign people have supposedly invested him. When his national function as ruler of the whole people is emphasized, he may lose credibility as the spokesman of other subjects in his local community. The fiction of representation has to sustain a continual strain from opposite directions.

The dimensions of the conflict have not always been apparent even to those engaged in it, but we may perceive it in operation at an early stage in the English republican theorist Algernon Sidney's explanation of the representative's national authority. "It is not," Sidney argued in the early 1680s,

> for Kent or Sussex, Lewis or Maidstone, but for the whole nation, that the members chosen in those places are sent to serve in Parliament; and though it be fit for them as friends and neighbours (so far as may be) to hearken to the opinions of the electors, for the information of their judgments, . . . yet they are not strictly and properly obliged to give account of their actions to any, unless the whole body of the nation for which they serve, and who are equally concerned in their resolutions, could be assembled. This being impracticable, the only punishment to which they are subject, if they betray their trust, is scorn, infamy, hatred, and an assurance of being rejected, when they shall again seek the same honour.

Sidney here takes pains to distinguish the representative's obligations to the whole nation from his obligations to the electors who choose him as their agent. Yet he relies on the electors to remove him if he betrays his trust. What trust? The trust reposed in him by Kent or Sussex, by

Lewis or Maidstone? No, the trust reposed in him by the whole body of the nation, which cannot be assembled for removing him—and by the same token was never assembled for entrusting him in the first place. If he betrays the trust so mysteriously placed in him, he is supposed to be subject to scorn, infamy, and hatred. But whose? Is it not likely that the man who wins scorn, infamy, and hatred from the rest of the nation may win praise, fame, and love in Kent or Sussex, in Lewis or Maidstone? And conversely the man who is faithful to his trust for the nation may win scorn, infamy, and hatred in Kent or Sussex, Lewis or Maidstone.

Sidney was not troubled by this contingency and would probably have responded to it, as he did to other objections, that while a representative assembly was not infallible, nevertheless "a house of commons composed of those who are best esteemed by their neighbours in all the towns and counties of England" would at least be less "subject to error or corruption than such a man, woman, or child as happens to be next in blood to the last king." In the worst possible case, in other words, a group of men popularly chosen, however strong their local attachments and whatever their weaknesses, are a safer repository of power than a hereditary king.

Because representative government rests on conflicting fictions, or on a single fiction with glaring internal contradictions, it has often required such left-handed defenses. It is a *pis aller*, better than the alternatives. But Sidney's ignoring of the possible conflict between local and national interests is a reminder that representative government, in order to work, in order to mute the conflict within the fiction, requires that the different communities represented be able and willing most of the time and on most issues to perceive their own local interests as being involved in, if not identical with, the interests of the larger society.

That perception was more easily sustained while the authority of government was derived from the king than when the representative body professed to derive it from the people at large. When authority came from the king, government was palpably something other, a force against which representatives protected their constituents or to whose actions they effectively bound themselves and their constituents. Representatives, like those they represented, could be thought of as acted upon rather than as actors.

Moreover, that authority itself was less likely to be swayed by any combination of local interests. A king might become a tyrant, pursuing his own interests rather than those of his subjects. But he was not as likely as the majority in a representative assembly to place the interests of particular parts of his realm above the interests of others or of the whole. Because the monarch was less likely to be geographically partial, there was less need than in popular governments for every community to have its own representatives to protect its special interests against those of other communities. Protection was needed, rather, against the more general danger of arbitrary government by the monarch, and this could be furnished by one set of representative subjects as effectively as by another.

Before representatives took over full command of government, there was accordingly little agitation by excluded communities for inclusion in the representative body. The great expansion of representation in Parliament in the sixteenth century came not because of demands by formerly excluded communities but because the rising and expanding gentry wanted seats in the House of Commons. Many of Parliament's so-called rotten boroughs were rotten at their creation, incorporated only to give some aspiring gentleman a seat. Similarly the expansion of the electorate in the seventeenth century was not the product of a demand by the unenfranchised. It was in part an accident of inflation, which reduced the value of the property qualification for voting (established in 1430) and in part the result of contests for seats, in which an ambitious candidate brought unqualified voters to the polls and then succeeded in having their votes legitimized by Parliament. In other words, while authority was derived from the king, the expansion both of the suffrage and of representation in Parliament came from the top down, through the desire of members of an elite class for a share in the king's authority. In the colonies, where the king's authority was diluted by distance and representatives were correspondingly more powerful (in fact if not in theory), there was somewhat more concern about extending representation equitably. But even here, in Pennsylvania and in the southern colonies, where representation was most inequitable, there seems to have been little concern about the matter until shortly before the Revolution.

When the king's authority was removed, as it was in England during the Commonwealth period (1649–60) and in America after 1776, the conflict of local interests with the sovereignty of the people at large became much more evident. In a Parliament where representatives chosen by a handful of voters had total authority over communities that could not vote at all, there were immediate demands for a more rational and equitable way of exercising the newfound sovereignty of the people. And a rational plan of parliamentary representation in England was in fact adopted in the Commonwealth period, only to be abandoned for nearly another two centuries after the restoration of the monarchy in 1660. And in the independent American states after 1776 the apportionment of representation became a major concern, because particular communities and regions feared that without adequate representation they would not be adequately protected from their sovereign compatriots.

In this transformation, government remained, as it had to, something other, something external to the local community; but that something was no longer a king. It was now the representative body itself, or at least the representatives of other localities, acting rather than acted upon, exercising an authority derived from a people who could not exercise it themselves. With the authority of representatives thus magnified, it became all the more important to each community that its particular representatives retain a local identity and outlook and all the more important to every community to have representatives. Thus, just when representatives assumed larger responsibilities and larger authority, they were brought under greater local pressures to retain their local, subject character.

The Commonwealth experiment in England was too brief and inconclusive to reveal fully the strains that popular sovereignty placed on the fiction of representation. Even so, James Harrington, the most astute, if the most tedious, political philosopher of the period, sensed the problem when he attempted to divide the functions of representation between two bodies, both elected by local constituencies. Harrington envisaged a small senate or upper house, which would have the sole power to formulate policy for the nation by initiating all legislation. A much larger lower house would then pass upon the senate's proposals, accepting or rejecting but with no power to alter or amend or to initiate legislation by itself. In effect, the senate would exercise the national, authoritarian function of representation—the powers that had once emanated from the king—while the lower house would exhibit the local, subject character.

Harrington's proposal was, of course, never tried in England, but it was attempted in the Carolinas and in Pennsylvania. It failed for the foreseeable reason that the lower house was in no case content with half of the representative functions. The conflict therefore remained, in the colonies as in England. In England it was successfully muted until the great reforms of the nineteenth century. And in the colonies it was easily contained while authority continued to derive from the king. But the American Revolution brought it to an acute stage. As soon as the colonies substituted the authority of the people for what was left of the king's authority, they had to contend with the danger that locally oriented representatives, in exercising the new authority, would favor one region over another or would sacrifice large-scale needs to parochial prejudice. And the danger was magnified by the nature of the quarrel with England that had preceded independence.

III

The Americans' quarrel with England began, as everyone knows, with the attempt of Parliament to tax the colonists. When the colonists insisted that they could not be taxed by a body in which they were not represented, England maintained that they *were* represented—represented by men whom they had never seen or heard of. People from Massachusetts to Georgia were represented by men chosen for them by a handful of voters in the boroughs and counties of England.

This was carrying the fiction of representation too far from the facts, destroying altogether its local character. The fiction collapsed, and with its collapse the local character of representation emerged as a cardinal American principle. In resolutions, declarations, and petitions the colonists reiterated their conviction that the people of a particular locality could be represented only by someone whom they themselves had elected and empowered. By the time the colonial assemblies threw off English control in 1776, they were so firmly committed to this principle that any attempt to temper it appeared as a betrayal of the Revolution.

To be sure, the several colonial assemblies had to act together on a continental scale in order to make their bid for independence. But the Continental Congress in which they joined to do it was not a representative assembly. Since most of the members were chosen by the state legislatures, both before and after the Articles of Confederation of 1781, the Congress was an assembly, not of representatives, but of representatives of representatives. Since representatives could not properly transfer their powers, the Congress did not and could not have the powers that only popular election could confer. The only true representatives in America sat in the state assemblies.

And there they displayed their local attachments all too clearly. In most states, after independence, the number of representatives in the assembly was increased and the size of constituencies reduced, thus weakening still further the orientation and obligation of each representative to the larger whole. As the number of a representative's constituents fell, representation became less fictional. Government moved closer to the people, but in doing so became less capable of exercising authority effectively, consistently, and sensibly for a whole colony, let alone a whole country.

Those who rescued American representative government from this predicament by means of the Constitution of 1787 restored the fictional purpose of representation—namely, to persuade the many to accept the government of the few. And they did it by an additional fiction. They invented the American people, a fictional body comprising all the people of the whole nation, endowed with sovereign powers superior to those of the people of any state or of all the states.

It was not one of those inventions for which the world was unprepared. The Revolution had created a fund of national feeling and a whole class of people who had committed their lives and fortunes to a common cause that seemed to be dissolving in victory. James Madison and his high Federalist friends at the Philadelphia convention drew on that feeling to gain credence for their new fiction—an American people capable of empowering an American national government.

Earlier efforts to correct the defects of the state governments had cen-

tered on giving greater powers to the upper houses of the bicameral legislatures, or to the executives, of the several states. But these had proved
ineffective. Representative assemblies still dominated the state governments and retained their ascendancy by virtue of their perceived close-
ness to their local constituents. It was the Federalists' aim to give to a
national government, led by a select few, a claim to higher representative power than the mobbish state assemblies possessed. In order to reach
their goal, they had to persuade Americans to accept representation on a
scale hitherto unknown. The representative assembly of the national government, directly elected by popular votes, would be smaller in size than
most of the state assemblies, 65 men to represent nearly 4 million. (Georgia, with a population of 82,000, had an assembly of 84 representatives;
Connecticut, with a population of 238,000, had an assembly of 171.) The
national representatives would have such large constituencies that they
would lose much of their local character—and would gain, it was hoped,
a larger vision along with larger power. With the authority of the newly
sovereign American people behind them, they would be able to overcome
the shortsightedness of the state governments.

It was touch-and-go whether Americans would accept the new con-
figurations of fictions. Antifederalists cried out that the new representation was no representation at all, that national representatives would be
too remote from their constituents, no better than the specious representatives the colonists had been told they had in Parliament. But the
Antifederalists lost. Americans suspended their disbelief. The idea of
representation recovered the fictional qualities it had been losing in the
state governments, and the few were thereby enabled to govern the many
without recourse to violence. The fictions of popular sovereignty embodied in the federal Constitution may have strained credulity, but they did
not break it. Madison's invention worked. It still does.

—1983

CHAPTER SIXTEEN

The Role of the Antifederalists

THE UNITED STATES CONSTITUTION has proved to be the most durable frame of government possessed by any major power in the world today, and it has furnished more reliable safeguards for human liberty than most other governments. The Constitution has been a success. All the more reason, then, for intellectual generosity toward those who feared that it would be a disaster and who helped to add to it some of the safeguards that have made it a success. The constitutional historian Herbert J. Storing admired the Constitution, but was so impressed with the quality of the initial opposition to it that he collected for republication the newspaper articles and pamphlets in which the so-called Antifederalists urged its rejection and demanded amendments.

What the collection makes plain is that the 1780s were a "critical period," perhaps (excluding the 1860s) *the* critical period of American history. The central issue was whether Americans would be one people with a national government or several peoples united in a limp federation that was steadily losing the powers it had exercised in the years before it was acknowledged to have any power at all (the Revolutionary War was nearly won before the Articles of Confederation were agreed to in 1781). It was not, however, simply a question of strengthening or creating a national government. The Antifederalists were prepared to strengthen the existing federation. What they feared was the annihilation of the state governments and of the popular liberties that they thought the state gov-

ernments could protect and that the proposed national government would
not or could not protect.

What the Antifederalists wanted was a union of states rather than of
people and a simple, minimal central government with wide popular participation and safeguards for traditional popular rights. But in order to
appreciate the Antifederalist position, it may here be worth recalling that
what the Antifederalists were for was not entirely synonymous with what
the Federalists were against. And what the Federalists were against animated both sides.

Since the Constitution was the product of compromises that blunted the
purpose of its principal authors, what the Federalists were against appears
more clearly in their writings and speeches than in the provisions of the
Constitution itself. The architect of the Constitution was James Madison,
and what moved Madison and his supporters at the Convention was not
merely the weakness of the national federation but the iniquity of the state
governments. Though he proposed a national government in part as an
end in itself, as the political expression and guardian of national identity, he
also proposed it and designed it as a means of curbing the vicious propensi-
ties of the states. If he and his friends had had their way, the national government would have had an absolute veto over all state laws.

What bothered the Federalists most about the state governments was
their failure to protect the rights of property, and in particular the rights
of creditors. After winning a war against British threats to American property through taxation, the states themselves seemed bent on destroying the
security of American property through laws that made depreciated paper
money a legal tender or that declared a moratorium on collection of debts.
And state governments that held firm against these destructive measures
were defied by mobs that closed the courts in order to stop collection of
debts. The Federalists wanted a national government that would be strong
enough to put down such insurrections and to see that state legislatures
did not yield to any other pressures inimical to property rights.

Madison, who not only designed the Constitution but wrote the classic defense of it in the *Federalist Papers*, was far less pleased with the finished document than he indicated in those essays. Writing to Jefferson
on September 6, 1787, just before the Convention broke up, he thought

that the Constitution, if adopted, would "neither effectually answer its national object nor prevent the local mischiefs which every where excite disgusts against the state governments." In a later letter, when the secrecy imposed by the Convention was lifted, he explained why: because the Convention had rejected his pleas for a veto power over state laws, the national government would not be able to prevent the local mischiefs. And he even went on to give his opinion that "the evils issuing from these sources [the state governments] contributed more to that uneasiness which produced the Convention, and prepared the public mind for a general reform, than those [evils] which accrued to our national character and interest from the inadequacy of the Confederation to its immediate objects." If Madison's opinion was correct, curbing the states was more important in the minds of Americans (as it seems to have been in his) than strengthening the union.

The principal evils that the Federalists (and many other Americans) were against, then, lay in the states and the state governments. Federalists were unable—and some would have been unwilling—to do away with the state governments altogether. But they wanted a central government strong enough to interdict state actions. Madison did not think that the Constitution would provide such a government. Neither did Hamilton. But they recognized that the Constitution would give them more leverage against the states than they had had in a Continental Congress with no coercive powers at all. They were willing to settle for what they could get.

In the light of what the Federalists had aimed at (which despite the secrecy of the Convention proceedings was widely known or suspected), the reaction of the Antifederalists will appear somewhat less paranoid than it does when one approaches their writings cold. They thought that the national government proposed in the Constitution would destroy the state governments and that that was the intention of the framers, as indeed it may have been of some. Madison did not get his veto over the states, but to the Antifederalists it looked as though he had got far too close to it. The Constitution made national laws and national treaties the supreme law of the land. Did that not amount to an overriding of state laws? The Constitution forbade the states to issue paper money or to make anything but gold and silver a legal tender or to pass laws impairing the obligation of contracts, but it did not forbid these things to the national government. Nor did it reserve to either the states or the people the powers not expressly delegated to the national government. There was no general bill of rights specifying what the national government could not do. In the absence of such a limitation and under cover of its constitutional authorization to provide for the general welfare and to do whatever was necessary and proper to carry out its functions, the national government would be able to do almost anything. And whatever it did would be the supreme law of the land. In the face of this leviathan, the state governments would be helpless. They would soon wither away, and liberty would wither with them.

Such fears were not groundless. And they were aggravated by the very widely publicized speech given in Pennsylvania by James Wilson, Madison's chief ally at the Convention. Wilson argued that the Constitution needed no bill of rights, because it specified the things that the national government could do, and thereby excluded the doing of anything unspecified. In every state the Antifederalists rose to demolish Wilson's argument by reversing it. The Constitution specifically prohibited some things to the national government, such as bills of attainder and ex post facto laws, and thereby (to follow Wilson's reasoning) permitted the doing of anything unspecified. By inference, the Constitution granted to the national government all powers not specifically excluded.

By their insistence on a bill of rights to limit the national government, the Antifederalists were able to add to the Constitution, in the first ten amendments, much of what they were for. But they thereby added little that the Federalists were against and nothing that removed their own deepest fears. Madison himself drafted the amendments. It was almost as though the Federalists had deliberately omitted a bill of rights in order to be able to disarm their opponents with this concession (there is no evidence that such a strategy was intended). What no bill of rights could answer was the fear of the most thoughtful Antifederalists that a national government by its very nature, by virtue of the size of the area it governed, would be incapable of recognizing, or responding to, the needs of the people it governed. In their ruminations on this danger, the Antifederalists went to the heart of the problems inherent in representative government, and it is here that their writings deserve closer attention.

It was a truism in eighteenth-century political thinking that republican government could not be extended over a large territory. Montesquieu, the political philosopher most frequently cited in support of this proposition, had argued that republican government thus extended would fall prey to factions and become aristocratic or oligarchic. If it escaped such a transformation, it would break up into a series of smaller republics. The only way to have republican government in a large territory was through a federation of such small republics, united only for dealing with countries outside the federation. That, of course, was what the United States already had under the Articles of Confederation.

As is well known, Madison was prepared to cope with Montesquieu's argument. Taking his cue from a casual remark of David Hume's, Madison turned the argument on its head, to show that republican government was better suited to a large territory than a small one. According to Madison, a large territory had two advantages over a small one: it would contain a larger number of able men from whom the inhabitants could select their governors, and it would contain such a variety of different and opposing interests (factions) so widely spaced that no combination of them would be able to agree on measures that might oppress the rest.

Madison's argument is perhaps the most significant contribution to political thought by any of the founding fathers, and it is the foundation of subsequent pluralist political thought. But it made small impression on the Antifederalists, who indeed took surprisingly little notice of it. While they occasionally cited Montesquieu in their arguments against the Constitution, they relied much more heavily on the long-cherished American conception of representative government that prompted and sustained colonial resistance to British taxation, and finally directed the formation of their new state governments. It was a conception that could not be squared with Madison's.

Representative government has always embodied a paradox, not to say a contradiction. Representatives were originally the agents of particular communities, empowered to meet with a superior governing power in order to convey the assent or dissent of their constituents to new laws and taxes imposed from above. Representatives were more the attorneys of other subjects than a part of the governing power. As representatives gradually assumed or usurped the powers of government (a process not yet complete in either England or America before 1776), they had to think and act as rulers, not only for the communities that chose them but for the whole society of which their communities were a part. Yet they remained the agents of their constituents; they had to think and act both as subjects in a local community and as rulers over a much larger society. The history of representative government is the history of the conflict between these two functions, neither of which can exclude the other.

Americans in 1787 were still close to the original representative function. A representative in American experience had almost always been someone who was familiar with the needs of his community, someone the people in it knew and trusted and sent off to the government to look after their interests. And a representative assembly was supposed to be a mirror of the various communities that participated in it. It was a substitute for an assemblage of the whole people. It should therefore be, as John Adams said, "in miniature, an exact portrait of the people at large. It should think, feel, reason, and act like them." When the British Parliament began taxing the colonies in 1764, Americans had accordingly complained not only that they *were* not represented in Parliament but that they *could* not be. Distance forbade it. They could not be represented, because a representative sent to London would be out of touch with his constituents and therefore unable properly to convey their views and look after their interests. He would not be able to think, feel, and act like them at so great a distance.

England actually had no intention of allowing Americans to send representatives (it was suggested but not seriously considered). Instead, England responded to the American charge by affirming in absolute terms the other aspect of representation, emphasizing the function of representatives as governors, as a kind of elective aristocracy. Americans, it was said, might not actually vote for members of the House of Commons, but they were nevertheless represented there in the same way as most other British subjects, most of whom could not vote: they were "virtually" represented. Virtual representation meant that every member was discharged from local responsibilities and charged with looking after the running of the whole society. He represented everybody. To Americans this was so ridiculous as to be scarcely worth an answer. One might as well say that Parliament represented the whole world (a proposition that may not have seemed wholly absurd to Englishmen of that day). And Americans declared in no uncertain terms that the only persons who represented them were those whom they had elected to their own representative assemblies.

The quarrel with England thus reinforced the Americans' emphasis on the local character of representation, the representative's attachment to the community that chose him. It was representatives schooled in this traditional concept who assumed nearly all powers of government in America, once the break with England was made. Fresh from proclaiming local autonomy against the superintending power of king, Parliament, royal governors, and governor's councils, they had now themselves to exercise or direct whatever overall superintending powers there might be. To the Continental Congress (which was not popularly elected and thus not a representative assembly), they would allow no coercive powers, and in the state governments they subordinated all other branches—governors, judiciary, and upper houses—to themselves in their representative assemblies. As a result, even at the state level, larger, long-term concerns were sacrificed, and at the national level the Continental Congress lost the grudging support given it under pressure of war. Hence the local mischiefs which troubled Madison and his friends so much, and which even the Antifederalists acknowledged.

What the Antifederalists would not acknowledge was that the way to overcome the mischiefs was through a supreme national government in which representation as Americans understood it would be nonexistent, a national government that might reduce the states to impotence and thus effectively demolish true representative government everywhere in the United States. The kind of representation proposed by the Constitution for the national government looked several degrees worse than what the colonists had renounced and denounced in the quarrel with England. If Americans could not be properly represented in the British House of Commons, no more could they be in a national House of Representatives. America was a large and growing country. The capital would be too far away for proper representation of most parts of it. And to compound the difficulty the Constitution proposed a House of Representatives so small as to suggest a deliberate repudiation of what Americans had always demanded in their governments. In the British House of Commons 558 members inadequately represented 6 million people. The Constitution provided for a House of Representatives that would initially contain only 65 members to represent 3 million people spread over a much larger territory than England, and future houses were not to contain more than one representative for every 30,000 persons. The first United States House of Representatives would be smaller in size than most of the state representative assemblies. Double the number, triple it, the situation would be improved, but not much. In order to have the ratio of representation Americans were accustomed to, the House would have to seat 2,000, a veritable mob, incapable of deliberating about anything.

As the Antifederalists saw it, the consequence of any attempt to extend representative government to so large a country as the United States had to be an instant aristocracy or oligarchy. Admit with Madison that there would be a large pool of talent from which to draw representatives; it was not talent, however, that was needed in a representative but familiarity with the situation of the people he represented. If he was going to think for them, he ought to think like them. And anyone who was well-enough known to 30,000 people to be elected to Congress was not going to be someone who would think like most of them. He was going to be a man of reputation, someone who had been born to wealth and position or who had climbed or clawed his way there over the bodies of people who did not think or feel like him.

Or admit with Madison that the United States contained a great variety of people with a great variety of interests, would that variety be embodied in a house of representatives of 65 men or 130 or even 200, a size that most Americans of the time seemed to consider maximum for effective deliberation? On the contrary, to the Antifederalists it seemed likely that they would be all of a kind, the kind that could be designated "natural aristocrats." The United States did not have and would not have a hereditary titled aristocracy. The proposed Constitution forbade it, just as the Articles of Confederation had forbidden it. But that did not mean that some men were not much richer, more powerful, more looked-up-to than the rest. The most thoughtful Antifederalist pamphleteer (the anonymous "Federal Farmer") estimated the number in the whole country at four or five thousand. From those five thousand, the Antifederalists predicted, the members of Congress would inevitably be drawn. Lesser men—the middling sort of farmers, mechanics, and tradesmen—would not be widely enough known outside their immediate neighborhoods to win the necessary votes. No representative would embody their interests. In order for a representative body to be a picture of the people represented, it had to be chosen from small districts, small enough that the people would all be acquainted, so that they could vote for men like themselves, whom they knew personally and not simply by reputation. Such small districts were possible in elections for a state legislature, but on a national scale they would produce too large an assembly to be workable. A national government, though representative in form, would have to be unrepresentative in fact. It ought not, therefore, to have the extensive powers that the Constitution proposed for it. It ought to be subordinate to the state governments.

Were the Antifederalists wrong? Was Madison right? Yes and no. Representative government of the kind the Antifederalists valued in the state governments was clearly what Madison did not want in the national government, and the fact that the size of the nation would eliminate that kind of representation was, for him, all to the good. Attachment to local interests was what he hoped the national government would overcome; natural aristocrats were just what he wanted in the national House of Representatives. But the men he encountered there a few years later were not quite what he had expected, and he was not altogether happy with the way they behaved. Nor did he find them as varied in their interests or as unable to agree in oppressing others as he had predicted. Fortunate for him that he did not succeed in securing a national veto over state legislation, for by 1798 he was trying for a state veto over national legislation.

Fortunately he did not succeed in that either. Representative government is bound to disappoint those who expect too much from it—or too little. It is merely not as bad as other, more rational kinds of government, whether in a small territory or a large one. It requires that representatives think sometimes the way Federalists wanted them to and at other times the way the Antifederalists wanted. And despite Antifederalist fears, national representatives have somehow managed to carry on this balancing act. They did not all turn out to be natural aristocrats (can we doubt that mediocrity is fully represented among them?). They did not annihilate the state governments. They did not become, in the long run, any more menacing to civil and political liberties than their counterparts in the state governments. Often they have protected those liberties when the states failed to. They did not, then, quite fulfill the Antifederalists' fears. Nor did they quite fulfill the Federalists' hopes. And just as well. In republican government a shutout victory is not a good thing.

—1982

The Genius of Perry Miller

Perry Miller, the Harvard professor who transformed our understanding of what the founders of New England founded, did not look like your usual professor. His manners were rough; his bearing was not quite the one expected of a professor; and his casual conversation was calculated to shock. He sometimes affected an uncouthness that made a perceptive listener at one of his lectures ask why he kept insisting that he was really a stevedore. The answer, perhaps, was that he feared dignity might not merely substitute for learning but overcome it. Indeed, his posture carried the suggestion that such a conquest had occurred in some academics whom he saw around him.

It did not occur in him. The seeming stevedore, with the best historical mind of his generation, perhaps of his century, devoted it earnestly, fruitfully, humbly, and unrelentingly to scholarship. His very industry was a rebuke to those of us with fewer talents, who had greater need to work but could not match his intensity. And he compounded the force of the rebuke by working at a subject cast aside by previous scholars as too arid to be worth investigating: Puritan theology. Even in his last years, when he often appeared to be in a state of collapse, he outdid persons of greater dignity who were granted higher honors by the scholarly world.

Miller's first book, *Orthodoxy in Massachusetts, 1630–1650*, which appeared in 1933, was itself an orthodox, if brilliant, piece of scholarship in which he had not yet hit his stride. It has been more widely read than his other works because it is more conventional. *Orthodoxy in Massachu-setts*, like most other scholarly monographs, can be summarized. In brief, it demonstrated what a few scholars had argued, though none so conclusively, that the founders of Massachusetts believed in a congregational ecclesiastical polity before they came to the New World, even though they had remained within the Church of England. It also described some of the problems they encountered in putting that polity into practice.

The only real hint of Miller's ultimate objective was the fact that the book gave so much attention to ideas. It was no novelty to be writing about the New England Puritans with respect. The denunciations of H. L. Mencken and James Truslow Adams had already been arrested, among historians at least, by Kenneth Murdock's *Increase Mather* and Samuel Eliot Morison's *Builders of the Bay Colony*. Miller had come to Cambridge to sit at the feet of Murdock and Morison, and seemed to be echoing their views in the preface when he hazarded the thesis "that whatever may be the case in other centuries, in the sixteenth and seventeenth certain men of decisive importance took religion seriously; that they often followed spiritual dictates in comparative disregard of ulterior considerations; that those who led the Great Migration to Massachusetts and who founded the colony were predominantly men of this stamp." He added, "I have simply endeavored to demonstrate that the narrative of the Bay Colony's early history can be strung on the thread of an idea."

Coming after the works of Murdock and Morison, the words did not sound especially daring, but probably no one realized, perhaps not even Miller, how much he meant by them. It was a time when religious ideas excited hardly anyone. Avant-garde intellectuals dismissed them as pie in the sky, and divinity schools busied themselves with the arduous problems of homiletics. Miller himself was an atheist and never pretended to be anything else. With a historian's objectivity he had shown that some people in the sixteenth and seventeenth centuries cared enough about religious ideas to act upon them. But it would have seemed a little ridiculous for an atheist to take religious ideas seriously except insofar as they affected action.

That, however, is precisely what Miller did. Meticulously, chronologically he read everything written by Puritans in England or New England in the seventeenth century (in his spare time he read American literature of the nineteenth century and regularly offered new lecture courses on the literature of the South and West, local color, industrialism, romanticism). In 1939, six years after *Orthodoxy in Massachusetts*, he published *The New England Mind: The Seventeenth Century*, a belated *summa theologica* of New England Puritanism. In this and his subsequent works, instead of treating ideas as they affected actions, Miller scarcely mentioned actions except as they affected ideas. And yet by spelling out the ideas through which people of the time understood what they were doing, he rewrote their history. In occasional sentences, as in an unembellished line drawing, he was able, almost casually, to reconstruct social, political, and even economic history. Once one had the scheme of the thing clear, he seemed to say, it was scarcely worth the trouble to paint in the details of who *did* what.

The academic world received *The New England Mind* with cautious, bewildered plaudits. It was difficult reading, and most readers attributed the difficulty to unskillful writing. Those who spent enough time at it recognized that the trouble did not come from the writing, which was always clear and usually brilliant, but from the complexity of the intellectual system that the book describes, and even more from the subtlety of the author's observations about that system. Miller saw in Puritan theology a vast apparatus for describing reality. He wished to delineate it without simplifications so that his contemporaries might compare it with their own systems, to which they too often attributed a greater degree of sophistication. But Miller could not be content with the role of expositor. He was forever poking the apparatus here to show how it responded there. And the result, to any but the most careful follower of the text, was confusing. It was difficult to see precisely how the parts were connected. And how could anything be so complicated? Where did the Puritans stop and Miller begin? An eminent historian once confessed to me that reading Miller was to him like watching Einstein at a blackboard: he was impressed, he recognized there was something deep going on, but he did not know what.

Actually it is not impossible to treat *The New England Mind* as conventional intellectual history. One can describe its findings like those of any other scholarly work: its discovery of hitherto unsuspected elements in Puritan thought, such as humanism, Scholasticism, and the logic of

the sixteenth-century philosopher Peter Ramus, its demonstration of
the central role played by the doctrine of the covenant. Yet to say this
is to say too little, for what Miller had done was to create a new genre
of intellectual history. His book was not a building block for that imaginary tower of learning to which historical labors are always said to offer
"contributions." Nor was it the end product of such contributions by others. Though Miller was always more than generous in acknowledging the
help he received from the work of other scholars, *The New England Mind*
in fact owed surprisingly little to anyone else's scholarship. It was an end
product produced at a single stroke, a work of synthesis created when
there were no contributions to synthesize. *The New England Mind* is both
a description of a complex system of thought and a translation of that system into a universal commentary on the human condition. It is at once a
work of history and a testament.

Miller had begun a second volume when the war interrupted him.
After the war, however, he turned first to a study of Jonathan Edwards.
In doing so, he was reaching ahead from the seventeenth century to the
individual who in the eighteenth had worked most creatively with the
intellectual problems that Miller had already identified and described. In
Edwards, Miller saw the most challenging intelligence of American history, and the way Miller accepted the challenge is indicated in his astonishing statement that the whole of Edwards's writing constituted a giant
cryptogram, which could be unraveled only by reading between the lines.

Previous scholars had recognized Edwards as a genius, but they had
usually been content to praise him and hurry on; for Edwards's writings,
though extraordinarily lucid as theological writing goes, were, like Miller's own, extraordinarily difficult to those not versed in theology and not
willing to give days and nights to them. Miller implied that Edwards's
writings were deceptively simple, and the message he decoded from them
was complex—an amalgam of Edwards's system and Miller's explorations
of its implications.

Again, it is possible to state the main point made, that Edwards had
recast the Puritan message in terms of Lockean psychology and Newto-
nian physics, that he had repudiated covenant theology and leapt into a
modern way of apprehending the world, leapt so far that the twentieth

century has not yet overtaken him. But again, to state the point is to state much less of the book than would be the case with another writer. The genius lies in the tissue of implications and overtones that Miller wove around his story. He had become so familiar with New England thought that he could see the radical purpose in a conventional sermon or catch the personal gibe hidden in a theological treatise. Though he scorned the writing of social history, he revealed, almost parenthetically, the inner workings of New England society in the family feuds, local quarrels, and political maneuvers that swirled around the ideas of Jonathan Edwards.

After writing *Edwards*, Miller resumed work on the second volume of *The New England Mind*, subtitled *From Colony to Province*. In the earlier volume, while describing the tensions and paradoxes of New England Puritanism, he had not attempted to trace their unfolding in time. In *Colony to Province*, he took up again the theme initiated in *Orthodoxy in Massachusetts*: the impact of time and of the American experience on the system of ideas the Puritans brought with them. This is perhaps his greatest work, showing how in the isolation of the New World paradox and tension turned to contradiction and generated personal rivalries and party splits within New England orthodoxy. The central figure of the book is Cotton Mather, who with his father represented a conservative effort to keep the system as closely knit as possible. Attacking the Mathers on the one side stood Solomon Stoddard and on the other John Wise. And attacking them in the center stood Miller himself, mercilessly laying bare the egotism behind their efforts to retain control.

In one passage Miller revealed something of his own technique. To understand the Mathers, he insisted (and for that matter the rest of New England as Miller saw it), it was necessary

that we appreciate the habit of speech that grew up in New England as an inevitable concomitant of the jeremiads: references had to be phrased in more and more generalized terms, names never explicitly named, so that we are obliged to decipher out of oblique insinuations what to contemporaries were broad designations. When ministers denounced "oppression" and "luxury," they meant certain people whom they did not have to specify. The controversy between moder-

ates and the charter party must be deduced from what seem like plati-
tudes in election sermons, where minor shifts of emphasis betrayed
party maneuvers. This habit of ambiguity, developed out of New
England's insecurity, out of its inability to face frankly its own internal divisions, out of its effort to maintain a semblance of unity even
while unanimity was crumbling—which became more elaborate and
disingenuous as internecine passions waxed—was to cling to the New
England mind for centuries. We look ahead to the decades in which
an emerging Unitarianism swathed itself in terms of studied vague-
ness; even after the split, the habit clung especially to the Unitarian
pulpit, many of whose brightest lights were proud that their sermons
never indicated any awareness of controversy. In Boston society today,
matters may be fully discussed which, to an outsider, seem never to be
mentioned at all. Such tribal reticence only an occasional Thoreau
was to defy or an Emily Dickinson to turn into secret triumph.

And we may add that among historians only a Miller would have the daring, the imagination, and the learning to penetrate that tribal reticence.
At the end of the volume we are ready for the unfolding of Edwards's
giant cryptogram.

By 1953, when *Colony to Province* appeared, Miller's years of reading
in later American history and literature were demanding more expression
than he could give them in his teaching, and he was again impatient to
reach ahead. He projected a large-scale study of American thought from
the Revolution to the Civil War, leaving behind for a time the interven-
ing history of New England. As usual, there were preliminary forays in
articles, monographs, anthologies, and even one lengthy book, *The Raven
and the Whale*, which he once referred to, while writing it, as a "comic
book." There was also an introduction to a newly discovered journal of
Henry Thoreau, as dazzling a piece as Miller ever wrote.

The new work was never finished. The scraps he had written were
published posthumously in 1965 as *The Life of the Mind in America: From
the Revolution to the Civil War*. Although this book won a Pulitzer Prize, it
was only a draft of what he was discovering about the replacement of theology by juristic and scientific thinking as a way of apprehending reality.

He had only begun to trace the new patterns of thought he saw emerging, when he died in 1963, at the age of fifty-eight.

Miller's distinction lay in an extraordinary ability to discover order where others saw chaos, and to express his deepest insights without uttering them, by tracing unsuspected patterns in the raw materials of the past. Only one who has studied the raw materials for himself can fully appreciate the beauty of those patterns in *The New England Mind* or how faithfully they encompass the materials. No one but Miller, in fact, has in our time known so well the materials of New England history during the period that he covered. But a few of us have studied some of them. To do so and then to read or reread Miller is to be stunned not only by his familiarity with the sources but by the way he has put into a paragraph interpretations and observations that one might expect to find as the conclusion of a whole monograph. And good monographs were written, are being written, and doubtless will be written to document in detail what Miller has already said and could himself have documented.

How, then, are we to assess his achievement? It is, of course, true that he has had a powerful influence of the kind that other great historians have had. He has changed in many ways the standard picture of early New England. Because of him we know now that the founders of Massachusetts were non-separating Congregationalists, that the exodus to Connecticut was not the result of a democratic impulse, that the antinomian controversy involved a dispute between John Cotton and other ministers in which Cotton was defeated and obliged to accept the doctrine of preparation, that New England theologians employed the logical system of Peter Ramus, that they made the covenant of grace the central doctrine of their system, and that Jonathan Edwards repudiated that doctrine. These and a great many other such propositions, which have found or will eventually find their way into the standard textbooks, can be counted as a heritage of Miller's work.

But to make such a statement is to reduce the man to the terms by which we measure other historians. One feels a similar incongruity in observing, what is true, that because of him a great many other scholars are now studying Puritanism. Some of these are his students, and it is more than a personal observation that Perry Miller was a great teacher. You could not be in his presence without feeling that he cared about you and your ideas. Indeed, he always saw so much more in your ideas than you had seen yourself that you were compelled to stretch your imagination and to reach beyond yourself. Something of this impetus was communicated by his writings to persons who never saw him. He was a man thinking, and the phenomenon is so rare that it cannot fail to affect everyone who sees it or hears of it. To be sure, it excited envy, mistrust, and dislike as well as imitation. People almost seemed to hope that he was drinking himself to stupefaction, so that his relentless creativity could not continue to chide. And when at last he was gone, one sensed a subdued relief at the funeral service. But there is no escape from his example. Such men do not live without effect.

Yet one remains in the end with the sense that his influence was incommensurate with his genius. Charles Beard and Frederick Jackson Turner, whose intellectual achievements were inferior to Miller's, had at least as great an influence on the study of history as Miller had or is likely to have. He was, in fact, not a leader of thought, because at the level he worked, thought will not bear leading. He raised a standard to which no one could rally. His true achievement lay not in altering the general picture of early New England, or in the encouragement he gave his students, or even in the example he set to men who would think. His achievement was a series of books the like of which had not been seen before, the record of a mind that craved reality and reached for it through history, as others have reached through religion or philosophy. Only when historians become philosophers and philosophers historians will the full significance of his achievement be understood.

—1964

ACKNOWLEDGMENTS

THIS BOOK EXISTS as a book because Robert Weil at W. W. Norton shared my view of what makes heroes and heroines. His editorial skills and those of Otto Sonntag have sharpened the language of all the essays. And I can recognize in all of them the guiding hands and historical insights of two people who have successively shaped my understanding of the past: Helen M. Morgan and Marie Morgan.

INDEX

ABOUT THE AUTHOR

EDMUND S. MORGAN, who received his Ph.D. at Harvard University studying with Perry Miller, was born in 1916 in Minneapolis. He has written for the *New York Review of Books* for over forty years and has published more than fifteen books, including *Benjamin Franklin*; *Inventing the People: The Rise of Popular Sovereignty in England and America*, which won Columbia University's Bancroft Prize in American History in 1989; and *American Slavery, American Freedom*, which won the Society of American Historians' Francis Parkman Prize, the Southern Historical Association's Charles S. Sydnor Prize, and the American Historical Association's Albert J. Beveridge Award.

Joining the faculty at Yale University in 1955, he trained a generation of students in early American history and was named a Sterling Professor in 1965, retiring over two decades later in 1986. In 1971 he was awarded the Yale Chapter of Phi Beta Kappa's William Clyde DeVane Medal for most outstanding teaching and scholarship, considered one of the most prestigious teaching prizes for Yale faculty. One year later, he became the first recipient of the Douglas Adair Memorial Award for scholarship in early American history, and in 1986 he received the Distinguished Scholar Award of the American Historical Association. Among other honors, he has received the National Humanities Medal in 2000, the 2006 Pulitzer Prize Special Citation, and the American Academy of Arts and Letters' 2008 Gold Medal for History. A woodturner and furniture craftsman of distinction, he lives in New Haven with his wife, Marie Morgan.